INDIAN KNOLL

INDIAN KNOLL

by William S. Webb

Introduction to the New Edition by
Howard D. Winters

THE UNIVERSITY OF TENNESSEE PRESS · KNOXVILLE

237991

Library of Congress Catalog Card Number A46-3963
International Standard Book Number 0-87049-150-4

[XI]

Reprinted by permission of the Department of Anthropology and
Archaeology, University of Kentucky, Lexington.

Originally published as *Indian Knoll, Site Oh 2, Ohio County,
Kentucky,* in *The University of Kentucky Reports in Anthropology
and Archaeology,* Volume IV, Number 3, Part 1 (Lexington, 1946).

Library of Congress Cataloging in Publication Data
Webb, William Snyder, 1882–1964.
  Indian Knoll.
  Reprint of the 1946 ed. published by University
of Kentucky, Lexington, which was issued as v. 4,
no. 3, pt. 1, of University of Kentucky reports in
anthropology and archaeology.
  Includes bibliographies.
  1. Indian Knoll site, Ky. I. Title.
II. Series: Kentucky. University. Dept. of
Anthropology. Reports in anthropology, v. 4, no. 3,
pt. 1.
E78.K3W42 1974   917.69'835   73-18473
ISBN 0-87049-150-4

Introduction to the New Edition
by Howard D. Winters

With the reprinting of *Indian Knoll,* a classic in archaeological literature, we are again reminded of the contributions to archaeology of
William S. Webb, one of the most productive and innovative minds
of a generation that established the base necessary for the development of a disciplined and scientific approach in New World archaeology. Douglas Schwartz (1968) has covered admirably the details
of Webb's career and his historic role in Midwestern archaeology,
and there is no need to repeat those details here. Instead, I shall attempt to discuss some of Webb's contributions to the understanding
of the Archaic and to assess the meaning of the Indian Knoll Culture
in terms of present-day problems.

Although Webb was little concerned with archaeological theory
per se, his ever increasing sophistication in the preparation of excavation reports has provided data that have been of considerable value
in recent years for studying problems ranging from settlement system
analysis (Fowler, 1959; Winters, 1969) to the interpretation of prehistoric procurement patterns of exotic commodities (Winters, 1968),
and analysis of traditions of the Archaic in the mid-continent area of
North America (Lewis and Kneberg, 1959).

The significance of Webb's work was recognized by W. W. Taylor
(1946), who, in casting a critical eye over the work of the eminent figures of the 1940s, remarked: "Before leaving this analysis of Webb's
contributions, I wish to state once again that I believe that he has
given us some of our best archeological reports. Although it is true
that he has failed to make the most of his opportunities, it is possible
to abstract more out of his publications than from those of the major-

ity of his colleagues. There seems to be no doubt that he has been influenced toward a purely time-and-space, comparative approach by the need to go along with his fellow archeologists and find a place for his discoveries within the Midwestern system. Perhaps this need has changed the course of a development that would have led to more detailed and refined cultural pictures and thus eventually to more detailed comparative studies. Perhaps if he had managed to carry on according to his own inclinations, he would not have become so concerned with presence-and-absence trait lists and comparative studies. As the matter now stands, Webb's contributions are considerable and he presents an enlightening paradox."

Rather than being led blindly down the path of trait-listing and the Midwestern Taxonomic System, Webb, at the time, probably perceived these pursuits as a means of bringing order to the chaotic accumulation of data from previous decades. His later work shows that he ultimately saw the futility of further wandering along the taxonomic road to nowhere. Certainly, by the 1950s, Webb's interests had turned to synthesis of data and interpretation of the lifeways of hunting-and-gathering populations in the Midwest, and he had completed a lengthy manuscript on this topic. He had also compiled a study of the atlatl, using previous reports on Kentucky shell middens. It is to be regretted that he deferred these projects to his waning years, when he could no longer bring to his writing the clarity of insight and acuity in analysis that marked the years of his peak productivity.

Little had been written about Archaic sites before Webb and his associates published their reports on Indian Knoll (see map, facing p. 119), other sites of the Indian Knoll Culture along the Green River and Cypress Creek in Kentucky, and numerous prepottery sites in the Tennessee Valley. *The Archeology of Eastern North America* (Griffin, 1952) shows that there were, of course, such notable works as Ritchie's report on the Lamoka site (Ritchie, 1932), in which he had applied the term *Archaic* to a prepottery site in New York, and his subsequent report on the excavations at Frontenac Island (Ritchie, 1945). But, in general, the literature was devoid of substantial references to Archaic sites or cultures, and in many published excavation reports the material pertaining to Archaic components was simply included with Woodland and later components on the site. Indeed, the putative assemblages from some of these sites were a melange of a bewildering number of artifactual styles that actually belonged to what are now known to be discrete Archaic and Woodland cultural units. Of course, such erroneous cultural attributions could scarcely have been avoided at that time. Archaeologists had excavated many shallow sites that contained the mixed deposits of thousands of years of occupation, but there was a dearth of the deep, stratified sites needed as a key for sorting out the artifacts. Significantly, Webb's reports on Carlson Annis (Webb, 1950a) and sites in the Tennessee Valley (Webb and DeJarnette, 1942; 1948a, b, c, d) were among the earliest to provide sufficient stratigraphic data to show that midden accumulations in eastern North America had resulted from the activities of many groups of people over long spans of time.

The considerable scope of Webb's excavation projects was made possible by an infusion of funds from such New Deal programs as the Works Progress Administration, which provided jobs for the vast numbers of unemployed in the 1930s; the Tennessee Valley Authority, which had embarked on a program of dam construction; and the Civilian Conservation Corps, which provided work for great numbers of the younger unemployed. And it was thus that Professor Webb was drawn to the planning and direction of excavation programs of a scope never before conceived in eastern North America. He had the organizational ability to keep numerous projects running concurrently under field supervisors, and he designed excavation procedures for mounds, cemeteries, middens, and villages that permitted standardized reporting over an area ranging from the Tennessee Valley in northern Alabama to sites along tributary streams of the Ohio River in Kentucky. One of the results of these coordinated programs was the accretion of a vast amount of data on what was then referred to as the Shell Mound Archaic, and Webb's publications have remained the principal sources on Archaic shell middens in mid-America, still constituting the largest and most comprehensive corpus of excavation derived data on Archaic sites in all of eastern North America. Oddly enough, while these sources are constantly cited, there has been relatively little use of them for further major synthesis and interpretation of late Archaic cultures. They deserve to be used for something better than the nebulosities of the trait list. Nor has there been much attempt to re-analyze the collections, with the exception of Martha Ann Rolingson's (1967) University of Michigan dissertation on sites in the Green River and Cypress Creek valleys and the publication by Rolingson and Schwartz (1966) on sites in western Kentucky. There is obviously still great research potential for a number of industrious archaeologists.

In addition to the vast array of data provided by Webb in describing excavation results, he also dealt with a number of special topics that are important as antecedents of contemporary areas of research. For example, today there is increasing concern with the problem of the functional identification of artifacts, and many traditional categories are beginning to be understood as far more complex than their titles indicate. Stemmed, chipped stone objects are not necessarily projectile points, since some categories are stemmed knives. Bone awls should not be categorized simply as perforators because of the variety of ways in which they were used: as basket-weaving implements, for skewering food, and for piercing hides—a use category to which all bone awls have been casually assigned in many reports. Scrapers can be identified much more specifically with functions such as woodworking and hide-working. And many of the objects designated as hammerstones were actually manos for processing plant foods.

Although the foregoing distinctions are not made in Webb's publications, one can readily appreciate that he was among the pioneers in functional analysis, having devoted a considerable amount of attention to identifying the component parts of Indian Knoll Culture atlatls, such as handles, hooks, and atlatl weights, or bannerstones, as they were fancifully called by most professional and amateur archaeologists. Although the function of atlatl weights is still unresolved, their association with atlatl shafts seems clear. Curiously, in undertaking his atlatl analyses (Webb and DeJarnette, 1942; Webb and Haag, 1939; Webb, 1946, 1950a, 1950b), Webb made evident one of the major defects of the trait list that is divided into categories, such as chipped stone, ground stone, copper, bone, antler, and shell artifacts, even though he does not seem to have recognized the implications of relying upon a classificatory system based solely on raw materials and manufacturing techniques. For example, if one were recording a complete atlatl, the dart point would appear under chipped stone, or possibly bone or antler; the atlatl and dart shafts under wood; the hook and handle under bone or antler; and the atlatl weight under ground stone or shell. The obvious result would be the fragmentation of a unitary implement into a set of scattered and unrelated artifacts.

Webb also investigated the manufacture of fish hooks by peoples of the Indian Knoll Culture (Webb, 1950a) and was able to present quite clearly the steps in manufacturing the various types and to pro-

vide information that permitted the identification of unfinished specimens and the residual material that was cast aside during the manufacturing process. Finally, Webb (1950a) made a notable contribution to functional analysis of Archaic materials in his discussion of
animal bones that may have been inclusions in medicine bags associated with burials.

Webb was also more thorough than most of his predecessors and
contemporaries in identifying sources of raw materials. There is cur-
rently much interest in this kind of information, which is useful in
working with problems ranging from manufacturing operations to
the study of procurement systems and trade, and even to the study
of differentials in status and role among prehistoric populations
(Rothschild, n.d.). For example, his publications provided the data
that were essential for my paper investigating the possibilities that
procurement systems underwent cyclical fluctuations and that different values were attached to particular classes of artifacts (Winters,
1968).

Although Webb did not devote much space to the delineation of
subsistence patterns, he did include in *Indian Knoll* a report by Miss
Opal Skaggs on the species contained in some 380 cartons of bone
(Webb, 1946, pp. 333-40). The totals for fragments identified and
numbers of deer bone have been recomputed, since the totals given
in the Indian Knoll report seem to be grossly in error, if the numerical
data on individual species are correct, and certain conclusions have
been reached about the subsistence pattern of the Indian Knoll Culture. Of the 28,263 mammal bones, 27,597, or 97.6 percent, are deer;
of the 1,536 bird bones, 1,281, or 83.4 percent, are those of turkey.
Reptiles and fish are present in insignificant numbers, although these
latter species may be inadequately represented in the sample since
there was no screening of the midden material. But, of the vertebrate
fauna, deer was the only quantitatively significant animal.

Another obvious item of importance in the diet, of course, was
mussels, the abundance of which was noted by Webb (1940, p. 108):
"In most heaps shells form at least 25% of the actual bulk of the site
. . . . That shell fish formed a large portion of their meat diet is quite
evident." Morse (1967) is probably correct, however, in his observation that deer was quantitatively a far more important element in the
diet than mussels. But it should also be remembered that bulk is not
the only factor in a subsistence analysis, another element being the
contribution by the food item of essential nutrients—trace elements,

vitamins, and protein, for example. Deer may be the main source of animal protein, but it has serious deficiencies in respect to other essential nutrients.

Plant foods must also have been important as attested by the very considerable numbers of pestles at Indian Knoll (1438), Carlson Annis (276), Ward (130), Kirkland (21), Read (214), Chiggerville (123), Barrett (58), and Butterfield (55). These numbers are at best minimal, since at many of the sites only unbroken specimens were reported in the trait lists. It is not improbable that nuts would have been the most important of these plant resources, since all of the Indian Knoll sites lie within relatively narrow valleys within the hill section of the western mesophytic forest, which consists predominantly of hardwood, nut-bearing trees (Braun, 1950). In support of this last surmise, Rolingson reports (1967, p. 99) that fragmentary and/or burned hickory nuts and a few occurrences of giant ragweed were found in soil samples from burial pits at the Kirkland site, one of the components of the Indian Knoll Culture, and nut hulls are mentioned in the field notes on some features.

If this interpretation of the nature of the Indian Knoll subsistence pattern is correct, the economy would have been of the narrow-spectrum Riverton type, or what I have called elsewhere a harvesting economy (Winters and Yarnell, n.d.). That is, the economy was based upon a few essential resources, which in this case would have been deer, mussels, and nuts—a triumvirate that has the admirable quality of supplying all known essential nutrients, with the exception of an adequate supply of vitamin C.

Societies with harvesting economies tend to be very complex and are important theoretically for reasons that I shall discuss below. Their characteristics are:

1. A highly developed technology, with plant processing equipment, woodworking equipment (usually), highly efficient hunting and/or fishing gear, and virtually all known items of fabricating and processing equipment for altering raw materials and manufacturing finished products therefrom.

2. Intensive exploitation of a small number of plant and animal species, i.e., a narrow-spectrum economy.

3. Division of labor beyond sex and age categories, which may be manifest in specialized economic activities, rudimentary craft specialization, ritual activities, etc.

4. Methods of banking (storage) through use of basketry and other containers, storage pits, and other preservation techniques. The result is a leveling out of subsistence crises in the annual cycle.

5. In many instances, there is a systematic procurement of or trade in foreign commodities. Presumably, a side effect would be a trend towards the breaking down of "tribal" barriers.

6. Denser concentrations of population in relatively small territorial units.

7. Leisure time might be expected in more predictable units, permitting, although not leading inevitably, to more effective planning in the allotment of the leisure time so abundantly available to most hunters and gatherers.

8. A settlement system that is marked by prolonged residence of several months at seasonally occupied sites covering several acres. Sites for specialized activities are ancillary to the main occupation areas.

9. In some instances, there is an unequal distribution and concentration of certain resources, such as marine shell and copper, hence the accretion of wealth and a rudimentary form of capital. It is even possible that some forms of wealth constituted a limited medium of exchange.

10. More complex expression of religious symbols, with religious ("ceremonial") paraphernalia appearing in special contexts.

11. There is some evidence for increased internal and external conflict. Some deaths in sites of the Indian Knoll Culture were caused by projectile points normally associated with alien cultures in the Tennessee Valley area, for example. At Riverton, on the other hand, one or more deaths in the small burial sample were caused by projectile points of local manufacture.

It is even possible to propose a hypothesis as to why conflict may have become an important factor in such societies. First of all, narrow-spectrum economies in the Midwest were concentrated in areas where all the necessary food sources were locally available. Such localities were infrequent in the tens of thousands of square miles in which these cultures developed. If, as is stated below, subsistence crises were brought about through natural fluctuations in the availability of the basic resources and through overexploitation of the resources during periods of declining productivity, one solution to the problem could have been an attempt to take over other such localities that could support an economy of this type, or, perhaps, to raid the sites in these localities for stored food reserves. Locally, as the subsistence crisis developed, one might expect increased competition within the group for the declining yields of essential foods. In other words, the rare localities with the potential for sustaining narrow-spectrum economies were analogous to the rarity of naturally suitable land in developing agricultural economies.

Any, or several, of the foregoing characteristics may appear, of course, in other types of social systems. But in previous and current research, it has been concluded that all were present in the Indian Knoll Culture, with their most complex expression at Indian Knoll itself.

If, as I believe, the Indian Knoll Culture is characterized by a harvesting economy, it joins a group of Midwestern cultures, such as Riverton, that are of considerable theoretical interest in that most social and cultural evidence of them disappeared between 2000 and 1000 B.C. These cultures either met extinction or underwent changes of such amplitude that the derivative cultures are no longer recognizable in terms of their earlier patterns. Yet, paradoxically, they all give evidence of being technologically elaborate, having a well developed pattern of seasonal sedentism, possessing very efficient techniques for exploiting their environments, and showing stable cultural configurations over several centuries. Their demise cannot be imputed to natural catastrophes, there being no evidence for such events. A more gradual change in climate, leading to the disappearance of mussels, could account for a change in subsistence patterns; again, however, no supporting evidence has come to light. Environmental degradation may have been an important factor, but it seems insufficient to explain the rather abrupt collapse of these flourishing societies. An important part of the process may well lie in ever amplifying fluctuations in the resources that were essential to maintaining the narrow-spectrum pattern in a given area, the fluctuations deriving from both natural cycles of expansion and contraction of the resource and overexploitation of the resources by the resident groups. It is not intended to imply that such societies must inevitably follow the path to extinction. There are patterns of change that would have permitted survival of the society, albeit frequently in very different form, and these alternative patterns will be discussed subsequently in another context.

Had Webb not provided quantitative data, it would have been impossible to make this preliminary interpretation of the Indian Knoll subsistence pattern and to relate it to the complex societies in which harvesting economies occurred. Simple lists of plant and animal species reveal very little about the economy of a society. One could, for example, have two identical lists of one hundred plant and animal species for two sites, and the economies could be totally different. In one instance, the economy might be linked to three species, with the remainder constituting variety, seasoning, or emergency rations. In the second, some twenty or thirty items might have been essential for the year-round survival of the group. In the case of the former, the resources had to be available either in nature or as stored commodities throughout the year, while in the latter instance, the broad-spectrum economy, the availability and importance of particular resources tended to change with the season. The result was very different types of societies, with different potentials for development. And the *potential* for developing agriculture lay with societies that had narrow-spectrum economies.

This statement may again sound paradoxical, since most of these groups in the Midwest seem to have become socially and culturally extinct. But it is probable that the potential for developing plant-tending and agriculture could be realized only when certain linked factors were present:

1. A narrow-spectrum economy, along with an adequate technology for processing and techniques for storing plant foods. The invention of the pebble mano by hunters and gatherers must have been one of the true technological revolutions of earlier times. The mano permitted effective exploitation of the hard-coated seeds of the weedy ancestors of the cereal grains and other domesticates, reducing to edible form large quantities of abundant and nutritious resources that would otherwise have been difficult to incorporate into the human diet.

2. The availability of easily controllable plants of the weedy type, particularly if the species were multiversant rather than pauciversant.

3. An adequate acreage of disturbed habitats so that such plants yielded enough annually to make them economically important. Disturbance, which may have resulted from the natural action of wind and water, seasonal flooding, fires, and the activities of man in the

sites that he occupied was important because it provided an environment especially conducive to the growth of weeds, which are the
sources of most of man's present-day cultigens.

In some soils the method of disturbance need not have been any
more complicated than that of the Natchez Indians in planting
choupichoul, a native grain which has never been satisfactorily identified in regard to species. Le Page du Pratz states (n.d., pp. 156-57),
"I ought not to omit mentioning here, that from the low lands of
Louisiana, the Mississippi has several shoal banks of sand in it, which
appear very dry upon the falling of the waters, after the inundations.
These banks extend more or less in length; some of them half a
league, and not without a considerable breadth. I have seen the
Natchez, and other Indians, sow a sort of grain, which they called
Choupichoul, on these dry sand-banks. This sand received no manner
of culture; and the women and children covered the grain any how
with their feet, without taking any great pains about it. After this sow-
ing, and manner of culture, they waited till autumn, when they gathered a great quantity of the grain." Perhaps the Natchez were simply
practicing an ancient mode of cultivation that was prevalent in North
America before the intensive cultivation of maize, which began sometime after A.D. 500 in the Deep South. And it does, in fact, sound very
much like a historic example of Stuart Struever's (1964) mud-flat
agriculture.

4. A relatively high population density within a small area and
general filling of alternative habitats, so that scheduling of the harvesting of potential cultigens was not only desirable but essential.

5. The addition of the deliberate disturbance of areas favorable to
the growth of economically important weeds to the pattern of
seasonal activities.

In such situations, while the development of plant-tending and
agriculture were not inevitable, their appearance was not unlikely.
Subsequently, we may expect the addition of specialized equipment
such as hoes, plows, diversified farming techniques (swidden system,
irrigation, dry-farming) and selection for more productive or successful varieties of the important species.

The foregoing facts serve to point out another reason why Indian
Knoll is fascinating. It appears that the Indian Knoll Culture, like
Riverton, was one of those cultures with harvesting economies that
could not have developed agriculture independently, since both

items three and four were inadequately represented in the total pattern. The area of naturally disturbed habitats in both areas was small. Hence, the potentially cultivatable weeds were economically unimportant, and scheduling emphasized, instead, the nut tree, a plant that was not easily controllable by hunting-and-gathering societies, the maturation time being too lengthy. One could scarcely expect that societies of the Indian Knoll and Riverton type, with their very successful adaptive systems, would foresee the vastly greater potential of turning their interest to their quantitatively insignificant local weeds. There would also have been considerable reluctance to create extensive, newly disturbed habitats in their narrow valleys since the most suitable areas would have been the forest fringes, the most rewarding area for harvesting nuts and acorns. To use Flannery's terms (1968), scheduling in this type of harvesting economy is a deviation-reducing factor. In other harvesting economies where all of the requisite elements are represented, scheduling could have been a deviation-amplifying factor leading in the direction of plant-tending and agriculture. It is to be hoped that there will be renewed field investigations of Indian Knoll subsistence patterns. We shall undoubtedly know more about this important subject when the results of Marquardt's (1972) recent tests at Carlson (Carlston) Annis become available.

Another sphere in which Webb made important contributions toward the raising of standards for archaeological reporting was in the incorporation of analyses and information provided by authorities from fields as diverse as geology, chemistry, zoology, malacology, dendrochronology, ethnobotany, and physical anthropology. Thus he foreshadowed the development of the 1950s that became fashionable under the rubric of the interdisciplinary approach, which initially seems to have produced considerable mystification among the many specialists who were being assiduously wooed regarding the relevance of their contributions to archaeological studies and the benefits that they might expect from their labors. Webb was frequently more successful in relating the data of the specialists to his own work, while later interdisciplinary efforts often resulted only in the addition of sundry appendages to a report, with little recognition of their existence in the report itself.

All in all, Webb left a legacy that can be profitably utilized for many purposes today. For example, several years ago, I followed in the footsteps of Fowler (1959) in characterizing various sites of the

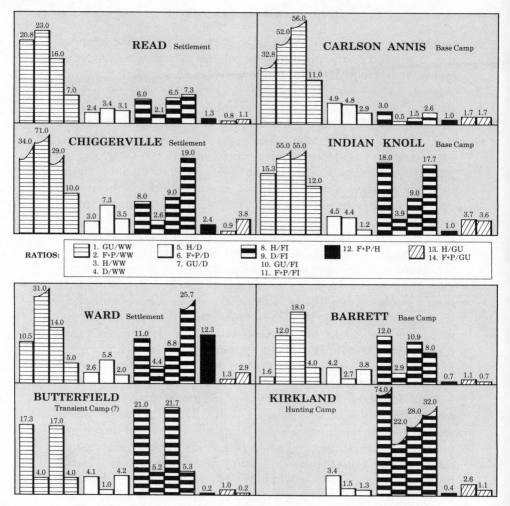

Relative importance of activities at sites of the Indian Knoll Culture as shown by ratios of selected functional categories: general utility (GU), woodworking (WW), fabricating and processing (F+P), hunting equipment (H), domestic implements (D), and fishing gear (FI). For example, among artifacts recovered from the Read site, there were 20.8 general utility tools for every woodworking tool.

Indian Knoll Culture as elements of a settlement system (Winters, 1969). Subsequently, to clarify the settlement system of Indian Knoll sites, I tried re-arranging the artifacts in Webb's trait list into functional categories and computing the ratios of the various categories to each other (see graph). Thus it was possible to show, albeit crudely, the relative importance of certain activities at Ward and Kirkland

(Webb and Haag, 1940), Chiggerville (Webb and Haag, 1939), Indian Knoll (Webb, 1946), Barrett and Butterfield (Webb and Haag, 1947), Carlson Annis (Webb, 1950a) and Read (Webb, 1950b).

Although there may have been errors in compiling the data, deriving from inadequate sampling in the field and from my interpretation of the function of some of the artifacts, the errors are consistent for all of the sites. Furthermore, although the sites are multicomponent, non-Indian Knoll components are statistically insignificant in terms of the vast number of items at each site that do belong with the Indian Knoll occupations. Hence, substantial quantitative differences in proportions must derive from something other than sampling and interpretative errors.

The graph is not intended as a conclusive statement about the Indian Knoll settlement system; instead, it is intended as an exploratory operation to determine whether further analysis of the settlement patterns and systems of the Indian Knoll Culture would be profitable. Careful inspection of the graph indicates that the establishment of such a research program should afford worthwhile results. There are notable differences, qualitatively, in the general patterning of the ratios and, quantitatively, in the numerical expression of the ratios. What I have called settlements and base camps are relatively more similar to each other in patterning, however, than either is to a transient or a hunting camp. Fabricating and processing activities, for example, were more important at settlements and base camps than at either the transient or the hunting camp. Fishing seems to have been only a minor activity and woodworking virtually irrelevant at the hunting camp. But I do not propose to develop any elaborate interpretations from this exploratory operation, which rests on defective data, including only a limited amount of stratigraphic data at two sites (Read and Carlson Annis) and none at the others. Clearly, relying only on the published material available, there is not much use in pursuing the settlement system studies further. Rather, for such research to be profitable would require the procurement of unpublished data on stratigraphy, re-analysis of the actual artifacts with the objective of defining specific functions, refinement of typologies, sorting of the material by components, study of the raw materials and their sources, and additional excavations at sites of the Indian Knoll Culture to obtain information on subsistence patterns, environment, and chronology. The latter is especially important since I feel that what have been termed the Ward, Read, and Chiggerville settlement units (Winters, 1968, p. 176) may not be entirely contemporaneous.

The existing radiocarbon dates from Indian Knoll and Carlson Annis are anything but satisfactory. Five samples of shell and antler from Carlson Annis gave dates of 4289 ± 300 B.P., 4333 ± 450 B.P., 4900 ± 250 B.P., 5149 ± 300 B.P., and 7374 ± 500 B.P. Three antler samples from Indian Knoll provided dates of 3963 ± 350 B.P., 4282 ± 250 B.P., and 5302 ± 300 B.P. (Johnson, 1951; Rolingson, 1967, app. C). All of these dates were obtained by the outmoded solid carbon method, and two of the Carlson Annis dates are from samples of fresh-water mussel shell, a material that is frequently unreliable by virtue of the incorporation of ancient carbonates carried in solution in the waters of the stream. While the samples are identified in regard to the level from which they came, their contexts are inadequate. The accretion of shell middens does not necessarily follow a classic "layer cake" pattern of deposition, and that there are components earlier and later than the Indian Knoll Culture at the two sites is evident from the presence of fluted, Dalton-Meserve, LeCroy, Kirk Serrated, Adena, and Madison points. The foregoing factors may explain why some dates are out of phase in the stratigraphic sequence, with early dates coming from strata above more recent dates.

Seven of the preceding dates can be corrected through dendrochronologic calibration of the C-14 time scale by means of a conversion table that covers the last 7,355 years B.P. (Damon, Long, and Wallick, 1972). The corrected dates for Carlson Annis and Indian Knoll are as follows, using a half life of 5,730 years:

Sample	Site	Depth	Old Date	Corrected Date	B.C.
C- 738	Carlson Annis	1.0′+	4289 ± 300 B.P.	4920 ± 340	2970 ± 340
C- 739	Carlson Annis	4.0′+	4333 ± 450 B.P.	4975 ± 475	3025 ± 475
C- 251	Carlson Annis	6.5′	4900 ± 250 B.P.	5658 ± 260	3708 ± 260
C- 116	Carlson Annis	6.5′	5149 ± 300 B.P.	5942 ± 310	3992 ± 310
C- 741	Indian Knoll	4.5′	3963 ± 350 B.P.	4508 ± 365	2558 ± 365
C- 740	Indian Knoll	1.0′	4282 ± 250 B.P.	4912 ± 295	2962 ± 295
C- 254	Indian Knoll	1.0′	5302 ± 300 B.P.	6100 ± 315	4160 ± 315

William Marquardt of Washington University has kindly made available two unpublished dates from samples obtained during his 1972 excavations at Carlson Annis:

Sample	Depth	Old Date	Corrected Date	B.C.
UCLA 1845B	1.4-1.6 m.	4040 ± 180 B.P.	4605 ± 210 B.P.	2655 ± 210 B.C.
UCLA 1845A	1.8-2.0 m.	4250 ± 80 B.P.	4874 ± 175 B.P.	2924 ± 175 B.C.

These dates from the bottom (Level 10) and the lower portion (Level 8) of the midden indicate that deposition began much later in the area of Marquardt's test pit than in the area of Webb's excavations. Caution should be used in attempting to interpret and relate the two sets of dates, however, since, as previously indicated, the Webb dates were determined by the outmoded solid-carbon method. But it would scarcely be surprising to learn that midden accumulations were expanding over time, with more peripheral areas dating later than the original core. Actually, any realistic interpretation of horizontal and vertical accumulation patterns in shell middens would have to be based on literally dozens of dated samples carefully chosen for a thorough sampling of the complex stratigraphy and probable discontinuities that typify large shell-midden accumulations.

But one obvious result of the conversion of Webb's dates, if they can be taken literally, is that both Indian Knoll and Carlson Annis seem to have had their beginnings sometime very late in the fifth millennium or early in the fourth millennium B.C., rather than very late in the fourth or very early in the third millennium. Nearly 2,000 years now separate the earliest dates of the Indian Knoll Culture from the earliest dates of the Riverton Culture, which are less drastically changed by the corrections, the dates now ranging from 3961 ± 140 B.P. to 3411 ± 235 B.P., or from 2011 ± 140 B.C. to 1461 ± 235 B.C. There are no adequate terminal dates for any of the Indian Knoll occupations, but we doubt that the span was much more than 1,500 years. Thus there may have been a gap of several hundred years between the end of the Indian Knoll Culture in the Green River Valley and the appearance of the Riverton Culture in the Wabash Valley. Such a temporal separation may explain one of the problems that has bothered me, i.e., why in some respects Riverton seems so much like Indian Knoll and differs in so many other respects. Over the course of several centuries, sufficient change may have taken place that the Indian Knoll Culture could even have been ancestral to an intervening culture that developed into Riverton.

Thus the importance of these new and revised dates is more than historical. In a preceding section mention was made of the considerable possibility that many of the societies with harvesting economies had become extinct in the Midwest. But there were also patterns of change that would permit the continuation of the traditional lifeway or the development of considerably different patterns. Summarized briefly, some of the possibilities were:

1. Removal to an unoccupied area where the essential resources were equivalent to those traditionally utilized in maintaining the economic system. Relatively little change might have been expected. This solution was probably comparatively rare in the Midwest, since the concentration of the essential resources tended to occur only in a few localities, and by 5000 B.C., most, if not all, had been appropriated by other societies, with the exception of a few niches that appeared at later dates in the northern part of the Midwest. The Indian Knoll Culture serves as a probable example of this point. Rolingson (1967, pp. 43-44, 97) summarizes the results of surveys on the upper Green River and its tributaries, the Rough, Nolin, and Barren rivers. No shell middens were reported, although there are mussel beds on both the upper Green and upper Barren rivers. I would attribute this anomaly to the reduced subsistence potential of the upper portion of the Green River system; i.e., a reduction in size of the areas for harvesting deer and nuts, the other essential elements of this particular system. One might say that this illustrates the principle that man cannot live by mussels alone. Taking over already occupied niches would have been difficult for any hunting-and-gathering society, since the people generally had neither the manpower nor the surplus for sustaining campaigns leading to the actual conquest or domination of areas occupied by societies with equivalent technologies and economies. Nor would raiding have been a very effective means of relieving subsistence crises. The vision of a small band of warriors staggering home with another group's nut harvest is somewhat mind-boggling. This is not to say that there were no attempts at implementing aggressive solutions, but simply that the attempts were probably unsuccessful. I do not know of any historic examples of hunters and gatherers who could be used as examples of this type of solution, but the peopling of unoccupied Pacific islands by Polynesian migrants might be roughly analogous.

2. Addition of land with other types of resources, thus inducing a shift toward a broad-spectrum economy. Such solutions were probably more frequently possible than the first example, but were probably not common in the Midwest. The territory surrounding the loci of Midwestern harvesting economies tended to consist of dense

forest in some instances, dense forest and prairies in others. Neither area would have added appreciably to plant and animal resources. Had the buffalo entered the Eastern prairies at an earlier date, the prairie areas might successfully have been incorporated into such an expanded subsistence zone, but their utility as a resource area would have been quite minimal prior to A.D. 1300.

3. Still another pattern of change would have involved movement into an area of lower carrying capacity. The effects of such moves could have been quite variable, but innovation would generally have been one of the effects of such relocations. If the new area was only slightly inferior to the original habitat, so that there were no radical disruptions to the traditional manner of life, one might expect changes along the lines postulated by Binford for the Near East (1968), where reduction in the subsistence base might have led to technological innovations and agriculture in an attempt to maintain a traditional life style. Or change might have been of the type that was associated with the removal of agricultural Bushmen into the Kalahari Desert, where they made a very successful transition to an economy based solely on hunting and gathering. This case is particularly interesting in the light of Lee's (1968) observation that the desert-dwelling Bushmen were able to maintain a higher subsistence level than their agricultural neighbors during periods unfavorable to the growth of domesticated plants.

The buffalo-hunting Plains tribes also exemplified adjustments of this type. Originally Woodland Indians with a mixed economy that included farming, they moved westward into areas that were probably increasingly ill suited for such mixed economies. By incorporating the horse and rifle into a pattern that emphasized buffalo-hunting, they developed a life pattern that differed radically from their former manner of existence. In a sense, however, they became agriculturists once removed since, in establishing an exchange system with and dominance over the sedentary Missouri Valley farmers, they were able to trade the products of their hunting for the agricultural products that they needed.

4. Trade in essential staples. The Plains buffalo hunters offer one example of this mechanism for alleviating deficiencies in the economy. A contemporary example can be found among the island populations of Melanesia, where inland people obtain essential meat

protein by trading local products with coastal people for fish and other commodities.

We do not know whether Archaic peoples were exchanging subsistence resources, but they were certainly involved in an extensive network that controlled the distribution of marine shell and copper. In historic times, there is ample evidence in the northern part of the Midwest of trade in maize, tobacco, furs, and other commodities (Wright, 1967, 1968).

5. Population reduction, either through the breaking away from the main group of small units or through internal conflict, might also have been a mechanism for making adjustments in the economic base.

6. Diffusion of new techniques for altering the economy to fit changed circumstances. In connection with this alternative, it is interesting that the greater number of seeming extinctions of shell midden cultures in the mid-continent area occurred in the central and northern reaches of that zone. In the southern part there is evidence for the continued accretion of shell middens well into Woodland times. The survival of the southern cultures might well have been the result of the diffusion of maize cultivation from meso-America sometime after 1000 B.C., although I doubt that they became effective agriculturists until much later.

The sites of the Indian Knoll Culture are close to ideal for studying the development and processes of change that a particular culture with a harvesting economy has undergone. Rather than having been eliminated from the cultural succession in the Midwest, the Indian Knoll Culture, in light of the corrected dates, may have been involved in patterns of change that could explain the development of such later cultures as Riverton, or even Lamoka. At present one can only point out the similarities and dissimilarities among these widely separated cultures that have so many features in common and so many characteristics that are specific to one particular culture. For example, Riverton is notable for the rarity of woodworking tools, particularly the grooved axes that are so characteristic of Indian Knoll and other Archaic cultures in the Midwest, and the virtual absence of the manufacturing of ground stone implements, both elements having been very important in Indian Knoll and variably represented in Lamoka.

But much can still be accomplished from use of the published sources, particularly when comparative data are needed. One valuable project would be the preparation of a statement on the material content of the Indian Knoll Culture and the ways in which the artifacts and their styles differ from other Midwestern Archaic cultures.

The information in Webb's publications can also be useful in dealing with another problem that is beginning to occupy the attention of archaeologists, namely, the utility of thinking of the Archaic as a developmental stage. We have long recognized the folly of attempting to characterize cultures as being agricultural and/or sedentary or nonagricultural and nonsedentary (Archaic) on the basis of the presence or absence of certain artifacts. Drawing in part on Alexander (1969), it can be shown that there are nonagricultural societies that possess digging sticks (Paiute, Bindibu, Vedda, Bushmen), metates (Paiute, Bindibu, Vedda, many Archaic cultures in North America), manos (numerous Archaic cultures in North America), ground stone tools (Warramunga, many Archaic cultures in North America), irrigation (Paiute), pottery (Andaman Islanders, Yokuts, Vedda, Capetown Bushmen), substantial housing (Adheulean at Terra Amata, Northwest Coast tribes, several North American Archaic cultures), and metal (Northwest Coast tribes, Old Copper Culture). On the other hand, some agricultural societies lack items that are normally associated with such societies in general. Pottery, although once made in many parts of Melanesia and Polynesia, is now totally lacking in the latter area. Metates are absent among the Ambo and in sub-Saharan Africa in general and among North American agricultural societies in the Deep South.

The term *Archaic* has long been defined in terms of the absence of pottery, burial mounds, agriculture, and settled village life, and the presence or absence of certain stone tools and preparation techniques thereof. And the general understanding of *Archaic* as a "stage" has long been a normative one, even though regional variants and such factors as seasonality have been recognized. Jennings (1968, p. 111) summarizes the normative view in his statement that, ". . . the Archaic can probably be best understood as a fundamental lifeway, not geared to any one ecosystem. Through this approach, regional differences are reduced in importance with the historical implications dominant." Obviously, it would be disastrous to apply such a view to the historic Paiute and Kwakiutl cultures, which in respect to subsistence and technology would have to be considered Archaic in terms of the traditional normative definitions. And it is equally disastrous to apply such an interpretation indiscriminately to the diverse prehistoric hunting-and-gathering societies that have been lumped under the heading Archaic. The range of variability of the prehistoric cultures may not have been as extreme as the historic examples that I have cited, but there is a considerable range in complexity of the various prehistoric societies. When one compares Indian Knoll and Riverton with some of the prehistoric Great Basin sites, there is a contrast in respect to the complexity of technology, extent of involvement in trading and procurement of exotic raw materials, average size of sites, and types of subsistence patterns, to name only a few of the variables. The Riverton settlement system is certainly closer to that of the Kwakiutl (Forde, 1963, pp. 72–73) than it is to that of the Paiute, which is probably true of many other aspects of the Riverton and Indian Knoll cultures. The view that there is a continent-wide Archaic stage leads only to the collecting of type fossils and contributes little to the understanding of the types of variation among these hunting-and-gathering societies and the reasons for the variations.

William S. Webb was a pioneer of the modern interpretation of the prehistory of North America. Dealing with data from a wide range of archaeological projects, he made significant contributions to the functional analysis of artifacts, the identification of the raw materials of excavated artifacts, and the study of settlement and subsistence patterns. But, even more important, Webb's *Indian Knoll* and other publications stand among the best archaeological reports of his time. Readers of this new printing of *Indian Knoll* should avail themselves of the abundant data assembled in Webb's publications and renew investigation of the Green River sites. As evidence concerning the life and death of a fascinating culture, they have much to offer the contemporary researcher.

Bibliography

Alexander, J.
   1969   The Indirect Evidence for Domestication. In *The Domestication and Exploitation of Plants and Animals,* ed. by Peter J. Ucko and G. W. Dimbleby. Aldine Publishing Co.

Binford, Lewis R.
  1968   Post-Pleistocene Adaptations. In *New Perspectives in Ar-
  cheology,* ed. by Sally R. Binford and Lewis R. Binford. Aldine
  Publishing Co.
Braun, E. Lucy.
  1950   Deciduous Forests of Eastern North America. The Blakiston
  Co.
Damon, Paul E., Austin Long, and Edward I. Wallick.
  1972   Dendrochronologic Calibration of the Carbon-14 Time
  Scale. *Contributions,* No. 57, Department of Geosciences, University of Arizona.
Flannery, Kent B.
  1968   Archeological Systems Theory and Early Mesoamerica. In
  Anthropological Archeology in the Americas, ed. by Betty J. Meg-
  gers. The Anthropological Society of Washington.
Forde, C. Daryll.
  1963   Habitat, Economy, and Society. E. P. Dutton and Co., Inc.
Fowler, Melvin L.
  1959   Summary Report of Modoc Rock Shelter. *Reports of Inves-
  tigations,* No. 8, Illinois State Museum.
Griffin, James B., ed.
  1952   Archeology of Eastern United States. University of Chicago
  Press.
Jennings, Jesse D.
  1968   Prehistory of North America. McGraw-Hill Book Co.
Johnson, Frederick.
  1951   Radiocarbon Dating. *Memoir,* No. 8, Society for American
  Archaeology.
Lee, Richard B.
  1968   What Hunters Do for a Living, or, How to Make Out on
  Scarce Resources. In *Man the Hunter,* ed. by Richard B. Lee and
  Irven DeVore. Aldine Publishing Co.
Le Page du Pratz, Antoine Simon.
  N.d.   The History of Louisiana. Pelican Press, Inc.
Lewis, Thomas M. N., and Madeline Kneberg.
  1959   The Archaic Culture in the Middle South. *American Antiq-
  uity,* Vol. 25, No. 2, Society for American Archaeology.
Marquardt, William H.
  1972   Recent Investigations in a Western Kentucky Shell Mound.

Research Report read May 4, 1972, at the Annual Meeting of the Society for American Archaeology, Miami Beach, Fla.

Morse, Dan Franklin.
1967   The Robinson Site and Shell Mound Archaic Culture in the Middle South. Ph. D. diss., University of Michigan.

Ritchie, William A.
1932   The Lamoka Lake Site. *Researches and Transactions,* Vol. 7, New York State Archaeological Association.
1945   An Early Site in Cayuga County, New York. *Research Records,* No. 7, Rochester Museum of Arts and Sciences.

Rolingson, Martha A.
1967   Temporal Perspective on the Archaic Cultures of the Middle Green River Region. Ph. D. diss., University of Michigan. University Microfilms.

Rolingson, Martha Ann, and Douglas W. Schwartz.
1966   Late Paleo-Indian and Early Archaic Manifestations in Western Kentucky. *Studies in Anthropology,* No. 3, University of Kentucky Press.

Rothschild, Nan A.
1972   Sex and Status: A Prehistoric Perspective. Paper read at the Annual Meeting of the American Anthropological Association, 1 December 1972, Toronto, Canada.

Schwartz, Douglas W.
1968   Conceptions of Kentucky Prehistory. University of Kentucky Press.

Struever, Stuart.
1964   The Hopewell Interaction Sphere in Riverine-western Great Lakes Culture History. In *Hopewellian Studies,* ed. by J. R. Caldwell and R. L. Hall, *Scientific Papers,* No. 12, Illinois State Museum.

Taylor, Walter W.
1948   A Study of Archaeology. *Memoir,* No. 69, American Anthropological Association.

Webb, William S.
1946   Indian Knoll. *Reports in Anthropology and Archaeology,* Vol. 4, No. 3, Pt. 1, University of Kentucky Press.
1950a   The Carlson Annis Mound. *Reports in Anthropology and Archaeology,* Vol. 7, No. 4, University of Kentucky Press.

1950b   The Read Shell Midden. *Reports in Anthropology and Archaeology,* Vol. 7, No. 5, University of Kentucky Press.

Webb, William S., and David L. DeJarnette.
1942   An Archaeological Survey of Pickwick Basin in the Adjacent Portions of Alabama, Mississippi, and Tennessee. *Bulletin,* No. 129, Bureau of American Ethnology.
1948a   The Flint River Site. *Museum Paper,* No. 23, Geological Survey of Alabama.
1948b   The Whitesburg Bridge Site. *Museum Paper,* No. 24, Geological Survey of Alabama.
1948c   The Perry Site. *Museum Paper,* No. 25, Geological Survey of Alabama.
1948d   Little Bear Creek. *Museum Paper,* No. 26, Geological Survey of Alabama.

Webb, William S., and William G. Haag.
1939   The Chiggerville Site. *Reports in Anthropology and Archaeology,* Vol. 4, No. 1, University of Kentucky Press.
1940   Cypress Creek Villages. *Reports in Anthropology and Archaeology,* Vol. 4, No. 2, University of Kentucky Press.
1947   Archaic Sites in McLean County, Kentucky. *Reports in Anthropology and Archaeology,* Vol. 7, No. 1, University of Kentucky Press.

Winters, Howard D.
1968   Value Systems and Trade Cycles of the Late Archaic in the Midwest. In *New Perspectives in Archeology,* ed. by S. R. Binford and L. R. Binford. Aldine Publishing Co.
1969   The Riverton Culture. *Monograph,* No. 1, Illinois Archaeological Survey.

Winters, Howard D., and Richard A. Yarnell.
N.d.   Plant Remains at the Riverton Site. Unpublished manuscript.

Wright, Gary A.
1967   Some Aspects of Early and Mid-seventeenth Century Exchange Networks in the Western Great Lakes. *The Michigan Archaeologist,* Vol. 13, No. 4, Michigan Archaeological Society.
1968   A Further Note on Trade Friendship and Gift Giving in the Western Great Lakes. *The Michigan Archaeologist,* Vol. 14, Nos. 3-4, Michigan Archaeological Society.

Table of Contents

INDIAN KNOLL

FOREWORD

This report constitutes Part 1 of Bulletin Number 3, Volume IV, devoted to the Shell Mound Complex of the Green River region. Part 1 deals with the archaeology of this site. Part 2, which is now being prepared by Dr. Charles E. Snow, will be devoted to a study of the skeletal material from this site. When published, the two parts will constitute Bulletin Number 3 which will complete Volume IV.

THE INDIAN KNOLL

Site Oh 2 Ohio County, Kentucky

INTRODUCTION

Ohio County in west-central Kentucky lies in the valley of
the Green River which forms the county's southwestern boundary
and separates it from the county of Muhlenburg to the southwest.
The Green River continues its general northwestward course
crossing McLean and Henderson Counties to empty into the Ohio
River near Henderson, Kentucky. The counties of McLean, Ohio,
Muhlenburg and Butler show much evidence of prehistoric occupancy. The region has long been known as the "shell mound
region of Kentucky," from the fact that the Aborigines living
on the banks of the Green River and its tributaries in early prehistoric times gathered great quantities of shell fish from the river,
both gastropods and pelecypods for use as food. The fish were
eaten and their shells discarded on the occupation site. Thus
large middens were accumulated along or near the banks of the
stream.

The large concentrations of shells on the river banks, mingled
with other forms of debris of an Indian occupation site, commonly
called shell mounds, are outstanding features of the river terrain
in this region of Green River. Their locations are well known to
the local inhabitants and in several instances, because the tops of
such shell mounds are the highest points in the vicinity they have
been selected as dwelling sites by modern man. They make a safe
refuge from floods in time of high water, and it often happens that a
farm dwelling, stables, cribs, and stock pens are erected on such
mounds. The Indian Knoll is one such shell midden, long recognized by the early settlers as a place of prehistoric habitation, hence
its name.

The "Knoll" was thus occupied by a dwelling house and out-
buildings up to the time of the very exceptional and disasterous
flood of 1937. At that time the dwelling house on the Knoll was
demolished by the flood and it was not later rebuilt. It was because of this fact that the site was available for excavation in
1939.

In the study of such a site, its probable topography when occupied by the aborigines, as revealed by present day conditions and the geology of the region are of such interest.

On these points, Mr. Marion H. Baugh, supervisor of this excavation, and a trained geologist makes the following observations:

TOPOGRAPHY

The general topography consists of fairly fertile bottom lands with rolling hills farther back from the drainage lines. These hills, especially when an outcropping of sandstone occurs, present rather steep faces, giving rise to many points along Green river known as "bluffs", although very few places show true bluff development. The relief is intermediate, a maximum being about 200 feet. Pool elevation of Green river at Paradise is approximately 370 feet above sea level.

Green river was dammed for navigation about 1830, and apparently this has had some effect on the drainage channels. Tributaries tend to meander and cut-off, an old-age aspect, due to the raising of their base level, but their valleys are still narrow enough to indicate mature erosion. Green river itself does not show pronounced meandering, but since the surrounding lowlands are filling with silt, its valley can be said to be in a fairly mature cycle of erosion. Much artificial drainage has been added to the numerous swamps of the area causing a ready run-off of rainfall and a consequent considerable variation between pool and flood stage in the main streams. Green river normally is sluggish but in flood time, especially during the winter months, carries a good volume of water.

As the present valley of the Green has some ox-bow lakes still retaining water, it is reasonable to suppose that at the time of aboriginal inhabitance, river conditions were quite different from what they are now. The major streams were probably more sluggish and meandering, and not very liable to floods. It is not to be assumed that the change from this supposed condition was caused by diastrophism, but rather by deforestation and artificial drainage channels dredged through the swamps and across the necks of meanders.

The linear rise of ground on which the Knoll is located is doubtless a natural levee. It is traceable for about a mile down-river and perhaps a half mile upstream from the site. The present river bank shows a considerable levee of this same type, with the lowest part of the bottoms being immediately below the Knoll. From this point the plain rises about four feet in the four or five hundred feet to the river bank. In the opposite direction from this low point the "second bank" rises at a considerable greater rate, perhaps fifteen feet in the hundred feet to its highest point. This fifteen feet does not include the five foot. deep accumulation of midden material making up the site proper. Continuing away from the "second bank", the bottoms slope very gently toward the channel of Pond Run, about a half mile from the river and paralleling it. Pond Run does not carry water at this point due to a ditch having been dredged between it and Green river about a mile above the site where the two streams are within 300 feet of each other. The channel is distinct, however, and can be traced to a point about one and a half miles below the site where it enters the river. These two streams, granting that Pond Run carried water in aboriginal times, enclosed an almost entirely water-locked area two miles long and a half mile wide, bordered on the southwest and southeast by Green river, and on the northwest by the creek. This area would contain approximately 700 acres of comparatively level plain not subject to floods to any considerable extent, an ideal location for a village of a hunting and fishing group.

As stated, the local topography indicates that the "second bank" on which the Knoll is located, is a natural levee. If this deduction is true, and there is considerable evidence, to show that it was at one time the main bank of the river, then it is also true that Green river did not assume its present channel by gradual sidewise cutting, but changed its course abruptly in time of flood, as is not uncommon in streams of old age. It is not possible to show that the main stream flowed immediately under the Knoll at the time of its occupation, but surely some body of water lay there as shown by sediments of a gumbo character mixed with the refuse on the river side of the site. This body of water may have been an ox-bow lake at the time, or even a cut-off meander, intermediate in age between main channel and ox-bow lake. This latter assumption seems most likely.

A twenty acre tract of timber lies immediately behind the site, reaching from a line 400 feet northeast of the crest of the "second bank" to a point beyond Pond Run. This tract has been left to act as a breakwater in time of floods, preventing Green river from cutting a new channel across this area. Considering this modern attempt to change course and the apparent natural levees, it is not improbable that the foregoing conclusions concerning the streams course during aboriginal times are true.

GEOLOGY

The area in question is on the southeast margin of the Illinois Basin. Outcropping rocks of sandstone and shale carry various commercial coals and frequent deposits of gravel of Pennsylvanian age of a workable character. Formations dip gently toward the west and north, as is to be expected. Faulting occurs to some extent, displacements as a rule being slight. All rocks are sedimentary, but the gravel deposits are made up of material transported from the Appalachian area and furnish various igneous and metamorphic rocks used by aboriginees for stone work. It is not to be concluded that all such foreign materials come from the gravel deposits, but certainly many specimens did. Others may have been traded into the area. Farther up the Green river drainage system occur sandstones of various ages saturated with the residue of an asphaltic crude oil. These formations do not produce oil, but are worked for rock asphalt. Commercially this asphalt consists of about 6% bituminous matter, although some of the richer areas show a higher percentage which must be mixed with weaker material to give the commercial grade. On exposure the mined rocks "bleed" the asphaltic contents—a film or drops of tar-like material form on their surfaces. This bituminous material, collected from the surface of streams or scraped from the rocks themselves, is the source of the "pitch" used in hafting tools and in making artifacts by the inhabitants of Indian Knoll.

A hematitic iron ore occurs in conjunction with some of the coal deposits but not in commercial grades or quantities. Shortly after the Civil War an affort was made to smelt the ore, but the enterprise was a failure. Remains of the smelter and engine house can be seen about a half mile downstream from Paradise on the Muhlenburg County side of the river. These deposits of iron ore furnished various colored iron oxide pigments, samples of which are found with burials in the Knoll.

Clays occur with the coals. These clays range in color from nearly white through gray to buff. Clayey shales also present sometimes are green in color. Such deposits are doubtless the source of pigments of these colors.

THE SITE

Indian Knoll lies on the southern edge of Ohio County, on the northeastern bank of Green River about a half mile up stream from the ferry landing at Paradise, Kentucky. The village of Paradise is on the southwestern bank of the river in Muhlenburg

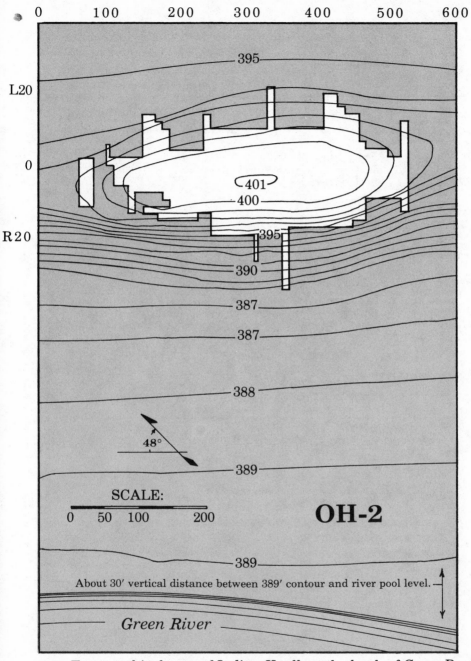

Fig. 1. Topographical map of Indian Knoll on the bank of Green R.

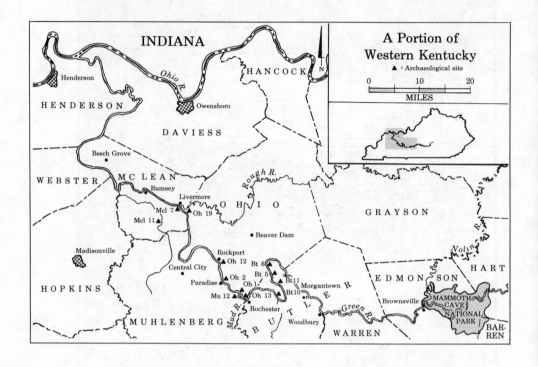

A Portion of Western Kentucky

▲ = Archaeological site

0   10   20
MILES

INDIANA

Henderson

Ohio R.

HANCOCK

N

Owensboro

HENDERSON

DAVIESS

Beech Grove

WEBSTER

MC LEAN

Rumsey

Livermore

Mcl 7   Oh 19

Mcl 11

OHIO

Rough R.

GRAYSON

Madisonville

Rockport   Oh 12

Bt 6

Bt 5

HART

HOPKINS

Central City

Paradise   Oh 2

Oh 1

Bt11

Morgantown

EDMONSON

Mu 12   Oh 13

Bt10

Brownsville

MAMMOTH
CAVE
NATIONAL
PARK

MUHLENBERG

Mud R.

Rochester

BUTLER

Woodbury

Green R.

Nol...

WARREN

BAR-
REN

Beaver Dam

County. The site is an ellipitical area about 450 feet long and about 220 feet wide, showing scattered shell on the surface. The long axis parallels the river and coincides with the "second bank" or natural levee, see Figure 1.

Over the "second bank" the shell was accumulated to a maximum depth of about 5 feet, thinning out at the edges. However, on the river side of the Knoll, due to the sloping of the original face of the bank toward the river and to the irregular surface, there were depths of shell deposit as much as 8 feet, see Figure 2. It appears that the first inhabitants of this site chose a section of the "second bank" not much higher than the bank elsewhere, and comparatively smooth on top. Then began the long continued deposit of shell mingled with the debris of an Indian village. The earth floor of a portion of this village site sloped toward the river, and was crossed by several ravines, as shown in Figure 2. Down this slope and into these depressions, the first deposits of debris accumulated, which had the effect of leveling up the site as occupancy continued. It seems certain that as this deposit continued, some of the debris on the side toward the River was pushed down the bank into a body of water. This conclusion is reached because on this side of the Knoll, the debris is mingled with silt deposits. Stratification in this deposit is hardly observable, suggesting that the site started on the bank of a slough or some slow moving body of water. This suggests that the inhabitants preferred to live on the bank of a cut-off meander where fishing would be good, and where the situation would be more sheltered than on the immediate bank of a large stream such as Green River. While the site here is a shell "mound," shell is by no means the major constituent in the accumulation. Except for a few thin clay layers, probably house floors, there is no evidence that earth in any considerable amount was ever carried upon the site; but much food, wood and other organic matter brought on the site resulted in a highly nitrogeneous soil very dark in color. In this black soil, shell was thoroughly scattered, together with many animal bones not yet fully decayed. Flint chips and broken stone artifacts were found and also much broken sandstone and many fractured river pebbles. These showed the effect of heat and immediately suggest their use in hot rock cooking.

Fig. 2. A trench profile on the river side of Indian Knoll. The trench is cut down to the old river bank on which the deposit began. Note the irregular surface crossed by ravines running toward Green River which lies just beyond the trees at the right, seen over the corn field in the rich bottom land.

PREVIOUS EXCAVATIONS

Indian Knoll as an important archaeological site was first brought to the attention of the scientific world by the excavations there in 1915 by C. B. Moore[1] for the Academy of Natural Sciences of Philadelphia. Following his usual method of field work, he came up Green River with his working crew by steamboat. The boat served as living quarters, laboratory, and store room as well as a convenient means of transportation. Moore stated that his crew of eight men devoted the equivalent of about 22.5 days to excavating this site. He reported the removal of 298 skeletons. This excavation by Moore was notable in that it was the first report of a non-pottery people in this region and was interesting because the cultural complex discovered was quite unlike any other previously found in the area. While his report of the site gave many details concerning burial customs, and was the first to report the association of antler hooks and so called "banner stones," he made no attempt to present data upon which a trait list defining this cultural complex could be prepared. After the discovery that shell mounds in Alabama[2] held a comparable cultural complex, the need of a trait list defining the characteristics of Kentucky shell mound dwellers became especially apparent. Since the Indian Knoll was the first site of this people excavated and since by the work of Moore it was so well known, it appeared highly desirable to attempt a second investigation of this key site, in the hope that enough of it still remained to enable a complete trait list to be determined. For somewhile it was impossible to obtain permission for this investigation, since for a time, title to the land was under the jurisdiction of the court. However, fate was kind. During the season of extraordinary river floods in the spring of 1937, the dwelling house and nearly all buildings on the site were destroyed. Shortly thereafter, the land came into the possession of a new owner, Mr. E. P. Williams of McHenry, Kentucky who kindly consented to this investigation.

ACKNOWLEDGMENTS

To Mr. Williams thanks are due for this permission to excavate the site. His cooperation and kindness made it possible to continue this excavation for nearly two years.

[1] Moore, Clarence B., 1916, p. 431.
[2] Fowke, Gerard, 1928, p. 73.
[3] Webb, Wm. S., 1939, p. 21.

Great credit is due to Mr. Marion H. Baugh, supervisor of the excavation, for the very excellent results obtained. Mr. Baugh thoroughly trained the crew in proper techniques, and so carefully supervised the work that much detailed information has been made available. The careful preservation of materials and an excellent photographic record are due to his industry. His critical observations on the geology of the region, the present topography, and suggestions on the probable conditions existing when the Knoll was occupied are quite valuable.

To Mr. Ralph Brown, state archaeological supervisor, our thanks are due for efficient conduct for administrative matters in connection with this long continued excavation. After the promotion and retirement of Mr. Brown as state supervisor, his place was ably filled by Mr. John G. Henson, who as state supervisor had charge of the administrative work in its closing phases.

Careful field work and complete field records would be of little value if they were not followed by equally efficient work in the laboratory for the processing of the material.

To Mr. Wm. G. Haag, Museum Curator and to Dr. Henry A. Carey, Supervisor of the Laboratory, acknowledgment is made of their efficient conduct of this considerable operation. The cleaning, restoration, repair, and catalogueing of more than 55,000 artifacts without serious damage to material or loss of records requires a high order of care and organization. This task, these gentlemen accomplished with the use of W. P. A. laborers who were largely unskilled and untrained except for the instruction received in the laboratory from these supervisors.

To Mr. Haag acknowledgment is also made for services in reading manuscripts and aid in working out many of the details in the preparation of this report. In particular he has counted and classified the same 800 pot sherds taken from the superficial portion of this site. While this pottery is not an integral portion of the shell mound complex, its description is important as presenting evidence which identifies later transcient visitors to this site. Mr. Haag's summary of this pottery published herein is a valuable addition to this report.

To Dr. Carey acknowledgment is also made for his aid in preparing drawings of atlatl restorations presented herein.

Miss Opal Skaggs, a graduate student in the Department of Anatomy and Physiology has made a study of the osteological remains of the Indian Dogs found at this site. Her report is published in the chapter entitled, "A study of the Dog Skeletons from Indian Knoll." Beside this study, she made a count of the identifiable animal bones taken from the general excavation of the midden. This necessitated the handling of a very large mass of material and the identification by comparison of hundreds of specimens. For this service this author is deeply grateful.

To Mr. George Neumann acknowledgment is made for his aid in determining the age and sex of skeletons deposited at the U. S. National Museum by Mr. C. B. Moore. This data has made possible comparisons with data taken in this recent excavation.

To Mr. Joseph H. Gardner, Graduate Assistant, Department of Anatomy and Physiology, acknowledgment is made of his service in studying the cause of bone staining which is quite prevalent on human and dog skeletons from this site. His findings, as the result of chemical analysis, published herein, are important as confirming the probable wide use of red ochre on bodies at the time of burial.

To Dr. A. Whetmore, Secretary of the Smithsonian Institution, acknowledgment is due for having identified animal and bird bones, on numerous occasions, and for the loan of type wolf skulls for comparison.

Acknowledgment is made to Dr. Henry van der Schalie of the Museum of Zoology of the University of Michigan for having determined the source of various shell artifacts.

EXCAVATION

It was feared that, after the excavation by Moore, very little of the site would be found undisturbed. It was hard to believe that after the removal of 298 burials, enough still remained to give a fair sample of the site. Determination to investigate again the Knoll, however, was made on the basis that even if but little remained undisturbed, that little might be enough to supplement the report of Moore and give a more adequate picture of this cultural complex. It was quite a surprise, therefore, to find soon after this excavation began that the site was much more extensive than it was previously thought to be, and that the excavation by

Fig. 3.   General view of part of excavation showing how strips 10 feet wide were cut down across the village, the slack earth being laid back on the last excavation area to avoid rehandling.

Moore so far from completely destroying the site, had in fact affected it only slightly. As a result of finding so extensive a site, 880 additional burials are reported herein, and they do not represent a total clearance of the site, since the closing of the work was not due to the completion of the excavation, but to administrative difficulties arising from a shortage in the W. P. A. labor quota in that County. However, this premature closing of the work at this site left only a very small portion of the mound unexplored.

The site was staked in the usual way in a rectangular grid of ten foot squares. A ten foot trench was opened along the site's major axis. This trench was cut down to undisturbed sand below the shell deposit, and the bottom surface was troweled in search of intrusive burials. Where pits in the sand were revealed, they were carefully excavated, see Figures 4 and 5. When the trench floor excavation was completed, the next ten foot section was cut down, the open trench being used as a place to deposit the slack earth. In this way rehandling of earth was reduced to a minimum. This method permitted a thorough and complete investigation of all the area covered. This method is illustrated in Figure 3. Here each 10 foot strip is still to be distinguished in the loose earth. This was continued from the top of the "second bank" toward the river to a point where the shell deposit became quite thin. In Figure 3 the distant line of trees to the right, marks the bank of Green River. The land beyond the excavation and to the right is the very fertile bottom land, which was just being prepared for spring planting when the picture was taken. Figure 2 shows how the original floor of the old village varied in elevation when the deposit of shell first began. In this figure is seen the original village floor, the amount of accumulated debris near the edge of the site where it was thinest. Note the rank stand of corn in midsummer and the dense foliage on the trees along the banks of Green River.

Next, the other northeastern side of the village was trenched in the same way to a point where the midden became thin and burials quite infrequent. The area excavated is shown in Figure 1, a topographic map of the site upon which has been superposed an outline of the trench system. The excavation covered the major portion of the existing midden and included the area investigated by Moore. It appears that in his excavations no well de-

Fig. 4.   Illustrating method of excavating pit burials.

fined trenches were dug, but that test pits were put down at random in that portion of the site available to him. He explained in his report that due to the occupancy of the site by houses and barns, only a portion of it could be investigated.

In the systematic trenching of the site in this investigation, the test pits of Moore were quite apparent. It appeared that these pits were not regular in size or location. Seemingly a pit was dug at random, and if it intersected no graves, it was refilled. If it cut into graves, it was exploited in any direction desired and enlarged by throwing out earth. In some cases the size of the excavation and its form suggested that single holes may have been enlarged until the slack earth surrounding the excavation became troublesome when a new pit would be opened. In the area showing previous excavations, there was a considerable amount of scattered human bone in the refilled earth, which seems to indicate that Moore, in many cases, did not remove the skeletons, but after this disturbance threw the bones back in the refill of the pits. Aboriginal disturbance of burials always accounts for some human bone scattered in the middens, but the amount of scattered human bone in Moore's recent pits obviously opened from the present surface, is much larger than in other portions of the midden. In this excavation, this recently disturbed human bone was sacked by squares and levels, but without assignment of a burial number. At the laboratory, it was often possible by using criteria as age, sex, color, texture and topography of bone, and location, to reassemble nearly complete skeletons. This was possible because of the very excellent preservation of most of the bone in this midden, and bone disturbed by Moore in 1915, if it was below the frost line, seems to have deteriorated very little in that time. In a number of cases of such "assembled" skeletons, where seemingly related bones of similar age, sex and condition were brought together, the only major portion of the skeleton which was absent was the skull. This leads one to suspect that Moore removed many skulls of individuals while the remainder of the skeleton was left in the midden. This may account for the fact as he stated that he sent to National Museum 66 skeletons—out of a total 298 burials found by him.

Univ.—2

Fig. 5.   Showing method of searching trench floor for deep burial pits.

SPECIAL FEATURES

While the burials at this site and their associations constitute the chief item of interest, yet much may be learned of the daily life of these people from the special features found in the midden as the result of this thorough investigation. The special features may be listed as follows:

Areas of fired clay in the shell midden	2
Areas with charred nuts in the debris	2
Cache of gastropod shells	2
Fireplaces, marked by ashes, charcoal and burned blocks of sandstone	6
Cache of flint points and knives	3
Cache of stone artifacts, pestles, hammerstones, grooved axes, nutstones and mortars	5
Total	20

While there was no evidence in the midden of any elaborate or permanent structure or dwelling, scattered individual postholes about fired areas seem to demonstrate that crude dwellings of a very simple kind may have been erected on the midden. Rarely, clean clay seems to have been brought from a distance and spread as a thick layer over an area about 15 feet in diameter, thus forming a floor upon which a fire was often built. About such a fire used for warmth as well as cooking, crude dwellings may have been erected. Walnuts, hickorynuts, and acorns were eaten in quantities and the shells accumulated as they were thrown out. Many may have decayed but those which had been later charred were preserved as found. Into these fires, sandstone blocks and river pebbles were placed to be heated, see Figures 6, A and C. When hot, they were probably dropped into a container filled with water. By repeating this process, the water could be boiled and food cooked. After much usage, the stone would break and either be left in the fireplace or thrown out in the midden. While fireplaces were marked by accumulation of such fired and broken sandstone, much of the same material is very uniformly scattered throughout the midden. About such fires, collections of small gastropods seemingly were boiled to extract their food value, and the shells if dumped in piles would produce such caches in the middens as have been found, see Figure 6 B. In the vicinity of every such dwelling and associated fireplace, the preparations of acorns, nuts, seeds and roots for food would require certain heavy artifacts as hammerstone, pestles, mortars, grooved axes, and pitted stones. These kitchen fireside tools would naturally be kept together for convenience, and if accidently covered by the shell midden, would remain as a cache, see Figures 6, E and G. Occasionally, groups of flint artifacts in excess of the immediate needs might be hidden about the house floors to be kept for future use, see Figures 6, D and F. All of these special features point to occupancy of the area as a dwelling site. All features found can easily be understood as the natural result of gathering, preparation and cooking of food on the site. Some have suggested that this evidence does not prove continuous occupancy of such shell midden sites, but may indicate *seasonal* occupancy at times when the dwellers were engaged in fishing. While it has been found that the people of the shell midden complex did sometimes live on hill tops[1] where there was little or no shell deposit, yet in the vicinity of Indian Knoll as in the case of many other shell mounds, there is no evidence of occupancy of this people elsewhere than on the middens, and thus, there is nothing to suggest *seasonal* occupancy.

Figure 6 shows a number of features which may be described as follows:

A. Feature 19 was a fireplace made near Burial 493. Note the deer antler to the left and the pitted stone in the distance. The fireplace is marked by sandstone rocks broken by heat. Burial 493 was apparently partly destroyed in the construction of the fireplace. The missing bones were not found.

B. Feature 12 consisted of a cache of gastropod shells. This may be a group of shells saved for some manufacturing purpose; however, artifacts made from this type of shell were not found in any grave association. The cache probably represents the residue of a quantity of the shell fish thrown out after heating in water to extract the edible portions.

C. Feature 5 was an area with a concentration of fired rock. Such sandstone blocks and river pebbles broken by heat mark fireplaces in the shell midden.

D. Feature 20. A cache of 10 flint knives.

E. Feature 11. A cache of two limestone pestles and a spherical hammerstone.

---

[1] Webb, Wm. S., and Haag, Wm. G. 1940, p. 70.

Fig. 6. Special Features. A, C, fire places; B, cache of gastropod shells; D, F, cache of flint blades; E, G, cache of heavy artifacts pestles and hammerstone.

F. Feature 10. A cache of five, well made, near triangular flint knives with straight bases.

G. Feature 9. A cache of three pestles.

DESCRIPTION OF BURIALS

By far the most important item of interest in this excavation is the burial complex which it revealed. It appears that burials were made in this midden during all stages of its formation. The very early burials at this site were of necessity made in the sandy second bank of the river. As the shell midden grew deeper, graves were dug from the surface of the midden as it existed at the time. When grave pits were dug in the sand, the sand was so compact that definite pit walls were formed. After the burial of the body, the pit was usually filled with the black midden debris quite in contrast in color and texture with the yellow sand in which the pit was dug. Even in cases where the sand from a pit was used in the refill, the original pit walls were firm and easily detected. As the midden grew and came to have a sufficient depth, a grave could be made without the excavation penetrating the sand under the midden. In such a case, the walls of the pits dug wholly in the midden would not stand. Due to the creeping qualities of the shell, these pits were little more than open basins. Into these a body might be placed and covered with the shell filled midden earth of exactly the same color and density as that removed from the excavation. In time, this earth would become consolidated and the pit wall would loose its identity, and could not easily be detected. Also in some graves in the shell midden, the body was laid in a depression in the shell accumulation, and was then covered by drawing together the shell midden earth about it. It thus happens that burials in the midden, and burials in the sand under the midden, present a very different general appearance. Thus burials in the midden generally show no pit walls and no definite form of a grave. In Figure 7 A and B, there is shown by contrast, the difference in appearance of the burials in pits in the sand (A), and burials in the shell midden (B).

Portions of Figure 7 are described in detail as follows:

A. Burials in pits were often independent, but closely spaced in the sand below the shell middens. At the right, Burials 266 and

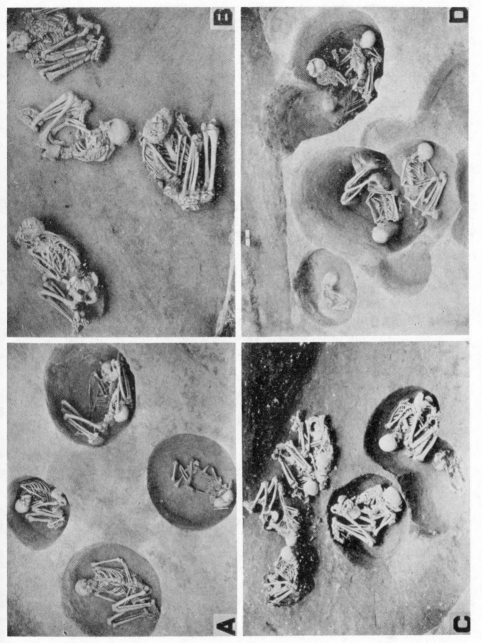

Fig. 7. Neighboring burials showing pits in subsoil, burials without pits in midden, and intrusions. Burial numbers as follows: A. (266-267), 268, 269, 270. B. 280, 281, 282, 283. C. 563, 564, 565, 566, 567, 568, 560, 569. D. 312, 310, 311, separately; and group, see Fig. 11.

267 are together in one pit, with burial 266 at the bottom. In the foreground is shown child Burial 268. Burial 269 is in the background and at the left is Burial 270. The bottom of these pits varied from 5.8 to 6.4 feet below the surface of the midden. These were all intruded into the sand below the shell midden.

B. When burials lay in the shell, usually no pit was observable. Such graves were necessarily not deeper than the shell middle at the point. Burials 280 to 283, inclusive were at depths of 2.9 to 3.3 feet below surface of the midden. At the left Burial 280 was fully flexed. Burial 281 is in the center and Burial 283 to the right. In the center foreground Burial 282 is shown. There were no artifacts.

C. In the background are shown, from left to right, Burials 563, 564, 565, 566, and 567. Of these, the last three are contemporary at a depth of 3.2 feet, but Burials 563 and 564 were not associated. All are in the shell just at the base of the midden. In the center of the illustration in a pit in the sand Burial 568 is 3.4 feet deep. In the pit to the right is Burial 560 and in the foreground is Burial 569.

D. This illustrates how in some burial areas pits were mutilated by the intrusion of later burials. In the pit at the left is Burial 312 at a depth of 5.7 feet. In the central pit Burial 309 lies on top of Burial 310, only a portion of which is to be seen. In the foreground is Burial 311 at a depth of 7.1 feet. The group burial to the right is presented in detail in Figure 11 C.

Due to the creeping of the shell midden matrix and to the shallow depth of the graves in the midden at the time some of them were made, many skeletons were crushed, and the large bones and the skull are often found badly broken. As a general rule, skeletons in the midden are poorly preserved, since the midden over them gives little or no support to them; however, the burials which were made in the sand, especially those where the grave pit attained a few feet in depth, are by contrast very well preserved. It happens that at this site, because such a large percentage of the burials were in pits in the sand, the preservations of the skeletal material from this site, as a whole, is little short of remarkable. At the site, in such pits, small bones, delicate bony tissues, and the skeletons of infants were often found in nearly perfect condition. Excavation thus was accomplished by running trenches 10 feet wide across the length of the site and carefully removing the 10 foot wide cut of the midden material to discover all burials and features, and to uncover the original sand surface of the old river bank. The surface of the original sand bank was carefully shaved by spade and trowel and investigated for intrusive pits. When found, such pits were carefully excavated from the original surface. This was difficult to accomplish as the pits were often small, quite deep, and the skeletal contents often in complicated positions. This could best be accomplished by workmen lying prone, and working with small tools as illustrated in Figures 4 and 5. Graves in pits were excavated by removal of the earth fill, carefully following the old pit wall in order to expose it without modification. The fill was so carefully removed that all skeletal material and artifacts were left undisturbed for photographing and drawing before being removed and packed for shipment.

ROUND GRAVES

The typical grave at this site may well be called a "Round Grave" as illustrated in Figure 8. Here burial pits were dug into the sand from different levels up in the midden. The pits extended into the sand for depths varying from a few inches to nearly 5 feet. These pits have nearly vertical walls, and usually a flat bottom. They vary from circular pits 2.1 feet in diameter to elliptical pits having maximum diameter from 2.4 to 3.1 feet. The skeleton in the typical round grave is flexed, folded, coiled or otherwise bent as shown in the illustrations so as to conform very exactly to the form of the pit. Some skeletons are so tightly flexed in these graves as to suggest that while in the flesh, the body was tied into a bundle, perhaps rolled in textiles into a bundle of the most compact form and placed in a pit only large enough to receive it. It is observed in Figure 8 that bodies were placed on either side, on the back, or twisted face downward. In the attempt to make the body conform to the shape and size of the pit, many very unusual and distorted positions were assumed by the skeleton. Such are illustrated in Figure 14 A, B and C. The form shown in Figure 14 F is the well known "sitting burial". Here the body placed in a sitting position in a small pit has slumped, allowing the skull to fall forward into the pelvic cavity, and the knees to remain elevated. There were not many burials of this

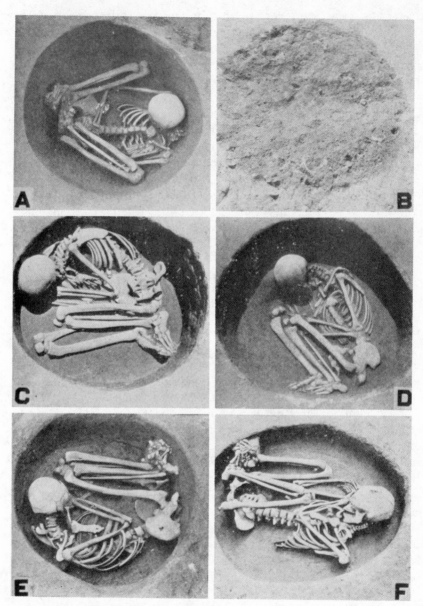

Fig. 8.   Round grave burials showing how grave pit was only large enough to receive a fully flexed burial.   B, shows the appearance of an unopened pit burial at level of old river bank.

type at the Knoll. The typical round grave thus occurs in the sand. Its contents as well as the pit is usually well preserved, and the grave usually contains no artifacts.

From the scores of round grave burials at this site, those appearing in Figure 8 have been selected as typical, and are described as follows:

A. Burial 501 is a typical round grave burial in a well formed pit, 2.3 feet in diameter and 1.1 feet deep. Base of pit is 6.2 feet below the midden surface. Body rests on its back, legs flexed on top, and head elevated because of the small pit diameter. Note disk beads at right forearm and at left elbow.

B. This shows the appearance of a typical burial pit in the sand below the midden before the pit was reopened in this excavation. This is pit of Burial 743, the bottom of which was 4.1 feet below the surface of the midden.

C. Burial 154 was in a pit, the bottom of which was 4.8 feet below the surface. The pit was 1.2 feet deep and 2.3 feet in diameter. No artifacts were found. Note how the body was arranged to fit the small diameter of pit, face down.

D. Burial 45 was in a pit in the sand 6.3 feet below the surface. The pit was 2.7 feet in diameter and 1.1 feet deep. This typical fully flexed burial was on the right side with shell beads at the neck.

E. Burial 168 was in a pit 4.8 feet below the surface. The pit was .8 of a foot deep and had a diameter of 2.1 feet. Note the curvature of the vertebral column, to make the body on the left side conform to the shape and size of the pit. No artifacts were found.

F. Burial 205 was in a pit 5.4 feet below the surface, lying on its back. The pit was only .5 of a foot deep, in the sand, and had a diameter varying from 2.4 to 3.1 feet.

INTRUSIVE BURIALS

When burials were made at this site, there seems to have been no attempt to mark their location. The area of the site was not large, and as stated, counting the burials removed by Moore, a total of 1178 burials have been recorded from this limited area. It is thus not surprising that later grave pits were ofttimes intruded into earlier graves. Due to the congestion of burials in parts of this area, intrusions were numerous. The business of living on the site required the digging of fire pits, rude fire basins, and occasional postholes as well as burial pits. The amount of this aboriginal digging was quite extensive, and resulted in the disturbance of many earlier burials by later pits. Figure 9 well illustrates the result of such practices, but gives only a faint idea of how much disturbance of burials was caused by intrusion. Often the intruded burial was not as deep as the original, and so but little damage was done the early burial, see C and E, Figure 9. However, if the early burial was somewhat shallow, its discovery by the aboriginal excavators of a new grave pit was no reason for discontinuing the excavation of the burial pit or changing its location. Usually the new pit was continued right through the old grave which happened to be in the path of the excavation. Often the earlier skeleton was cut away in part as shown in Figure 9 D and Figure 19 A. Frequently the disturbed portion of the skeleton was removed, and was not to be found in this investigation. Sometimes the excavated bones were later scattered in the fill of the recent pit. In a few cases, the disturbed bones were placed in a neat pile in the new grave along side the new skeleton. In some portions of this site, burials were so close together that disturbance by intrusion was the rule. This is illustrated by Figure 9 C and D.

Figure 9 may be described in detail as follows:

A. Burial 290 in foreground is shown to be intruded to a depth of 7.0 feet into a pit 7.9 feet deep containing Burial 291, which rested on top of Burial 292, only the skull of which is visible. In the digging of the intruded pit for Burial 290, slight disturbance of Burial 291 occurred.

B. Here Burial 60 fully flexed at a depth of 5.4 was intruded into an earlier Burial 61, which was not disturbed, not being reached by the later pit.

C. Burial 578, an adult, shown in foreground was intruded to a depth of 4.3 feet into the burial pit of a child Burial 579 which was at a depth of 4.9 feet. The pit of Burial 579 had in turn been intersected by a pit for Burial 580, which went to a depth of 5.9 feet. The order of burials in time, therefore, was 579, 580 and last 578. Burial associations of Burial 579 are shown in Figure 20 F.

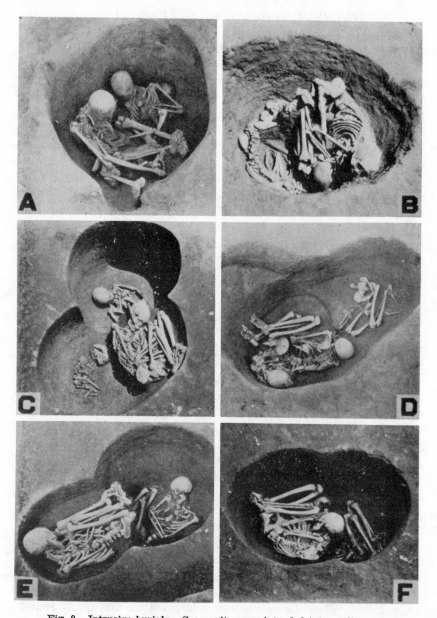

Fig. 9. Intrusive burials. Grave pits were intruded into earlier graves.

D. Burial 218 fully flexed, with artifacts which are shown in Figure 17 F, was made in a pit at a depth of 7.2 feet, which was intruded into Burial 219, which had been previously buried at a depth of 6.6 feet. The later burial pit cut through Burial 219. The pelvis, legs and right forearm of Burial 219, with beads about the wrist, were left in situ, in anatomical order. The other portions of the skeleton including skull, vertebral column and long bones, were removed, and after the placement of Burial 218, these bones were placed at the back of this burial in a pile against the pit wall.

E. Burial 590 fully flexed on left side at a depth of 3.1 feet was intruded into grave pit of Burial 591 which lay as shown at a depth of 4.8 feet below the surface.

F. Burial 475 fully flexed on right side at a depth of 5.5 feet was intruded into Burial 476 at a depth of 6.1 feet and covered the head and upper portion of the skeleton of Burial 476. Note how the burial pits intersected.

MULTIPLE BURIALS

The burial of more than one body in the same grave at the same time was quite a common practice. Here the general form of the grave was not changed. Often two bodies were placed in a pit in no way different from that of a single burial. See Figure 10. Where more than two bodies were to be buried, the pit usually remained circular, but was dug a little deeper and somewhat larger, see Figure 10 A, which is a pit containing six skeletons (Burials 370 to 375, inclusive). In many multiple burials, the grave is devoid of artifacts, as is the usual custom of single burials, but with this exception, multiple burials often show flint projectile points associated with the bones of the torso, but not imbedded in the bones. This suggests that these projectile points may have been imbedded in the flesh at the time of burial. This often repeated occurrence of single projectile points mingled with the bones of the torso suggests violent death, as a common experience at the Knoll, and may account for the frequency of multiple burials. In some cases the form of pit was modified into an elliptical pit made considerably larger than the usual round grave pit. Two or more bodies buried in these elliptical pits had much more room for placement, but burial position of the individual

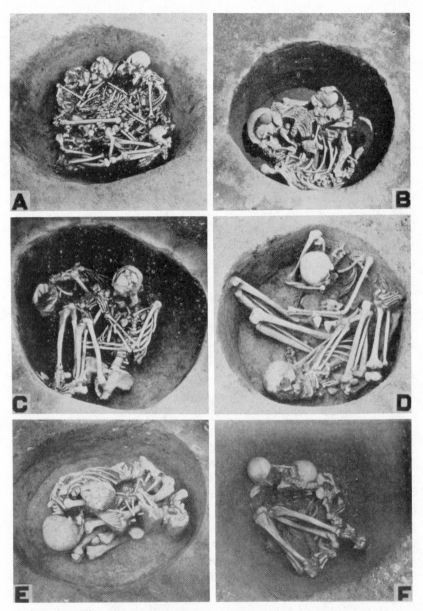

Fig. 10. Multiple burials. These occur frequently at this site and in such cases there is often evidence that the individuals died a violent death.

skeletons was much the same as in single graves, except that they were often piled one on top of the other, see Figure 11. The frequency of multiple burials is shown in "Burial Statistics".

The multiple burials illustrated in Figure 10 may be described in detail as follows:

A. In a pit, the bottom of which was 7.4 feet below the surface, there were placed six individuals numbered from left to right 370 to 375, inclusive. The skulls of Burials 370, 371, 372 and 373 are shown in a row in order. The jaw of Burial 374 may be seen below the skull of Burial 373. Burial 375 not visible was under Burials 370 and 371. No artifacts were with these burials save a small pestle which may be a chance inclusion in the grave fill and a single flint projectile point. This was found point upward by the side of the vertebral column of Burial 374. This may be significant as indicating the means of death of this individual, and suggest that all may have met violent death at the same time, and hence were buried together.

B. A young adult female Burial 514 was buried in a well formed pit 4.6 feet deep. This was a typical round grave burial. A child Burial 513 was placed on top. Note the stone pendant lying on two flint points near the center of the grave.

C. In a pit 4.1 feet below the surface, a young adult female Burial 525 was made. At the same level, and at the right side of Burial 525, a child Burial 526 was made. An infant Burial 527 was placed over the right arm of Burial 525.

D. These Burials 66 (in foreground) and 67 were placed in a pit at a depth of 6.3 feet. Note the black spot under the left eye socket of Burial 66. This hole indicates position of a flint projectile point which seems to have entered from the right, rear, under and inside the angle of the jaw. It cut through the back of the palate and lodged in the left maxillary sinus. It penetrated far enough to have the tip of the point emerge in the face below the eye socket. Another flint point was found among the ribs of this individual. Burial 67 seems to have been placed in a sitting position, the body resting against the side wall of the pit in a nearly vertical position. The knees were probably elevated. Due to slumping of the body, the knees fell to the right, and the head fell forward and rests face down on the lumbar region while the cervical vertebrae in anatomical order still rest against the pit

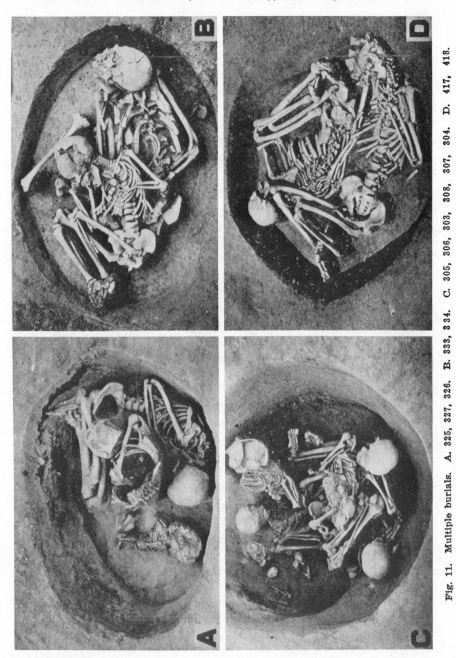

Fig. 11. Multiple burials. A. 325, 327, 226. B. 333, 334. C. 305, 306, 303, 308, 307, 304. D. 417, 418.

wall. Note the antler spear-point under the left humerus near the left elbow of Burial 67. This may well have been within the flesh at the time of burial.

E. In a pit 4.1 feet deep an adult Burial 272 was placed with the burial of a child, Burial 271 on top. A flint blank lay at the right tibia of Burial 272.

F. Burials 452 (right) and 453 (left) in pit at depth of 6.7 feet. An antler hook and handle were found near left arm in alignment. There were also two flint drills, a bone awl, and two worked stones.

Multiple graves in elliptical pits are illustrated in Figure 11, which are described as follows:

A. In a pit some 4 feet in diameter and at a depth of 3.9 feet, three burials were placed. Burial 325 was that of a child (left) and Burial 327 an adult placed on the left side, close to the right hand side of the pit, so bent as to conform to the pit wall. In the center of this pit, between two burials, Burial 326 was placed in a sitting posture. When the body slumped, the knees were displaced and the head became detached from the spinal column and fell over on the lumbar region of Burial 327. The remaining portion of the vertebral column being somewhat erect and above the other portions of the grave was further disturbed, probably by aboriginal occupancy above it. There were no artifacts.

B. Burials 333 and 334 were placed in a shallow pit at a depth of 4.6 feet. It is possible that Burial 333 was intruded into the burial pit of 334 after some time had elapsed. This would account for the partial disturbance of Burial 334. However, there appeared to be but a single burial pit.

C. In a pit some 5.4 feet in diameter and 7.9 feet deep at the deepest part, six burials were placed. In the foreground on the left, skull of Burial 306 and on the right foreground, skull of Burial 305 are shown. These two bodies completely flexed bore upon them the infant skeleton Burial 303. In the background on the right is the child Burial 308, the skull of which has an atlatl weight near it. Burial 307 lies on the same level and Burial 304 is to the right and slightly above. Note the cut maxillae (nostrum) of a carnivore protruding from under the right side of the skull of Burial 305. This carnivore has been identified as Martes pennati, (Fisher).

D. In a pit at a depth of 4.2 feet, Burial 418 was placed partially flexed, with its knees resting on the neck of Burial 417, which was fully flexed. There were no artifacts.

UNUSUAL BURIAL POSITIONS

As has been shown, most individual round grave burials at this site follow a very definite pattern. This seems to indicate that the body was rolled into a bundle—possibly tied in place by some kind of wrappings, and placed in a relatively small, circular pit. It may be possible that the body was encased in textiles or skins, or other covering so that the orientation of the body in the bundle could not be identified at the time of deposit in the pit. This might be expected to lead to peculiar and unusual placements of bodies in some cases. Whatever the reason, whether accident or intention, some skeletons are found in distorted and unusual positions in what would otherwise be typical round graves. Some of these are illustrated in Figure 12, which are described in detail as follows:

A. Burial 44, a partially flexed burial was in an elliptical pit 4.6 feet below the surface. Note that the body was twisted at the pelvis so that the ventral side was down, and the head was folded back under the body. This is the more peculiar since the size of the pit did not require this arrangement. However, the walls of the pit were not vertical. There were no artifacts.

B. Burial 398 was in a pit, 4.2 feet below the surface. Note the body was twisted at the hips and oriented dorsal side up. Note elevated scapula and head folded down under.

C. Burial 316 was in a well formed pit at a depth of 3.6 feet below the surface. Note how the body conforms to the pit wall, and is twisted so that the head is covered by the lower limbs.

D. Burials 55, 56, 57 and 58 are designated from left to right. Burials 57 and 58, both headless, were placed in an elliptical pit at a depth of 5.5 feet. This pit was intruded into an earlier pit containing Burials 55 and 56. In Burial 55 were two large bone awls and a stone bar atlatl weight. Under Burial 56 were found an antler hook and an atlatl composit shell weight of eleven segments not in alignment. With Burial 57 were two turtle carapace rattles and two flint points. With Burial 58 there were shell disk beads, an antler hook, and a shell composit atlatl weight. These

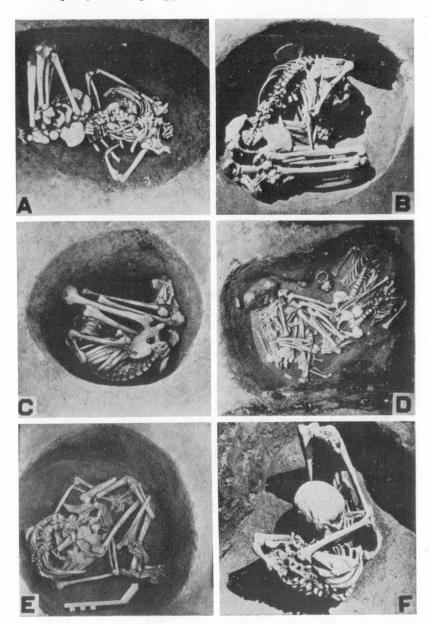

Fig. 12. Unusual burial positions. Such positions seem to indicate that body was rolled and tied into a bundle, possibly wrapped with textiles or other cover and placed in pit in peculiar position.

last were in alignment, and lay near the left pelvis. This atlatl weight was unusual in that it was made of ten equal sections, two of red stone and eight of shell. It is shown also in Figure 51 D. The stones constituted the third and ninth sections of the group of ten.

E. Burial 635 was in a pit at a depth of 4.3 feet. This body apparently was placed with head down and with pelvis high. The knees and head were on the floor of the pit. The feet were against the side of the pit wall. The body probably was rolled into a bundle, and either wrapped or tied in a bundle to hold the parts together to obtain this placement. After collapse of the body, the pelvis was upside down, and on top of the head which is on back, face up. The lumbar region of vertebra is dorsal side up, curving over and down the pit wall to the neck. In the collapse of the leg bones many large bones were broken.

F. Burial 100 was in the shell midden 5.2 feet deep with no evidence of any pit. It was clearly placed in a sitting position with knees elevated. When the body collapsed, the head fell forward into the pelvic cavity. There were no artifacts.

UNUSUAL GRAVES

The usual posture of the body as indicated by the position of the skeletons in the grave is properly described as "fully flexed". In some cases, however, where size of the grave permitted, the body was "partially flexed"—indicating less constraint at the time of burial, both from the walls of the grave or from any possible bindings or wrappings which it might have had. Bodies buried "fully extended" were so rare at this site (see Burial Statistics) as to be quite unusual. In the few cases of this occurrence, an elliptical pit was dug, see Figure 13 A, of sufficient length to accommodate the extended burial. Even in these few extended burials, multiple burials occurred, and even in this form of burial, the habit of piling one body on top of another still persisted, see Figure 13 C. In so large a number of burials as were found at this site it might be expected that a few would be so unusual as to conform to no pattern. Burial 368, illustrated in Figure 13 D, is such a burial. Figures 13 and 14, which show unusual graves, are described in detail as follows:

A. Burial 571 was one of the few fully extended burials at this site. It was a well formed elliptical pit at a depth of 3.7 feet

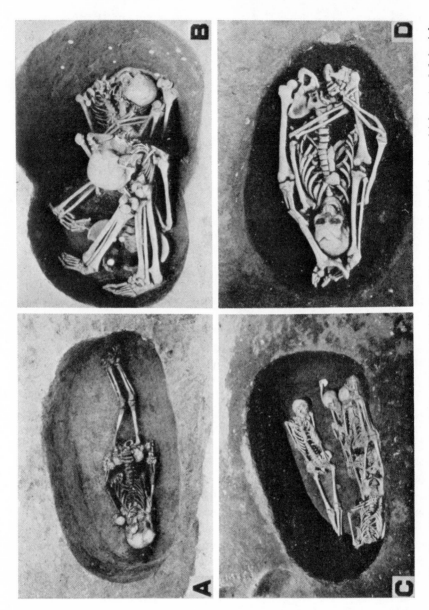

Fig. 13.   Unusual graves. A, single extended burial; B, sitting posture burial; C, multiple extended burial; D, ligaments severed at hips and legs folded over body.

below the surface.   Note the Anculosa beads at the left arm, the disk beads at right arm and pelvis and the ring-like shell beads and disk beads at neck.   At the left shoulder there was a pestle.

B.   Burial 642 in a pit was 4.8 feet below the surface.   It was a sitting burial which had slumped into the position as shown. Its pit had been intruded into an earlier pit containing Burial 643, which was at a depth of 6.5 feet.   Because Burial 643 lay at a greater depth, it was not disturbed.   Burial 642 in its sitting posture rested its back against that part of its pit wall which lay within the pit of Burial 643.   Thus, when the pit fill of Burial 643 further settled, Burial 642 could not retain its vertical position, but its vertebral column inclined outward into the older grave pit, and came to rest outside of its own pit wall.

C.   In this oval pit 6.4 feet long by 3.9 feet wide at a depth of 4.7 feet were placed four extended burials.   The separate burial was designated No. 611.   Burial 612 is next to it, lying in the same orientation and Burial 614 lies nearly on top of Burial 613, with the feet of Burial 614 on top of the skull of Burial 613.

The artifacts of flint and shell were numerous, but few can be seen in the photographs since most of them are obscured by bones.   Note the quantity of Anculosa beads at the pelvis of Burial 613.

D.   Burial 368 was in a shallow pit in the shell midden at a depth of 2.2 feet.   It is notable because of the very unusual disposition of the body at burial ,which suggests that the body may have been tied in a bundle in this form before deposit in the pit. Possibly the ligaments of the legs had to be cut to permit this position.   There were no artifacts.

A.   This shows how the burial pit of Burial 121 was intruded through Burial 120 at a higher level.   A portion of the skeleton of 120 was cut away by the aboriginal excavators of the pit for Burial 121.   Aboriginal disturbance of graves by later burials is quite common.   This would seem to indicate that graves were not marked, and if when a burial pit was being excavated, it was found to enter an earlier grave, that fact was not sufficient reason for a change in position of the pit.

B.   Burial 31 was placed face down on the bottom of a pit at a depth of 4.9 feet.   The head was bent backward with its arms

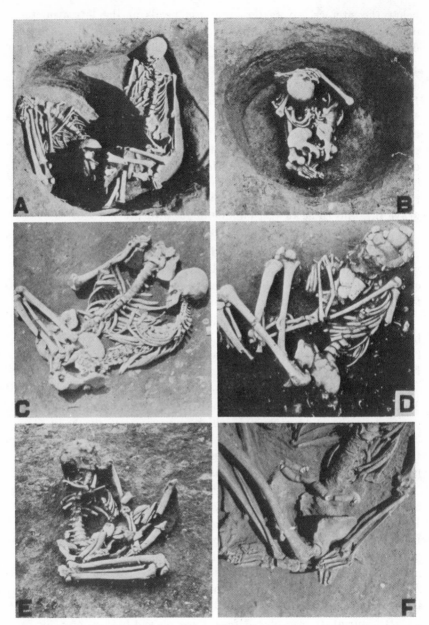

Fig. 14.   Unusual graves.   These illustrate intrusion, dismemberment and unusual burial associations.

about it, which reduced it to the smallest possible volume. The body does not nearly fill the pit dug to receive it, which suggests that the body in this form was wrapped in cordage or rolled in textiles or otherwise tide in a bundle and when buried, was placed ventral side down in the pit.

C. Burials 639 and 640 were in the shell midden at a depth of 1.7 feet. There was no evidence of aboriginal disturbance after burial; hence, the conclusion is forced that these bodies were partly dismembered before burial. Burial 639 to the right had lost both arms and the left leg. Burial 640 had lost both legs save the left femur, which had been broken and healed, and both arms were missing. The skull which lay under the right leg of Burial 639 was crushed.

D. Burial 395 was a partially flexed burial 2.1 feet deep in the shell midden. There were three conch shell gorgets under the chin, six bone pins below forearm and a beaver incisor tooth.

E. Burial 827 was a partially disturbed burial 2.2 feet deep in the shell midden. Near the center of the body were three mussel shells, three antler tines, six flint points, and shell pendants in imitation of animal teeth.

F. Burial 233 was placed in the shell midden at a depth of 2.6 feet. About the waist was a string of beads made of shell disk beads, strung between larger beads as shown. Two of these were stone, and two were cannel coal. All were barrel shaped. The fifth large bead was of bone and was cylindrical in form.

DISMEMBERED BURIALS

Disturbance of burials by the intrusion of later burial pits and by aboriginal digging in the midden incident to the normal life at this site has been discussed. As explained, this disturbance of burials resulted in the loss, by removal, of parts of many skeletons. When incomplete skeletons were thus formed, it was possible in many cases to attribute the incompleteness to aboriginal disturbance, which was usually obvious. However, in many graves where no intrusion was observable and where every indication pointed to no disturbance since burial, skeletons were found with some parts missing. This leads to the definite conclusion that some bodies were dismembered before burial, or possibly mutilated by

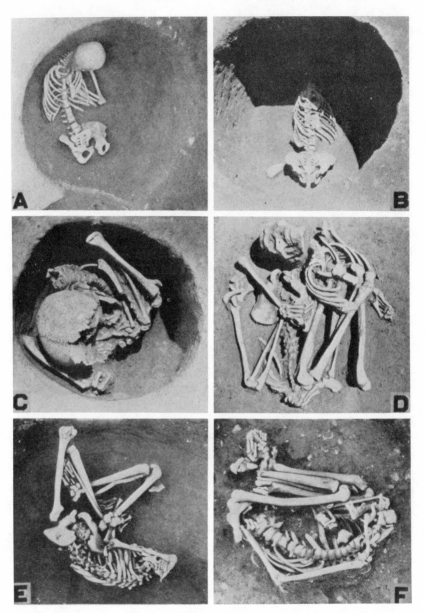

Fig. 15. Dismembered burial. The dismemberment and mutilation of bodies before burial was frequently found.

the destruction, or removal of parts at the time of death. Decapitation was fairly common, see Figure 15 E and F, but the loss of arms or legs, or both, was also found, see Figures 14 C and 15 A and B. Sometimes the torso was cut in two and the parts buried in non-anatomical order. Dismembered burials are usually without artifacts, except that they may have projectile points in association. The association in every case is such as to suggest that the projectile point may have been the cause of death. Burial 537, see Figure 15 B, which was without skull, arms or legs, had a conical antler projectile point lodged in the spinal column between the sixth and seventh cervical vertebrae, which by cutting the spinal cord probably would have produced death instantly. Thus the evidence of associated artifacts, in many cases of dismemberment, suggest that dismemberment was the result of mutilation of bodies at the time of violent death, possibly by enemies in combat. All dismembered burials were more or less incomplete; that is, in no case was a body dismembered merely to allow all parts of it to be placed in the grave. Always some parts were missing, usually some extremeties.

Figure 15 illustrates various forms of dismemberment which are described in detail as follows:

A. Burial 536, age 21 years, female. Both clavicles and all long bones were missing, except left humerus. The pelvis, vertebrae, ribs and sternum were all in position. Skull lies face downward inclined to the left. Burial was in a pit at a depth of 4.7 feet. There were no artifacts and no evidence of aboriginal disturbance.

B. Burial 537, age 26-28 years, male. Skull-less and all long bones missing except the left clavicle. Pelvis, vertebral column, ribs, and sternum were all in position. Note the lipped edges of the lower vertebrae suggesting arthritis. Pestle near pelvis. Conical antler spearpoint lodged between 6th and 7th cervical vertebrae, see Figure 29 D. Burial was in pit at a depth of 4.8 feet.

C. Burial 655. Child, six to seven years, male. Body severed through the lower back region at the level of the 5th lumbar vertebrae, dividing the body into two halves. The lower extremities and the hip region was disposed of elsewhere as only the upper half with the neck and skull were found in the grave. The arms with both shoulder girdles are in anatomical position along with chest cavity. Possibly the neck was also cut through at its base about the level of the 6th cervical vertebrae, and the head with the attached neck bones placed on the torso. Possibly due to natural slumping, the head and neck bones may have fallen forward onto the trunk, face downward. It is more likely, however, that the neck was intentionally cut through, which facilitated its placement as found since the body had been dismembered before the upper body parts were placed in the pit where found. The pit was 3.8 feet deep.

D. Burial 34, adult male. Clearly a case of dismemberment. First the body appears to have been cut through in the upper chest region at the level of the 6th-7th thoracic vertebrae, breaking the right collar bone in front at the point of greatest anterior curve. The legs were separated from the severed trunk at the hip joints and the trunk with attached pelvis and left shoulder blade placed abdomen downward with the upper parts bent to the left. Next, perhaps the arms were laid on, the left one first, flexed sharply at the elbow and placed to the left of the trunk in such a way that the right hand lay palm down on the left elbow. The severed legs were placed next, each bent upon itself at the knees. The left leg was placed first with the foot end at the top of the trunk and the thigh bone lying with its head at the heel. The right leg was placed in the opposite manner, the thigh bone laid against the left arm and on the hand, the head extending beyond the lower end of the trunk. The knee-joint was sharply bent so that the right foot lay above the left knee. Last the head with its severed neck and upper trunk section was placed obliquely across the lower end of the trunk with the upper chest section lying on the ends of the leg bones which were at the side of the lower trunk section. The curves of the spinal column sections and the flexure of the limbs suggest that force was required to achieve this curious arrangement. The body lay on the sand at the base of the shell midden at a depth of 5.8 feet.

E. Burial 383. Skull-less burial placed neck first in pit. The left arm is in position, slightly bent at the elbow. The spinal column is curved to the left and twisted from the lower back and pelvic region which lies abdominal surface downward, to a sideways position at the top of the rib cage. Both legs remained in position, articulated with the pelvis and trunk section and are both tightly flexed at the knees. The lower legs and feet are crossed so that the right foot lies under the left hip joint in front on the lower side and the left leg under the right knee joint. Body is in the shell midden at a depth of 2.5 feet.

F. Burial 197, a young adult male Skull-less burial (lower jaw in place) placed on the right side with the right arm and both legs tightly flexed. The feet were brought tightly up against the buttocks, the knees resting against the chest. The left arm is slightly bent at the elbow with the hand lying on the lower abdominal region. Later the hand bones fell into the empty pelvic cavity. Body was in shell midden at a depth of 2.7 feet.

DOG BURIALS

Many dog burials were found in this midden. It appears that many dogs were buried with the same degree of attention to grave pits, and placement of body as was accorded to their human contemporaries. In some cases, the dog was buried in human graves, in such close association as to indicate simultaneous interment. Sometimes two dogs were placed in the same grave. This form of burial association is illustrated in Figure 16. Note how in some cases, Figure 16 A and D, the dog is placed at the foot of the body, sometimes at the side as in Figure 16 B, C and F, and sometimes on top of the human body, Figure 16 E. Burials with dogs in association usually are devoid of artifacts.

A total of 21 dog burials were found during this excavation under conditions as follows:

Single dog burials in their own graves, not associated with human remains 8
Single dog burials in human graves 9
Double dog burials in each of two single human graves, dogs 4

                    Total 21

Thus of 13 dogs buried in human graves:

3 males, aged 23 to 28, had one dog each 3
3 females, aged 23 to 25, had one dog each 3
1 disturbed burial, undetermined sex and age, had one dog 1

2 males, aged 7 and 9 years, had one dog each 2

2 females, aged 1 and 3 years, had two dogs each 4

Total 13

While statistically the data is too meager to yield highly valid conclusions, it seems to point to the burial of dogs with females as often as with males, and to association with children as well as adults. Seemingly female children were the only ones having two dogs in a single grave.

In the following tabulation there is shown the age and sex of the human skeletons having 13 dogs in association. Their age and sex determinations are estimates made by Dr. Charles E. Snow after a careful study of the skeleton material:

Human Burial No.	Age in Years	Sex	Dog Burial No.	Total Dogs
73	26	M	4	1
115	28	M	7	1
152	1	F?	8, 9	2
232	7	M?	11	1
245	9	M	13	1
319	25	F	14	1
393		Indeterminate	15	1
505	3	F?	16, 17	2
652	24	F	18	1
732	23	F	19	1
817	23	M	21	1
				13

From such definite evidence of intentional association as is presented in Figure 16, described in detail below, one must conclude that dogs were often killed at the time of burial of their owner, and buried with them perhaps as a symbol of continued association in the spirit world. From the general excavation of this midden, a large amount of animal bone was taken from the debris. This mass of bone revealed that deer were eaten by the hundreds. Such bones occur in quantities on occupation levels, about camp fires, or scattered through the midden. Along with the bones of deer and other animals, undoubtedly used for food, were found the bones of dogs. These dog bones, occurring scattered

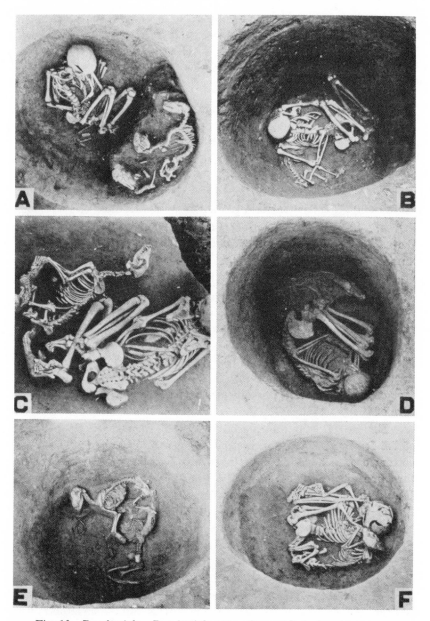

Fig. 16. Dog burials. Dog burials were often made in human graves.

in the midden and about fireplaces, in precisely the same situations as the bones of deer, wild turkey, and fish bones, seem to suggest that the dogs were also eaten on occasion by these people, and the bones thrown out in the debris along with those of other animals.

Figure 16, illustrating the burial of dogs in human graves, may be described in detail as follows:

A. Burial 245 was in a pit at a depth of 4.9 feet below surface. Dog burial conforms to the same pit wall, but at a slightly higher elevation, indicating that the burial pit was partly filled when the dog burial was made. They were, however, buried at the same time as there is no evidence of later disturbance or intrusion.

B. Burial 115 was in a pit at the depth of 7.8 feet below the surface. The dog was first laid on the floor of this pit and human body placed on top.

C. Burial 562 was laid in the shell at a depth of 1.7 feet. The dog was laid at the right side at the feet. These burials were made at the same level and at the same time. They were clearly associated as there was no evidence of later disturbance or intrusion.

D. Burial 319 was laid in a pit, completely flexed at a depth of 6.3 feet. The dog was laid on the floor of the pit at the foot of the burial and its body arranged to conform to the curvature of the pit wall.

E. Burial 505 was placed in a well formed pit at a depth of 7.2 feet. The body of this very young person was placed on the bottom of the pit and about the head, Dog burial 16 was laid on the same level. A second dog (Dog burial 17) was laid on Dog burial 16 and the legs extended over the head and shoulders of the human Burial 505. The human burial and the two dogs were evidently placed in the pit at the same time.

F. Burial 232 was in a pit 3.1 feet deep below the surface of the midden. The body was fully flexed on the right side. The body of a dog fully flexed was laid on its right side just at the back of Burial 232. It appears that the dog's body was intentionally arranged to take a position similar to the human skeleton. The left foot and nose of the dog skeleton rests upon the left shoulder of the human skeleton.

BURIALS SHOWING ATLATL HOOKS AND WEIGHTS IN ASSOCIATION

One of the most important problems connected with the study of the shell mound cultural complex is the occurrence and use of associated antler hooks and drilled stone and shell prismatic forms, believed to be atlatl hooks and weights, which together constituted throwing sticks. Evidence for this belief has been previously presented.[1] One of the important reasons for excavating the Indian Knoll was to obtain as *exact* and as *extensive* information as possible on the actual occurrence in burial association of these artifacts. Some 43 burials furnished evidence on this important problem, which will be further discussed later in this report. It is not possible to produce illustrations of every such occurrence, but in Figures 17 to 20, inclusive, numerous illustrations are presented, which portray the wide variation in the manner of occurrence of these implements in the graves. It is hoped that each burial, which is presented showing this association, is described in sufficient detail to enable the critical student to assess properly the value of the evidence presented.

A detailed description of Figure 17 is as follows:

A.   Burial 561, a male, estimated age 24 years, lay in a pit the bottom of which was 6.7 feet below the surface. There were two atlatl weights, one a stone prism broken longitudinally and the other a composit weight of eight shell sections. Both lay together in front of the body under the arm bones. One antler hook points toward the pelvis, and the other may be seen lying by the side of the shell composite weight. It appears that the wooden shaft of the atlatl which had the shell weight was broken in two, and the weight, with its hook, was laid side by side in the grave before the body was deposited, for the arms lie on top of these artifacts. The atlatl with the stone weight was deposited after the body was laid down. The weight was broken, ceremonially, and hook and weight deposited separately. With this burial were shell disk beads, and two shell ornaments at the neck, and a bone pin near the right hand.

B.   Burial 560, a female, estimated age 22 years, was in a pit the bottom of which was 6.0 feet below the surface. Lying on the chest of this skeleton was a composit shell atlatl weight and as

---

[1] Webb, Wm. S. and Haag, Wm. G., 1939, p. 50.

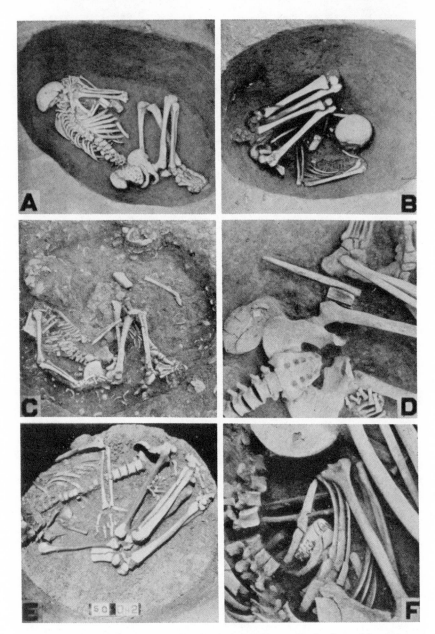

Fig. 17. Burials with associated atlatl weights, antler hooks and handles.

shown, an antler hook nearly in alignment, and at the correct distance apart, which is taken to indicate that an unbroken atlatl had been laid across the body. The slumping of the body allowed one end of the hook to fall slightly.

C.   Burial 785, a male child 6-7 years old, lay in the shell at a depth of 3.5 feet. Near the body and in front of it lay an antler handle and an antler hook. The alignment is not good, but the displacement is no more than could be possible in shifting shell at that depth. It is, therefore, considered that handle and hook, when deposited, were united and in line. The terrapin carapace shown close by within the pit was a rattle, and between the knees and the skull, a considerable body of woven textiles had been placed. This had been reduced to dust; only its form was observable.

D.   Burial 217, a male, estimated age 21 years, lay in a pit at a depth of 4.8 feet below the surface. Note the terrapin carapace rattle and the antler hook near left hip, with the broken atlatl weight. Both segments of the weight lay together, parallel to and touching the hook. The weight which had been split longitudinally was broken *before* being deposited. It could not have attained the position as found by being split by natural forces *after* it was deposited. It is believed that the atlatl was broken and all parts piled together in the burial pit *before* the body was laid down. The clearance between heel and hip when the body was in the flesh was insufficient to have permitted placement of artifacts after the burial of the body.

E.   Burial 69, a male, estimated age 21 years, was in a pit the bottom of which was 8.5 feet below the surface. There is shown an atlatl stone weight at knees. This weight is split longitudinally, but appears to have fractured after it was deposited. Just inside the right arm may be seen an antler hook. The displacement of the weight and hook is no more than what could have been expected had this atlatl been laid on top of this body. This is taken to represent a complete atlatl at time of deposit. However, when the skeleton was lifted a second antler hook and a stone bar atlatl weight were found together under the skeleton, which indicates an atlatl broken and parts placed together before the body was deposited. There was a trace of red ochre in this grave, and many other artifacts, among them a carapace rattle.

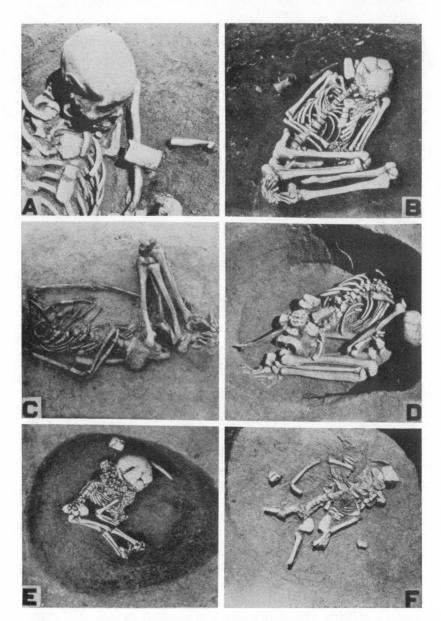

Fig. 18.   Burials with associate atlatl parts in situ.

F. This is a "close-up" of Burial 218, a male of estimated age of 37 years. This was a pit the bottom of which was 7.2 feet below the surface. Note the 8 segmented shell atlatl weight showing under the ribs. Note the antler hook under the leg bones. These artifacts were in alignment, and the atlatl of which they were part was surely placed in the pit before the burial was made. The composit shell weight had asphalt attached to it, which apparently was used to cement the hook, weight and shaft together.

Illustrations presented in Figure 18 may be described as follows:

A. This is a close up of Burial 39, a male, estimated age 17 years, which was in a pit the botttom which was in the sand 6.7 feet below the surface. There were disk shell beads about the neck, red ochre in the grave pit, and a stone atlatl weight with antler hook in near alignment and with their ends close together. The weight lay nearly balanced on the left humerus.

B. Burial 495, a male of estimated age 17-18 years old, was in the shell midden only two feet below the surface. There were large disk shell beads and two stone beads under the chin, and an antler hook near the left shoulder. Nearly in alignment and separated about 5 inches from it was the antler handle as shown. This is in the theoretically correct position for it if a complete atlatl had been laid in the grave. The subrectangular bar just above the left shoulder, had it been found out of association, would hardly have been regarded as an artifact since it is crudely finished. However, in this association, it seems surely to be a bar atlatl weight, probably part of the implement laid in this grave.

C. Burial 353, a female of estimated age of 18 years, was in the shell midden at a depth of 4.1 feet below the surface. At the right side above the pelvis and under the right forearm was an antler handle and antler hook in alignment, and about the proper distance apart to constitute the residue of an unbroken atlatl. It lay under the right arm and might have been so laid after the placement of the body, but its placement probably preceeded that of the body.

D. Burial 124, a male of estimated age 28 years, was in a pit at a depth of 5.8 feet below the surface. The only artifacts were an antler handle and an antler hook as shown. These are in alignment, but handle seems to have turned end for end. The atlatl may

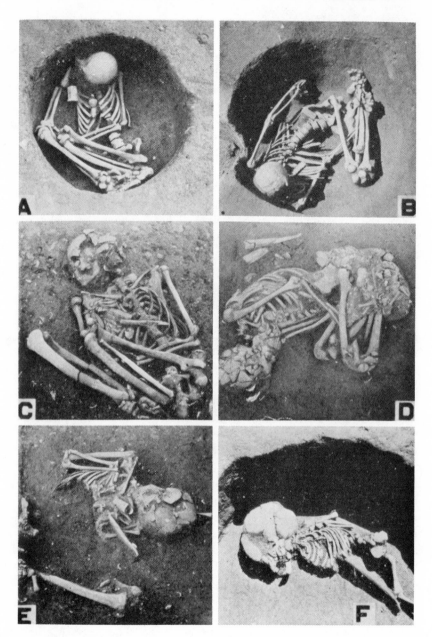

Fig. 19. Burials with associated atlatl parts in situ.

have been intentionally broken, or it seems possible that since it was laid on top of the body, the handle may have become reversed during the slumping of the body.

E. Burial 396 appears to be that of a male infant between 1.5 and 2 years of age, which was in a pit the bottom of which was 4 feet below the surface. There is shown a quantity of Anculosa beads about the thorax and a large stone bead and a few shell disk beads under the neck. Above the head there was a stone atlatl weight in alignment with an antler hook. These certainly are in correct position to indicate the deposit of an atlatl, and seem possibly to have been placed in the grave before the burial.

F. Burial 158, a male of an estimate age of 3 years, was in a pit the bottom of which was 6.8 feet below the surface. Note the disk shell beads in lines indicating they were once on a string, and the animal jaws. The nose portion of the skull, identified as Martes pennati· (Fisher), was with this burial. There was a stain of red ochre in the pit and as shown, the body lay upon an antler hook and a stone atlatl weight in near alignment, and the correct distance apart to indicate the deposit of a complete atlatl in the grave before the placement of the body.

Further illustrations of the occurrence of atlatl parts in burial association presented in Figure 19 may be described in detail as follows:

A. Burial 798, a male, estimated age 15 years, was in a pit in the sand at a depth of 4.3 feet. Note stone atlatl weight near chin, and antler handle and hook placed along the right humerus.

B. Burial 518, a female of estimated age 21 years, was in a pit at a depth of 4.0 feet. Note atlatl weight at left side of pelvis, and an antler hook under right shoulder. In the photo the hook seen over the right shoulder forms a line with the right humerus. The hook end was broken. This appeared to be an old fracture, i.e., hook was broken before placement in the grave. There were no other artifacts.

C. Burial 796, a male, estimated age 13 years, lay in the shell midden at a depth of 2.5 feet. Note antler hook and stone atlatl weight (broken) lying on chest. Weight was broken before placement.

D. Burial 754, a male, estimated age 15 years, lay in the

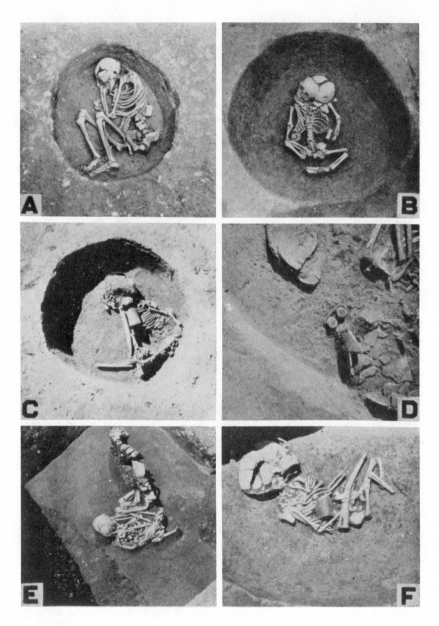

Fig. 20. Burials with associated atlatl parts. D, shows a copper ornament in situ.

shell midden at a depth of 3.9 feet. Note antler handle, antler hook (broken) and fragments of atlatl weight piled together at upper left. The fragments of the stone were scattered, but all were found and the stone was completely restored in the laboratory.

E. Burial 766, a young adult male, was at a depth of 2.9 feet in the midden. Note bone pin (hairpin) at back of head, and antler handle and antler hook in front of the face. Disturbance of the burial was caused by two recent postholes passing through the skeleton. This excavation disturbed the antler hook and left it upright, with drilled end up as shown.

F. Burial 92, a male infant, estimated age 8 months, was in a pit at a depth of 4.6 feet. Note the antler hook at the knee. An atlatl weight was found broken with fragments scattered in the fill of the pit overlying this burial.

Illustrations presented in Figure 20 may be described as follows:

A. Burial 140, a female, estimated age 22 years, was in a pit near the base of the midden at a depth of 4.2 feet. Note the stone atlatl weight in the left lumbar region. When the skeleton was removed, an antler hook was found under the vertebral column, lying by the side of and parallel to the perforation of the hole in the stone weight. This seems to indicate an atlatl was broken in two, and the parts deposited side by side on the pit bottom, before the placement of the body.

B. Burial 654, a male infant of estimated age 2 years, was in a pit at a depth of 3.8 feet. There were shell disk beads about the neck. A stone atlatl weight had been split longitudinally and deposited one half near the left hand, and the other near the left foot. This may indicate a ceremonial breaking.

C. Burial 743, a male infant of estimated age 8 months, was in a pit at a depth of 4.1 feet below the surface. There was, as shown, a hollow bonê tube 135 mm. long, and on top of the body a stone atlatl weight and antler hook lay side by side. This seems to indicate that an atlatl was broken into two parts and the portions deposited in the graves.

D. This is a close up of Burial 248, showing an unusual arifact made of bent cooper bar and six shell disk beads. This Burial was in a pit 4.4 feet deep. The copper artifact is shown separately in Figure 26 D.

E.   Burial 148, a male of estimated age 35 years, was in the shell midden 4.3 feet below the surface. Note stone weight and antler hook in alignment at the back near pelvis.

F.   Burial 579, a female, estimated age 9 months, was in a pit in the sand at a depth of 4.9 feet. There were two disk beads and two shell strip pendants. An atlatl weight and antler hook lay close together side by side, nearly parallel. That an atlatl was here broken in two and the parts deposited together is further supported by the fact that the antler hook was also fractured about midway. Antlers are tough and hard to break transversely. There was nothing in the grave to cause it to break in this way, and the fracture is not due to decay. Although the hook was bent until it partially fractured, the parts did not separate, as is shown. Further, the base of the hook is split longitudinally and a portion of the wall was removed as if it had been subjected to transverse pressure while the wooden handle was still inserted in the conically reamed perforation in the base. This particular hook is somewhat longer than usual. It is shown in Figure 26 A-F.

BURIALS SHOWING SHELL ARTIFACTS IN ASSOCIATION

Shell was by far the most abundant material found in burial association. Much of it was from large marine forms like Busycon perversum. This shell was often converted into a cup or other vessel by cutting out the central columella. Sections of this shell were often cut into pointed triangular pendants suspended singly or in pairs on strings of disk beads hung about the neck. Often larger shell gorgets 10 cm. broad with two perforations for suspension near one edge and a single perforation near the center are found in groups of four in the same grave. The columella of Busycon perversum and other large marine gastropods were often made into cylindrical beads and sometimes into large pendants or pins. Sometimes curved sections of heavy thick shell are cut and perforated in imitation of drilled animal teeth. Occasionally, the end whorl of large shells is made into a pendant. Attention has already been called to the use of shell in construction of composite shell atlatl weights. Anculosa shells were used as beads, sewed on garments.

Figure 21 presents a few selected burials showing shell artifacts in situ, which are described in detail as follows:

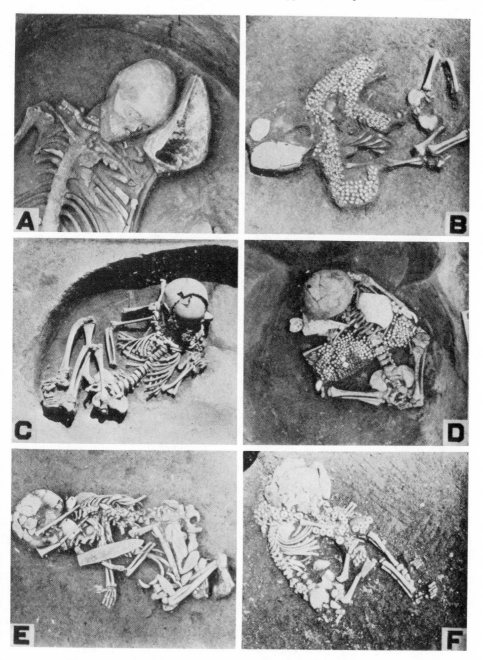

Fig. 21. Shell artifacts in burial association. Burial numbers as follows: A. 310, B. 116, C. 515, D. 610, E. 339, F. 20.

A.   This is a "close-up" of Burial 310 showing a shell cup made by cutting out the central column of Busycon perversum, and a string of large disk beads worn about the neck.

B.   This shows Burial 116. Note that the shells (Anculosa) are in groups with cut faces all down or all up. This shows the shells were sewed on a strip of cloth or leather, and the strip twisted and folded on itself was laid over the body in the grave. It is little short of remarkable that this ordered regularity should have been preserved. This shows that in pit burials, the fill did not shift position as did the covering of burials made in the shell midden.

C.   Burial 515 had a conch shell pendant under left side of skull, two columella shell pins at right of skull, 264 shell disk beads, and one cannel coal bead at the neck, and a bone awl paralleling the right humerus. These are shown in Figure 24 A.

D.   Burial 610, had two large sections of conch shell, 161 disk shell beads, one stone bead, two curved strips of shell, a bone drift, many square blocks of shell, some drilled and many shell fragments. The shell sections seem to represent all stages of the manufacture of shell beads and suggest this individual was a maker of shell beads. The Anculosa beads show by their placement that they were sewed on a garment in a band of nine parallel rows, and that the garment was wrapped about the central portion of the body before its placement in the grave. The band showing the shells with perforated side up passes under the spinal column. See Figure 23 A for photograph of artifacts from Burial 610.

E.   Burial 339 is shown with many artifacts scattered over the body. A large flint blade lies across the arms, perforated shell pendants are under the chin, two long bone hairpins lie on the skull and many drilled animal canine teeth are at the knees. A beaver incisor, many flint points and a broken antler hook lie under the flint point at knees. See Figure 24 B for photograph of some of these artifacts.

F.   This is burial 20 showing Anculosa beads, large and small disk shell beads and just above the knees a large barrel shaped cannel coal bead.

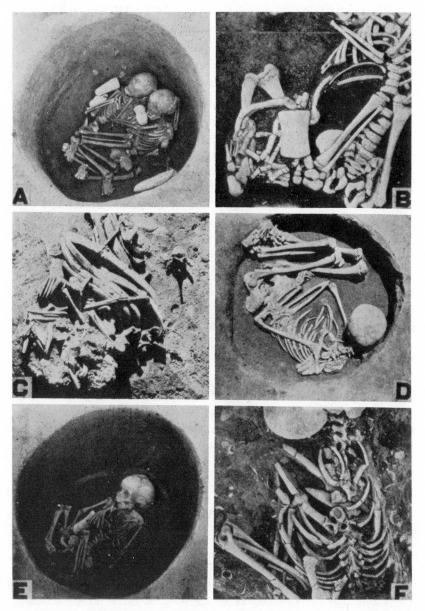

Fig. 22. Burials with artifacts. Burial numbers as follows: A. 253, 254, B. 544, C. 708, D. 153, E. 622, F. 295.

BURIALS SHOWING STONE ARTIFACTS IN ASSOCIATION

Excluding atlatl weights to be described later, stone artifacts were not numerous in burial association. Heavy stone artifacts like bell-shaped pestles, cylindrical pestles, hammer stones and fully grooved axes were only rarely put into the graves.

Figure 22 presents some unusual grave associations which may be described as follows:

A. Burial 253 (left) and 254 (right) were placed in a pit the bottom of which was 7.4 feet below the midden surface. Note the two fully grooved axes and two pestles. A drilled animal tooth and the point of a bone hairpin show between the skulls. There were flint scrapers and two flint projectile points at the left side of Burial 254. An antler hook lay on the chest of Burial 253, and two antler tines near the long pestle at the left of Burial 254.

B. A close up of the pelvic region of Burial 544 showing a much entwined string of disk shell beads with several beads of cannel coal. On this string was, as shown, a very fine specimen of granite atlatl weight. The size of the drilling in this weight permitted the shell disk beads to pass through it, but the larger coal beads, as shown, could not pass. This is the only known instance where an atlatl weight has been found strung or definitely associated with shell beads.

C. Burial 708 was a partially disturbed burial only 3.7 feet deep in the shell midden. Many of the associated artifacts can be seen piled over the bones. The following were with this burial: 3 antler tines, 7 flint pieces, 20 bone pins, 7 split bone splinters, a flint scraper, 11 drilled canine teeth, animal vertebrae and textile fragments.

D. Burial 153 was in a pit in the sand the bottom of which was 4.7 feet below the surface. At the left shoulder there was a necklace of 20 drilled canine teeth. With these were a few anculosa beads.

E. Burial 622 was in a well formed pit, the bottom of which was 4.8 feet below the midden surface. Note the pestle at the right side and the grooved ax under left shoulder. These artifacts seem definitely to have been placed in the pit before the body was laid there.

F. A close up of the vertebral column of Burial 295. Note the large flint spearpoint lodged in the vertebral column. It cut and fractured two vertebrae and doubtless caused the death of the individual. It is shown also in Figure 29 D.

BURIAL DATA

Having excavated 880 burials at this site, it is obvious that it is quite impossible to describe each burial in detail. However, because of the importance of this site as a key site in the shell mound complex, critical students of the future may desire statistical data, the nature of which is not now apparent. For this reason, burial data *for all burials* have been tabulated, and thus compressed into the smallest possible space which would still permit recording of much basic information.

In this tabulation certain symbols are used to permit the compression of data on a single burial to one line in most cases. The key of this symbolization is as follows:

Age Group:
    Nb = Newborn
     I = Infant   x– 3 years
     C = Child   4–12 years
     A = Adolescent   13–17 years
    SA = Sub Adult   18–20 years
    YA = Young Adult   21–35 years
    MA = Middle Aged   36–55 years
    OA = Old Adult   56–x years
           Age is expressed in years unless indicated
             in months (Mo.)

Sex:
     F = Female
    M = Male
     ? = Uncertain
    — = Unknown

Burial Form:
    D = Disturbed
    F = Fully flexed
    P = Partially flexed
    E = Extended

Body Position:
    B = On back

        R = On right side
        L = On left side
        F = On face
        S = Sitting

Burial Placement:
        X = In midden
        O = In pit in hardpan

Below Surface:
        Depth is in feet below surface of midden at
        point of burial.

Remarks:
        a b = Associated burial
        d s b = Disk shell beads
        b s b = Barrel-shaped beads
        sh = Shell
        bd = Beads
        a s b = Anculosa shell beads
        bs = Black stain on bones
        fl = flint

Burial Number	Age Group	Sex Evaluation	Estimated Age	Burial Form	Burial Position	Burial Placement	Depth Below Surface	Illustration Figure No.	Remarks
1	Nb	?	—	D		X	.5		42 d s b; 38 Olivella bd; A b 2.
2	Nb	?	—	D		X	.5		a b 1.
3	C	M	12	F	B	X	1,5		9 disc beads; work bone at neck.
4	I	?	2	P	B	X	1.6		
5	SA	M	19	P	B	X	2.1		7 d s b; fl spear point.
6		—	—	F	B	X	.8		No bones saved, decayed.
7	I	M?	4	D		X	.8		
8	I	F?	2 Mo	P	L	X	2.6		
9	YA	F	22	F	L	X	3.9		
10	YA	F	22	P	F	X	2.1		100 d s b at right arm and neck.
11	YA	M	32	D		X	1.3		9 fl pieces, 2 notched.
12	YA	F	22	F	B	X	2.1		1 carapace rattle at back of head.
13	YA	F	22	F	L	X	2.7		
14	I	F?	3 Mo	F	R	X	3.0		
15	YA	F	22	E	B	X	2.9		
16		—	—	D		X	3.1		No bones saved, decayed.
17	YA	F	23	P	B	X	4.3		
18		—	—	D		X	2.9		No bones saved, decayed; 1 carapace rattle.
19		—	—	D		X	3.1		No bones, saved, decayed.
20	I	M	6 Mo	P	L	X	3.0	21	444 d s b; 1 a s b; 1 bead cannel coal.
21		—	—	D		X	2.6		No bones saved, decayed.
22	YA	F	23	F	R	O	6.6		
23	YA	F	25	D		X	4.1		Only skull saved.
24		—	—	F	R	X	3.9		No bones saved, decayed.
25	I	F?	7 Mo	P	B	X	3.6		
26	I	M	4 Mo	P	L	X	4.0		
27	I	F?	5 Mo	P	L	O	4.4		
28	YA	M	26	F	R	O	3.9		
29	I	F?	2 Mo	P	B	O	3.8		1 carapace rattle at left shoulder.
30	YA	F	22	F	R	O	4.6		b s, red ochre.
31	YA	M	34	F	B	O	4.9	14	b s.
32	YA	M	33	F	L	X	4.3		
33	I	M?	2 Mo	P	L	O	4.8		Small shell pendant.
34	YA	M	24	F	B	X	5.8	15	Dismembered before burial.
35	I	M?	3	F	L	O	4.9		
36	I	F?	2 Mo	P	B	X	3.5		
37	C	M?	9	F	L	O	5.7		81 d s b; 66 medium disk beads about waist.
38	—	—	—	P	L	X	.9		No bones saved, decayed.
39	A	M	17	F	L	O	6.7	18	7 d s b; atlatl stone weight; antler hook; red ochre; beads at neck.
40	I	M?	3 Mo	P	B	X	4.1		

Burial Number	Age Group	Sex Evaluation	Estimated Age	Burial Form	Burial Position	Burial Placement	Depth Below Surface	Illustration Figure No.	Remarks
41	YA	M	32	F	B	O	4.6		
42	YA	M	25	E	B	O	6.3		287 d s b; 848 a s b at neck and plevis, 1 tubular bead stone.
43	MA	M	40	F	R	O	6.1		a b 44.
44	YA	M	27	F	R	O	6.2	12	a b 43.
45	MA	M	50	F	L	O	5.3	8	
46	SA	M	19	P	R	O	4.3		
47	A	F?	13	F	L	O	5.7		11 d s b; 11 sh rings, 20 mm dia. 13 mm hole; 3 pieces fl.
48	I	F?	3	P	B	O	5.7		a s b; d s b.
49	YA	F	21	F	L	X	2.3		221 a s b.
50	YA	M	22	F	R	X	2.3		b s.
51	C	M?	8	P	L	X	2.6		
52	YA	F	22	F	R	O	6.0		
53	A	M	14	D		X	3.3		
54	C	M	5	F	B	O	6.1		10 d s b at pelvis
55	YA	M	21	P	L	O	6.3	12 24	Stone bar atlatl weight, 2 shell pendants, 2 flat broad awls, 33 cm long made from human femora; bone fish hook, antler drift a b 55, 56, 57, 58.
56	YA	F	21	F	R	O	6.3	12	a s b; antler hook, atlatl shell weight, 11 segments.
57	YA	M	30	P	B	O	6.4	12	Headless; 2 carapace rattles, 2 fl points, 73 pebbles.
58	YA	M	22	P	B	O	6.4	12	Headless; d s b; atlatl shell weight of 8 shells and 2 stone segments, nearly aligned with antler hook.
59	C	F	12	F	L	O	7.3		Extra bones of Grus amercanus (Whooping Crane) in pit; a b 869.
60	YA	F	35	F	L	O	5.4	9	a b 61.
61	YA	M	32	F	R	O	6.5	9	a b 60.
62	I	M?	7 Mo	P	B	O	5.1		
63	I	M?	2	F	B	X	2.9		965 d s b at neck; 9 pearl beads.
64	YA	F	22	F	B	X	2.9		
65	I	M	3 Mo	F	B	X	1.9		
66	MA	M	40	F	R	O	6.3	10	Fl point at ribs and inside skull below eye socket; a b 67.
67	YA	M	28	F	S	O	6.3	10	Antler point; fl point; a b 66.
68	YA	F	21	F	B	O	6.1		
69	YA	M	21	F	B	O	8.5	17	2 antler hooks; rattle carapace; red ochre; 9 bone hairpins, fl drill, fl scraper, 1 atlatl prism weight and 1 flat bar; turkey leg bone; chunk of asphalt with incisor tooth imbedded in it; hollow bone 25 cm long worked.

Burial Number	Age Group	Sex Evaluation	Estimated Age	Burial Form	Burial Position	Burial Placement	Depth Below Surface	Illustration Figure No.	Remarks
70	YA	F	23	F	R	X	3.9		Fl point.
71	YA	M	35	F	L	O	4.9		
72	YA	F	24	F	L	O	4.4		
73	YA	M	26	F	R	X	3.8		Dog burial (4).
74	Nb	F?		F	R	X	4.4		
75	SA	F	20	F	R	X	1.9		
76	Nb	F?		P	B	X	1.8		
77	I	M?	1	F	B	O	5.5		
78	I	F?	3	F	L	X	2.2		
79	YA	M	22	P	B	X	1.5		
80	A	M	14	F	B	X	2.8		2 d s b.
81	YA	M	22	F	B	X	3.8		
82	YA	M	26	F	L	X	3.5		
83	YA	M	30	F	B	X	4.1		33 gastropod shell beads at right elbow.
84	Nb	F?		D		X	2.3		
85	C	M	10	F	L	O	5.3		
86	C	M?	5	F	L	X	3.1		
87	YA	M	21	P	R	O	6.7		33 a s b at neck; flat stone pebble at pelvis.
88	YA	F	26	F	B	X	3.6		
89	I	F?	5 Mo	F	B	O	6.9		2 d s b; red ochre found under head; large beads at neck.
90	YA	F	22	F	R	O	5.1		
91	I	F?	3 Mo	P	B	X	1.9		
92	I	M?	8 Mo	P	R	O	4.6	19	Atlatl stone weight; occurred in fragments scattered through pit; antler hook.
93	YA	M	24	P	B	O	7.2		Dismembered head, lower arms and legs missing.
94	I	M?	7 Mo	P	R	O	6.4		
95	A	M	16	F	B	O	6.5		
96	YA	M	33	F	B	O	4.3		Intruded into Burial 111.
97	A	M	17	F	B	O	6.6		5 d s b; a b 97, 98, 99.
98	YA	M	24	F	B	O	6.7		Skulless; dismembered lower arms, legs; head missing.
99	YA	M	22	F	B	O	6.7		104 d s b; skulless, legs missing; a b 97, 98, 99.
100	YA	M	35	F	S	X	5.2	12	
101	YA	F	23	P	B	O	7.5		47 d s b; 1 stone bead; a b 102.
102	I	?		P	B	O	7.5		No bones saved, decayed; a b 101.
103	YA	F	22	F	B	O	5.5		a b 104.
104	Nb	?		D		O	5.5		a b 103.
105	YA	M	37	F	B	O	7.1		54 d s b under head; red ochre.

Burial Number	Age Group	Sex Evaluation	Estimated Age	Burial Form	Burial Position	Burial Placement	Depth Below Surface	Illustration Figure No.	Remarks
106	YA	M	35	F	R	O	4.6		Intruded into Burial 111.
107	YA	F	22	F	R	O	5.9		
108	MA	M	37	F	R	O	8.1		b s.
109	YA	M?	25	F	L	O	6.4		37 d s b at left wrist.
110	YA	F	28	F	R	X	2.7		
111	YA	M	30	F	R	O	7.0		Pits of Burials 106, 96 intruded into Burial 111.
112	I	F?	1	P	R	X	2.1		
113	YA	M	25	P	B	O	5.6		
114	I	M?	1 Mo	D		X	1.1		
115	YA	M	28	F	B	O	7.8	16	Dog Burial 7 under head.
116	I	M?	5 Mo	P	B	O	6.1		463 a s b arranged to indicate pattern.
117	YA	F	22	F	B	O	7.6		
118	I	F?	3	P	B	O	6.2		31 d s b at neck; b s.
119	I	M?	8 Mo	P	B	O	5.6		
120	YA	F	22	P	B	O	5.8	14	Disturbed by intrusion of Burial 121; a b 870.
121	YA	M	22	F	B	O	6.0	14	89 d s b; hairpin of bone, pitch and shell; antler point.
122	YA	M	23	F	F	O	6.4		
123	SA	M	19	P	B	O	6.1		Shell pendant.
124	YA	M	28	F	L	O	5.8	18	Antler hook; bone atlatl handle.
125	A	M?	15	F	L	O	7.9		
126	YA	F	22	P	B	O	6.0		
127	A	F	15	F	R	O	6.8		A trace of red ochre in grave.
128	YA	F	22	F	L	O	4.5		
129	C	F?	6	F	R	X	.7		Atlatl stone weight broken.
130	I	M?	6 Mo	P	B	X	1.2		
131	SA	M	19	P	B	X	2.0		
132	Nb	?		D		X	2.6		
133	YA	F	21	F	B	O	3.1		Red ochre, 4 inch hollow bone tube (handle of graver).
134	YA	M	25	F	L	O	3.5		
135	YA	M	22	F	B	X	1.6		44 d s b; 1 cannon bone awl (hairpin), 1 bone pin.
136	A	M	13	F	L	X	2.9		b s.
137	I	F?	10 Mo	P	B	O	4.7		
138	C	M?	12	F	L	X	3.3		
139	I	M?	2	P	B	O	4.7		
140	YA	F	22	F	R	O	4.2	20	Atlatl stone weight; and antler hook laid parallel under spine.
141	MA	M	38	F	L	O	3.6		
142	YA	M	32	F	L	O	4.0		
143	OA	M	60	F	L	X	3.9		
144	—	—	—	D		X	1.0		a b 145; no bones saved.
145	—	—	—	D		X	1.0		a b 144; no bones saved.

Burial Number	Age Group	Sex Evaluation	Estimated Age	Burial Form	Burial Position	Burial Placement	Depth Below Surface	Illustration Figure No.	Remarks
146	YA	F	24	P	B	O	7.5		64 d s b at neck; 2 cut animal jaws; a b 147.
147	Nb	F?		D		O	7.5		a b 146.
148	YA	M	35	F	L	X	4.3	20	Atlatl stone weight and antler hook.
149	I	F?	13 Mo	P	B	O	4.4		b s; 1 bone cylinder (handle of graver) 2.5 cm long.
150	YA	F	22	F	L	O	7.1		
151	I	F?	7 Mo	P	B	X	3.7		
152	I	F?	1	P	B	O	4.4		Red ochre; dog Burials 8, 9.
153	A	F?	13	F	R	O	4.7	22	a s b; 22 drilled canine teeth; b s, back of head.
154	MA	M	37	F	R	O	4.8	8	
155	I	?	6 Mo	D		O	7.3		3 carapace rattles, pebbles for rattles, stone disc whetstone.
156	MA	M	37	F	L	O	4.5		b s.
157	—	—	—	F	L	X	1.0		No bones saved.
158	I	M?	3	P	B	O	6.8	18	d s b; 2 lower jaws cut and nostrum of Martes pennati (Fisher); a stain or red ochre; atlatl stone weight; antler hook.
159	I	M?	1	F	L	X	2.6		20 d s b; 1 b s b.
160	YA	F	22	F	L	X	2.1		Atlatl stone weight on sacrum.
161	I	?	1 Mo	P	R	X	1.9		
162	I	F?	2	P	F	X	2.6		
163	Nb	M?		P	L	X	3.5		
164	I	F?	4 Mo	P	R	X	3.2		
165	I	M?	3	D		X	4.2		Separate skull.
166	MA	M	37	F	R	O	4.3		
167	YA	M	22	D		X	3.1		
168	YA	F	22	F	L	O	4.8	8	Red ochre; b s.
169	A	M	14	F	R	O	5.9		
170	A	F?	15	F	B	O	3.9		
171	I	F?	1 Mo	P	B	X	3.8		38 shell beads, left shoulder, legs and arm missing.
172	C	M?	6	F	R	O	4.9		1 carapace rattle; pebbles found in carapace; left hand missing.
173	I	M?	1 Mo	D		X	1.7		
174	I	F?	1 Mo	D		X	1.8		Flint point.
175	OA	M	60	F	R	X	4.0		
176	I	M?	18 Mo	P	B	O	5.1		
177	C	M	8	F	L	O	5.3		155 beads at left wrist and neck; red ochre on front teeth.
178	—	—	—	D		X	4.8		No bones saved.
179	YA	M	24	F	L	X	3.4		
180	YA	F	22	F	L	X	.8		

Burial Number	Age Group	Sex Evaluation	Estimated Age	Burial Form	Burial Position	Burial Placement	Depth Below Surface	Illustration Figure No.	Remarks
181	—	—	—	D		O	4.7		No bones saved.
182	I	M?	5 Mo	P	L	O	4.9		
183	YA	F	22	F	R	X	2.8		2 fl points at left hand.
184	SA	M	19	F	R	O	4.6		
185	YA	M	24	P	B	O	4.8		Fl point at right elbow.
186	YA	F	24	F	L	X	4.8		
187	I	F?	9 Mo	F	B	X	4.5		
188	I	F?	5 Mo	D		X	4.5		
189	I	F?	7 Mo	D		X	4.5		1 d s b.
190	YA	M	22	P	B	X	2.6		3 fl points against spine, inside body at burial; bone awl on shoulder.
191	YA	F	21	F	R	X	4.9		25 d s b; 1 stone bead on chest.
192	—	—	—	D		X	1.2		No bones saved.
193	Nb	F?		F	B	X	2.1		
194	—	—	—	D		X	1.3		No bones saved, decayed.
195	Nb	F?		F	S	X	1.2		
196	I	F?	3	D		X	2.9		
197	YA	M	30	F	R	X	2.7	15	Head removed above lower jaw.
198	I	F?	4 Mo	F	B	X	3.2		27 d s b; 1 cannel coal bead at top of head.
199	I	M?	3	P	L	X	3.5		
200	—	—	—	P	B	X	2.7		A stain of red ochre found in grave. No bones saved, decayed.
201	Nb	?		D		X	2.3		
202	I	F?	7 Mo	P	E	X	3.9		Red and yellow ochre pebble.
203	YA	F	23	F	B	X	3.9		Head of Lepisosteus osseus (Garpike) at right shoulder; bone awls near pelvis; bone hair pin.
204	I	M?	6 Mo	D		X	4.0		
205	YA	F	22	F	R	O	5.4		
206	—	—	—	D		X	3.9		No bones saved.
207	I	F?	2 Mo	P	B	X	1.7		
208	YA	F	22	F	B	X	2.2	8	5 d s b; 125 a s b at pelvis.
209	—	—	—	P	R	X	2.5		12 d s b; 1 stone bead; tubular beads, barrel shaped, found under head. No bones saved.
210	Nb	F?		P	B	X	3.2		
211	I	F?	3	P	B	X	4.4		
212	—	—	—	F	R	X	3.2		No bones saved.
213	Nb	M?		F	B	X	3.4		
214	I	F?	1	F	R	X	3.8		
215	A	M?	17	F	L	O	5.7		95 d s b at neck; 1 tubular stone bead.
216	MA	M	47	D		X	4.2		Skull only.

Burial Number	Age Group	Sex Evaluation	Estimated Age	Burial Form	Burial Position	Burial Placement	Depth Below Surface	Illustration Figure No.	Remarks
217	YA	M	21	P	B	O	4.8	17	17 d s b; atlatl stone weight; antler hook; rattle carapace and pebbles; 2 stone beads; cannel coal bd at neck.
218	MA	M	37	F	L	O	7.2	9 17	Pit intruded into Burial 219; shell weight 8 segments; cemented with pitch; aligned with antler hook.
219	C	F	12	D		O	6.6	9	Disturbed by Burial 218; d s b at wrist.
220	YA	F	22	F	B	X	4.5		
221	I	F?	2	F	B	O	5.2		b s.
222	Nb	F?		P	L	X	2.4		a b 223.
223	I	M?	3 Mo	P	B	X	2.4		a b 222.
224	I	F?	3	F	B	X	3.1		b s.
225	I	F?	3	F	B	O	7.6		51 d s b at neck, left pelvis, right forearm.
226	Nb	?		P	L	X	5.3		3 d s b at neck.
227	YA	M?	27	F	R	X	2.0		
228	—	—	—	P	F	X	1.7		13 d s b; fl point lodged in vertebrae above sacrum; fl point, same type, at right side; no bones removed.
229	YA	F	22	F	L	X	1.1		
230	MA	M?	45	F	R	X	1.9		
231	Nb			D		X	2.4		Legs missing.
232	C	M?	7	F	R	O	4.2	16	Dog Burial 11.
233	YA	F	21	P	B	X	2.6	14	14 d s b; carapace rattle; 2 cannel coal beads; 2 barrel shaped stone beads; 1 bone bd, at waist.
234	YA	F	25	F	B	O	3.3		
235	YA	M	28	P	F	X	3.0		2 animal incisor teeth at face.
236	A	M	15	F	F	X	3.2		3493 d s b; 2 animal incisor teeth at face; b s; 4 small shell pendants; a b 237.
237	YA	F	22	P	B	X	3.0	25 30	a b 236; 36 large, 1136 small d s b; 504 a s b; 38 tubular bds; 2 bone awls, cut conch shell; 2 stone bd; 1 cannel coal bd (all barrel shaped), 3 animal teeth, perforated.
238	YA	F	23	F	B	X	3.5		
239	I	?	4 Mo	D		X	3.0		
240	YA	F	21	F	B	O	3.9		Infant under left foot; a b 241; b s.
241	Nb	?		D		O	3.9		a b 240.
242	YA	F	22	P	B	O	3.8		Infant in pelvic cavity, unborn; a b 243.
243	Nb	F?		D		O	3.7		a b 242.
244	C	M	7	P	B	O	4.9		

Burial Number	Age Group	Sex Evaluation	Estimated Age	Burial Form	Burial Position	Burial Placement	Depth Below Surface	Illustration Figure No.	Remarks
245	C	M	9	F	B	Q	4.3	16	314 d s b; fl point; stone bd at face; dog Burial 13.
246	I	F?	3 Mo	P	B	O	3.5		307 d s b; cannel coal bds at neck.
247	YA	M?	32	F	R	O	4.4		
248	I	M?	3	P	B	O	4.4	20	5 d s b at left head; ornament of copper; a b 249 and 250.
249	I	F	2 Mo	D		O	4.3		Burial 248 intruded into Burial 249.
250	YA	F	22	D		O	4.4		Burial 249 intruded into Burial 250; b s.
251	YA	F	21	F	B	O	5.9		Bone awl has pitch on point.
252	MA	F	37	F	L	X	2.7		
253	A	M?	13	F	B	O	7.4	22	a b 254; pestle, 2 fl points, axe, 3 fl scrapers, drilled canine teeth, bone hairpin; antler hook on breast.
254	C	F?	10	F	R	O	7.4	22	a b 253; axe, 2 fl points, 2 deer tines, 2 pestles.
255	A	M	17	F	L	X	3:1		
256	YA	M	24	F	L	O	3.7		
257	I	F?	3 Mo	F	L	O	4.1		2 curved shell pendants at right arm.
258	YA	M	35	F	L	O	4.5		
259	YA	F	23	F	R	X	3.0		
260	YA	F	26	F	R	O	7.9		
261	YA	F	25	F	B	O	4.5		
262	YA	M	24	F	B	O	4.3		b s.
263	YA	M	22	P	B	X	3.1		b s.
264	I	M	1.5	F	B	X	5.3		66 d s b.
265	I	F?	1.5	P	B	X	3.3		
266	MA	M	40	F	R	O	6.4	7	a b 267.
267	YA	F	26	F	R	O	5.8	7	a b 266.
268	I	M?	3	F	B	O	6.1	7	186 d s b at neck; bone awl at head.
269	YA	F	22	F	R	O	6.3		
270	YA	M	29	F	B	O	5.8	7	
271	I	F	2	F	B	O	3.7	10	a b 272; red ochre on bones.
272	YA	M	35	F	R	O	4.1	10	a b 271; fl blank at right tibia.
273	MA	M	40	P	R	O	3.7		
274	I	M?	2	F	L	X	2.3		
275	Nb	F?		P	R	X	2.5		a b 276.
276	C	F?	4	F	R	X	2.5		a b 275.
277	YA	F	23	F	F	X	3.2		
278	C	M?	12	F	R	O	3.6		Red ochre on bones.
279	I	M?	2	P	B	O	6.5		134 d s b at neck.
280	YA	M	24	F	R	X	2.9	7	b s.

Burial Number	Age Group	Sex Evaluation	Estimated Age	Burial Form	Burial Position	Burial Placement	Depth Below Surface	Illustration Figure No.	Remarks
281	YA	M	33	F	R	X	3.3	7	
282	YA	M	32	F	L	X	3.1	7	
283	YA	M	24	F	R	X	3.3	7	
284	YA	F	24	F	B	O	6.5		
285	YA	F	22	F	L	O	7.2		
286	I	F?	3	P	F	O	6.6		
287	I	M?	2	P	L	O	6.5		
288	YA	M	27	P	B	O	7.7		
289	A	F?	17	F	L	O	7.1		
290	YA	M	22	F	L	O	7.0	9	
291	YA	F	21	P	B	O	7.4	9	Very small adult.
292	YA	M	28	P	B	O	7.9	9	
293	YA	M	26	F	R	O	6.9		
294	YA	M	24	F	R	O	7.3		
295	YA	M	22	P	F	X	1.8	22	Fl point cut spinal cord and lodged in vertebral column.
296	MA	M	45	F	B	O	6.6		
297	YA	M	25	F	B	X	3.1		37 d s b; 3 carapace rattle; pebbles; 3 drilled canine teeth under head.
298	YA	M	33	F	R	O	3.3		b s.
299	YA	M	22	F	L	O	7.2		
300	I	F?	8 Mo	F	B	O	5.9		
301	YA	F	21	F	B	X	2.6		
302	SA	F	18	F	R	O	3.7		
303	I	F?	9 Mo	F	R	O	6.8	11	a b 304, 305, 306, 307, 308.
304	I	F?	3	F	B	O	7.1	11	a b 303, 305, 306, 307, 308; b s.
305	YA	M	28	F	B	O	7.4	11	a b 303, 304, 306, 307, 308; cut maxilla (nostrum) of carnivora, Martes pennati (Fisher).
306	YA	M	30	F	B	O	7.6	11	a b 303, 304, 305, 307, 308.
307	YA	M	21	F	B	O	7.9	11	a b 303, 304, 305, 306, 308; b s.
308	—	—	—	F	F	O	7.9	11	a b 303, 304, 305, 306, 307; atlatl stone weight; no bones saved.
309	YA	M	32	F	B	O	7.9	7	a b 310.
310	YA	M	28	F	B	O	8.3	21	a b 309; 257 d s b at back of neck; conch shell at left side.
311	YA	F	21	F	L	O	7.1	7	
312	I	F?	1	F	B	O	5.7	7	130 d s b at neck.
313	—	—	—	F	R	X	1.7		No bones saved.
314	YA	F	22	F	L	X	2.7		b s.
315	A	F	17	F	B	X	2.0		9 d s b; 14 tubular shell bds; 3 conch pendants at back of head; b s.
316	YA	M	31	F	L	O	3.8	12	
317	—	—	—	F	L	X	3.1		No bones saved.

Burial Number	Age Group	Sex Evaluation	Estimated Age	Burial Form	Burial Position	Burial Placement	Depth Below Surface	Illustration Figure No.	Remarks
318	I	M?	3	F	L	X	1.2		
319	YA	F	25	F	R	O	6.3	16	Dog Burial 14, at feet.
320	I	M?	4 Mo	P	B	X	3.2		
321	I	F?	1	P	R	O	3.8		29 a s b at neck; b s.
322	YA	M	22	F	L	O	3.7		a b 323; 4 antler pieces.
323	YA	M	25	P	F	O	3.7		a b 322.
324	SA	F	20	P	L	O	3.1		b s.
325	I	F?	1	F	R	O	3.9	11	a b 326, 327.
326	YA	M	24	D		O	3.5	11	a b 325, 327; b s.
327	MA	M	40	P	L	O	3.9	11	a b 325, 326.
328	YA	F	22	F	F	O	6.0		32 d s b at left wrist; b s.
329	—	—	—	F	R	X	2.4		No bones saved.
330	YA	M	24	F	B	O	3.4		
331	YA	M	24	F	R	O	3.3		
332	YA	M?	30	F	L	O	3.1		
333	C	M	8	F	R	O	4.3	11	a b 334.
334	YA	M	30	F	F	O	4.6	11	a b 333.
335	—	—	—	P	R	X	3.0		No bones saved, decayed.
336	—	—	—	P	F	X	3.1		No bones saved, decayed.
337	I	M?	2	P	R	X	2.1		Conch shell pendant, 2 holes; b s.
338	YA	F	22	F	L	O	5.4		
339	I	M?	3	F	R	X	3.5	21	5 d s b; 3 beaver incisors (Castor canadensis), 4 drilled canine teeth; fl knife; 5 fl pts.; 3 bone awls; 4 shell pendants; antler proj. pt.; antler hook broken; b s.
340	SA	F	18	F	L	X	3.3		a b 341; unborn child in pelvis; b s.
341	Nb	?	—	D		X			a b 340.
342	YA	M	22	F	R	O	7.1		
343	YA	M	33	F	R	O	2.4		
344	I	M	2	F	R	O	4.2		b s.
345	YA	F?	23	F	B	O	6.2		d s b.
346	YA	F	21	P	B	O	8.2		
347	YA	M	28	F	L	O	6.7		Atlatl stone weight; at back of head, antler hook found under right femur, point toward spine.
348	—	—	—	F	L	X	2.3		No bones saved; 6 d s b in body area.
349	YA	M?	24	F	L	X	2.2		
350	C	M	12	F	B	X	3.9		b s.
351	I	F	2	F	B	X	3.6		Bone pin across chest.
352	MA	M	36	F	L	O	8.3		450 a s b found on leg.
353	SA	F	18	F	B	X	4.1	18	Antler handle and antler hook, in line, found at right side.

Burial Number	Age Group	Sex Evaluation	Estimated Age	Form Burial	Burial Position	Burial Placement	Depth Below Surface	Illustration Figure No.	Remarks
354	C	F?	10	F	R	O	7.1		Canch shell; b s.
355	C	M?	12	F	F	X	.9		
356	A	F	13	F	L	X	1.5		
357	YA	M	35	F	R	X	1.4		d s b at elbow; 4 ground hog jaws (Marmota monax).
358	I	F?	2 Mo	F	B	O	5.3		130 d s b (2 strands) at neck.
359	I	F?	1 Mo.	F	R	O	5.3		b s; 44 a s b; bone tube 13 cm. long across left leg.
360	I	M?	1 Mo	F	R	O	5.1		b s.
361	A	M?	15	F	R	O	5.0		b s.
362	Nb	M?	—	F	L	O	5.2		
363	YA	M	32	F	R	X	2.3		Carapace rattle found at back of head; b s.
364	YA	M	33	F	B	X	1.2		
365	YA	F	28	F	L	O	6.8		a b 366.
366	SA	F	20	F	B	O	6.9		a b 365.
367	I	M?	2	F	F	X	5.5		Beaver tooth; bone awl; block of sandy pitch; 4 antler tines; b s.
368	YA	M	25	P	B	O	2.2	13	Very unusual disposition.
369	—	—	—	F	R	X	.5		No bones saved, decayed.
370	C	M?	8	F	B	O	7.4	10	a b 371, 372, 373, 374, 375; small limestone pestle; also bones of disturbed Burial 879 in same pit.
371	C	M	7	F	L	O	7.4	10	a b 370, 372, 373, 374, 375.
372	C	M	1	F	B	O	7.4	10	a b 370, 371, 373, 374, 375; b s.
373	YA	F	28	F	B	O	7.4	10	a b 370, 371, 372, 374, 375.
374	YA	M	22	F	B	O	7.4	10	a b 370, 371, 372, 373, 375; projectile pt., at left side,, touches vertebrae; b s.
375	I	M?	3	F	B	O	7.4	10	a b 370, 371, 372, 373, 374.
376	YA	F	22	F	R	X	1.8		
377	YA	M	35	F	B	O	6.2		b s.
378	—	—	—	D		X	.7		a b 379; preservation poor, no bones saved.
379	YA	F	21	F	L	X	1.3		a b 378; red ochre near pelvis; b s on forehead.
380	I	F?	3	F	L	X	2.9		82 d s b on left hand; 33 d s b at neck; Lithasia obovata Say.; b s.
381	A	F	17	F	B	X	3.1		
382	YA	F	22	F	B	O	4.2		
383	YA	M	32	F	R	X	2.5	15	Headless.
384	C	F?	10	F	L	X	1.6		a b 385; b s.
385	YA	F	22	F	L	O	2.1		a b 384.
386	C	F?	5	F	B	X	1.4		
387	I	F?	1	F	B	X	5.3		Red ochre on legs; b s.

Burial Number	Age Group	Sex Evaluation	Estimated Age	Burial Form	Burial Position	Burial Placement	Depth Below Surface	Illustration Figure No.	Remarks
388	C	M	8	D		X	2.3		a b 871.
389	I	F?	4 Mo	F	L	O	3.6		
390	YA	F	22	F	R	O	3.8		Antler tine, pestle iron carbonate, barrel-shaped stone bead, broken fl point.
391	SA	F	19	F	R	O	3.9		b s.
392	I	?	9 Mo	F	B	X	2.9		b s.
393	—	—	—	F	B	X	2.9		Dog Burial 15; preservation poor; no bones saved.
394	I	F?	2	F	L	O	3.4		d s b.
395	A	M	13	P	R	X	2.1		4 drilled conch pendants; beaver incisor; bundle of 6 bone pins below forearm; b s.
396	I	M?	2	F	L	O	4.0	18	6 d s b; 689 a s b; atlatl stone weight; antler hook; in alignment; 1 stone bd back of neck; b s.
397	YA	M	27	F	L	O	5.1		
398	YA	F	21	F	F	O	4.2	12	
399	A	M	13	F	R	O	5.3		b s.
400	YA	F	22	F	B	O	4.3		
401	YA	M	21	F	B	O	6.6		
402	YA	M	24	F	L	X	1.5		b s.
403	SA	F	20	F	R	X	1.2		
404	YA	F	22	F	F	O	3.1		b s.
405	C	M?	9	F	B	X	2.2		
406	YA	M	30	F	B	O	4.5		
407	YA	F	22	F	R	O	3.1		b s.
408	YA	M	24	F	F	O	4.5		b s.
409	YA	M	22	F	B	O	6.8		Fl blade; 19 drilled canine teeth at neck.
410	YA	M	28	F	L	O	3.6		b s.
411	YA	F	22	F	F	O	3.1		Red ochre and b s.
412	C	M?	7	F	R	X	2.0		4 teeth (incisor of ground hog) back of spine; 5 bone hairpins, back of spine; b s.
413	YA	M	28	F	B	X	2.6		2 bone hairpins beside head
414	A	M	13	F	F	O	4.6		b s.
415	I	M?	1	F	L	O	4.4		Carapace rattle; red ochre stains about skull; b s.
416	C	M?	7	F	B	X	1.9		3 fl points; 3 broken points; 4 bone awls; misc. flint pieces; 2 antler tips; animal bones near right side; b s.
417	YA	F	22	F	L	O	4.2		a b 418; broken right knee.
418	YA	F	22	P	R	O	4.2		a b 417.
419	I	M?	3	F	B	O	2.7		b s.
420	I	M?	2	F	L	X	4.8		b s.

Burial Number	Age Group	Sex Evaluation	Estimated Age	Burial Form	Burial Position	Burial Placement	Depth Below Surface	Illustration Figure No.	Remarks
421	—	—	—	F	F	O	4.1		a b 422; no bones saved, decayed.
422	—	—	—	F	B	O	4.3		a b 421; no bones saved, decayed.
423	YA	F	22	F	R	O	3.7		b s.
424	YA	M	28	F	L	X	2.3		b s.
425	YA	F	22	F	R	X	5.8		Red ocre on skull.
426	C	M	7	F	R	X	6.2		
427	Nb	F?	—	F	B	O	5.8		
428	C	F	11	F	L	O	7.8		
429	SA	M	20	F	B	O	7.8		a b 430; b s.
430	YA	M	35	F	R	O	7.9		a b 429.
431	I	M?	3	F	L	O	7.7		a b 432.
432	I	M?	2	P	B	O	7.7		a b 431; skulless.
433	A	F	15	P	B	O	7.8		
434	Nb	M?	—	F	B	X	1.9		d s b; bone awl; beaver incisor; curved shell ornament; b s.
435	I	M?	2	P	R	X	2.2		b s.
436	YA	M	29	F	L	O	7.1		Fl blade near right hand.
437	I	M?	3	F	R	X	1.3		
438	A	M	13	D		X	3.2		
439	C	M	13	F	L	X	2.9		92 d s b; 2 conch shells; b s.
440	YA	F	21	F	B	O	5.1		b s.
441	MA	M	40	P	R	X	2.3		Left arm missing; b s.
442	I	M?	1	P	L	O	3.6		
443	I	F?	4 Mo	F	R	O	4.9		
444	C	M?	8	F	B	O	5.4		b s on skull.
445	I	F?	1 Mo	F	L	O	6.8		53 d s b; 2 shell strip pendants; 2 tubular sh. bds; stone bead at neck.
446	MA	M	50	F	R	X	4.3		
447	YA	M	28	F	R	O	3.9		b s.
448	I	M?	1	F	L	O	4.0		b s.
449	YA	M	22	F	L	O	4.8		Well preserved large mussel shell; b s.
450	Nb	?	—	F	F	O	5.6		136 d s b; double strand around neck; 1 stone bead; b s.
451	YA	M	30	F	R	O	5.3		b s.
452	MA	M	50	F	R	O	6.9		a b 453; atlatl stone weight in alignment with antler hook; 2 fl drills; unfinished pestle; bone awl; antler drift; use of pitch.
453	C	F?	5	F	F	O	6.7	10	a b 452.
454	YA	M	23	F	R	X	4.1		b s.
455	YA	M	25	F	L	O	5.6		
456	YA	F	24	F	F	X	2.4		Antler tine near back of head.
457	YA	M	32	F	L	O	5.0		

Burial Number	Age Group	Sex Evaluation	Estimated Age	Burial Form	Burial Position	Burial Placement	Depth Below Surface	Illustration Figure No.	Remarks
458	C	M?	12	F	R	O	5.8		b s.
459	I	M?	5 Mo	F	R	O	5.4		82 b s b; 1 cannel coal bd at neck; b s.
460	I	M?	9 Mo	F	B	O	5.9		b s.
461	YA	M	32	F	B	O	6.5		
462	YA	M	22	F	R	O	5.6		23 d s b around neck; b s.
463	MA	M	37	F	B	X	4.3		Roughly chipped stone bar near head.
464	YA	F	22	F	R	X	4.7		b s.
465	YA	M?	28	F	L	O	7.2		3 carapace rattles; 2 fl scrapers; 4 pestles; cannon bone awl; red ochre.
466	MA	M	40	F	R	O	4.1		
467	YA	M	28	P	B	X	2.6		32 d s b around neck.
468	I	M?	1	P	L	O	6.1		b s.
469	I	F?	1	P	L	O	5.8		52 d s b around neck.
470	YA	F	21	F	R	O	5.9		61 d s b at right arm; b s.
471	YA	M	28	F	L	O	7.8		Pestle, plummet; fl scraper near hand; hammer stone.
472	C	M	8	F	R	O	5.1		
473	YA	F	21	F	B	O	6.2		
474	YA	F	21	F	B	O	7.4		38 d s b; 2 stone bd at left arm.
475	YA	M	28	F	R	O	5.5	9	Intruded into pit of Burial 476.
476	YA	M	25	F	B	O	6.1	9	b s.
477	MA	M	45	F	R	O	7.9		105 d s b; 500 a s b at waist and neck.
478	A	M	13	F	L	O	6.0		
479	C	F?	11	F	F	O	7.6		a b 480; 2 d s b used as head of hairpin, each had a dome of pitch on it.
480	YA	F	22	F	L	O	7.5		a b 479.
481	YA	M	22	F	F	O	7.5		589 d s b about waist; b s.
482	Nb	F?	—	P	R	X	1.2		
483	A	F	13	F	B	O	6.8		b s.
484	YA	F	22	F	B	O	5.4		b s.
485	YA	F	23	F	R	X	1.2		
486	YA	F	33	F	B	X	1.2		Antler projectile pt. at feet.
487	YA	M	35	F	L	X	2.2		Deer jaw; 2 bone hairpins at back of neck; b s.
488	A	F	17	F	F	X	1.9		b s.
489	YA	M	29	F	F	O	6.7		Bone hair pins with bds attached by pitch, at head; b s.
490	YA	F	22	F	F	O	4.8		
491	YA	F	24	F	R	O	4.6		
492	YA	M	30	P	B	O	8.4		d s b stone; 6 jaws of Lynx rufus (Bobcat) and a fragment of fossil tooth—(next to the last upper left molar of **Tapirus haysii** Leidy); b s.

Burial Number	Age Group	Sex Evaluation	Estimated Age	Burial Form	Burial Position	Burial Placement	Depth Below Surface	Illustration Figure No.	Remarks
493	YA	M	25	D		X	2.2		b s.
494	YA	F	22	F	B	O	4.9		85 d s b at back of head; 1 cannel coal bd; b s.
495	SA	M?	18	F	B	X	2.0	18	31 d s b; stone atlatl bar weight; 2 antler tips; 2 stone bd near neck; antler handle aligned with antler hook; b s.
496	YA	M	23	F	B	X	2.1		
497	Nb	F?	—	P	L	X	2.2		
498	Nb	F?	—	F	L	O	2.9		10 d s b at face.
499	MA	M	50	F	L	X	1.8		
500	A	F	13	F	F	X	2.5		b s.
501	A	F	17	F	B	O	6.2	8	61 d s b at right arm and left elbow.
502	A	F?	13	F	R	X	1.8		b s.
503	C	M?	4	F	L	X	3.2		Beaver incisor; 2 tubular columella bds; bone awl; block of pitch; stone bar, flat; antler tine; b s.
504	I	M?	2 Mo	F	R	O	4.4		
505	I	F?	3	P	F	O	7.2	16	2 dog Burials 16, 17.
506	I	M?	1	F	B	O	4.6		Tubular bone bd; 2 lumps red ochre; carapace rattle; b s.
507	YA	F	22	F	F	O	5.0		b s.
508	YA	M	28	F	R	O	6.1		
509	YA	M	22	F	R	X	3.6		202 a s b; fl scraper; 8 crinoid ring bds; thin cannel coal pendant; antler handle.
510	YA	F	28	F	B	O	2.9		b s.
511	I	M?	2	F	L	O	4.7		b s.
512	I	F?	1	P	B	O	5.1		d s b at neck; conch shell pendant.
513	I	F?	10 Mo	F	B	O	4.4	10	a b 514; slate pendant; 2 fl pt. at elbow.
514	YA	F	28	F	F	O	4.7	10	a b 513; b s.
515	C	F	4	F	B	O	4.6	21	264 d s b; conch shell pendant; 2 columella pins; stone bead; bone awl.
516	YA	M	32	F	L	O	4.6		b s.
517	I	M?	3	F	F	O	4.7		494 d s b; 4 cannel coal beads; stone bd; 4 shell tubular; 1 canine tooth at back under body.
518	YA	F	21	F	R	O	4.0	19	Atlatl stone weight; antler hook; fl point; b s.
519	YA	F	23	F	B	O	4.6		b s.
520	YA	F	22	F	B	O	3.7		
521	I	M?	1	P	F	O	3.5		b s.
522	YA	F	22	F	R	O	4.6		b s.

Burial Number	Age Group	Sex Evaluation	Estimated Age	Burial Form	Burial Position	Burial Placement	Depth Below Surface	Illustration Figure No.	Remarks
523	C	M?	7	F	R	X	3.1		Pestle at feet; antler drift.
524	I	F?	2	F	B	X	4.3		
525	YA	F	21	F	R	O	4.1	10	a b 526, 527; b s.
526	Nb	F?	—	F	L	O	3.9	10	a b 525, 527.
527	YA	M	22	F	R	O	4.1	10	a b 525, 526; b s.
528	YA	M	32	F	L	O	4.9		
529	YA	M	22	F	R	O	5.0		13 d s b; 3 jaws; Lynx rufus (Bobcat); b s.
530	C	F?	4	F	L	O	4.9		b s.
531	I	M?	1	F	L	O	4.5		14 d s b at neck; fl point; b s.
532	YA	F	22	F	B	O	4.1		
533	I	F?	9 Mo	F	B	O			
534	Nb	M?	—	F	R	O	3.8		b s.
535	I	F?	3 Mo	P	B	O	3.6		
536	YA	F	21	D		O	4.7	15	Dismembered; right arm and lower left arm and legs missing.
537	YA	M	32	D		O	4.8	15	Antler projectile point lodged in neck vertebrae; dismembered head and arms; legs missing; pestle at pelvis.
538	I	M	2	P	L	X	3.8		b s.
539	MA	M	37	F	R	O	4.9		
540	YA	M	32	P	R	O	4.0		162 d s b at back of neck; b s.
541	YA	F	22	F	B	O	5.0		b s.
542	YA	F	22	F	R	O	6.1		
543	YA	M	26	F	F	O	4.3		Perforated shell scraper; digging tool used to make grave.
544	I	M?	3	P	B	O	5.1	22 23	225 d s b; atlatl stone weight; 2 cannel coal beads; atlatl weight strung on strand of beads; b s.
545	YA	F	21	P	R	O	5.7		
546	YA	M	26	F	R	O	6.4		
547	YA	M	28	F	R	O	4.8		b s.
548	YA	M	31	F	R	O	3.9		b s.
549	A	M?	14	F	L	O	6.0		b s.
550	I	F?	1	F	B	X	3.5		
551	YA	M	28	F	B	O	4.8		
552	YA	M	22	F	B	O	4.3		b s.
553	I	F?	1	P	B	O	3.5		54 d s b at neck; b s.
554	I	F?	4 Mo	F	B	X	3.1		b s.
555	YA	F	22	P	R	X	4.0		b s.
556	I	M?	9 Mo	P	L	X	3.4		
557	I	F?	1	F	B	O	6.0		b s.
558	YA	M	25	F	L	O	6.3		
559	YA	M	29	F	R	O	4.8		b s.

Burial Number	Age Group	Sex Evaluation	Estimated Age	Form Burial	Burial Position	Burial Placement	Depth Below Surface	Illustration Figure No.	Remarks
560	YA	F	22	F	R	O	6.0	7 17	Antler hook in alignment with composite shell weight of 8 segmented, near left hand; b s.
561	YA	M	24	P	L	O	6.7	7 17	38 d s b; 25 a s b; atlatl shell weight; atlatl stone weight; 2 antler hooks; bone hair pins at face; 2 shell ornaments at neck; 2 antler tips; hole through left parietal.
562	OA	M	60	F	F	X	2.9	16	b s.
563	A	F	14	F	L	X	2.4	7	b s.
564	YA	F	22	P	R	X	2.7	7	a b 565, 566.
565	YA	F	22	F	B	X	3.2		a b 564, 566; b s.
566	C	M	8	F	R	X	3.2	7	a b 564, 565; b s.
567	SA	M	19	F	L	X	3.2	7	b s.
568	YA	M	23	F	L	O	3.4	7	b s.
569	I	F?	2	P	B	O	4.2	7	b s.
570	YA	F	21	F	R	O	3.8		
571	C	F?	7	E	B	O	3.7	13	259 d s b; 17 Marginella apicina (Menke) bds at left wrist; 7 b s b stone; 10 sh ring bds; 1 pestle; 1 animal tooth; 51 tubular sh bd; b s.
572	I	F	3	F	B	O	6.5		5 animal canines near right hand; red ochre; 1 tooth, human; carpace rattle.
573	I	F?	2 Mo	F	R	O	4.4		b s.
574	YA	M	28	F	R	O	7.1		
575	YA	M	22	F	L	O	5.6		99 d s b and 2 tusk-shaped shell ornaments at neck; b s.
576	SA	F	19	F	B	O	5.1		35 drilled canine teeth at neck; b s.
577	YA	M	22	F	F	O	5.9		Atlatl stone weight broken elsewhere; b s.
578	YA	M	28	F	L	O	4.3	9	Bone awl near head; b s.
579	I	F?	1	F	L	O	4.9	9–20	2 d s b; 2 sh pendants; atlatl stone weight; antler hook; b s.
580	I	M?	3	F	R	O	5.9	9	
581	I	M?	3	F	B	X	3.0		a b 872.
582	Nb	F?	—	P	B	X	3.5		4 d s b at neck.
583	C	M?	6	F	L	X	1.7		a b 873.
584	YA	F	23	F	B	O	4.9		
585	YA	M	23	P	B	O	6.3		52 d s b at neck.
586	YA	F	22	F	L	X	1.1		13 d s b; b s.
587	YA	M	23	F	L	X	6.6		8 d s b at right arm; b s; fl point at left forearm.
588	A	F	17	F	B	X	7.2		129 d s b; bone tube, wild turkey, Meleagris galapavo; fl blade.

Burial Number	Age Group	Sex Evaluation	Estimated Age	Burial Form	Burial Position	Burial Placement	Depth Below Surface	Illustration Figure No.	Remarks
589	A	F	17	F	F	X	2.2		b s.
590	YA	F	22	F	L	O	3.1	9	b s.
591	YA	F	22	F	R	O	4.8	9	
592	YA	F	22	F	R	O	4.3		
593	A	M	14	F	R	X	1.9		Fl point in upper end of right humerous.
594	Nb	F?	—	P	B	X	3.9		b s.
595	YA	F	24	F	R	X	2.1		
596	SA	M	18	P	R	X	2.2		33 d s b; 1 cannel coal bd under head.
597	YA	F	22	F	L	O	3.3		
598	YA	F	22	F	L	O	8.0		a b 874.
599	C	M	7	F	L	O	5.1		75 d s b and 1 stone bd at neck.
600	YA	M	28	F	B	O	4.1		
601	YA	F	22	F	B	O	4.3		
602	YA	M	35	F	F	O	4.3		b s.
603	YA	M	21	F	R	O	3.8		
604	YA	M	28	F	L	O	6.3		16 d s b at right wrist.
605	YA	M	24	F	L	X	2.1		b s.
606	I	F?	1	D		O	3.6		a b 607; 2 d s b, bones from 3 feet of Bobcat.
607	Nb	F?	—	P	R	O	4.2		a b 606; 10 d s b; carapace rattle, ceremonially broken?; pebbles; fl scraper; red ochre; b s.
608	YA	F	23	F	F	O	4.2		b s.
609	I	M	9 Mo	P	B	O	4.3		a b 610; 8 d s b; b s.
610	I	M	3	F	B	O	5.0	21 23	a b 609; 161 d s b; 572 a s b; fl reamer; 2 strips and 33 square sections of conch shell, 2 large conch sections 2 end; antler spatula; unfinished beads; b s.
611	YA	M	25	E	B	O	4.7	13	a b 612, 613, 614; 528 d s b; 4 stone bd; large mussel shell; 3 groups of foot bones; Lynx rufus (Bobcat); b s.
612	YA	M	22	E	B	O	4.7	13	a b 611, 613, 614, 431 d s b; 205 a s b; Lampois ovata, Say; 3 stone bds; 4 fl long points; antler flaker; antler projectile pt. and antler hook; b s.
613	YA	M	22	E	B	O	4.5	13	a b 611, 612, 614; 720 a s b; Anculosa praerosa, Say; fl drill; 2 bone pins; fish hook; antler drift; b s.
614	SA	M	19	E	B	O	4.4	14	a b 611, 612, 613; fl point; fl drill; long fish hook; 2 bone pins; Meleagris galaporo; headless; b s.

Burial Number	Age Group	Sex Evaluation	Estimated Age	Burial Form	Burial Position	Burial Placement	Depth Below Surface	Illustration Figure No.	Remarks
615	I	F	3 Mo	P	B	X	2.3		b s.
616	I	F	1	F	L	O	3.6		b s.
617	YA	F	26	F	R	O	3.7		3 carapace rattles; 2 large mussel shells; b s.
618	A	F	17	P	R	X	1.3		2100 very tiny d s b at neck; b s.
619	YA	M	22	F	B	O	6.9		Probably killed by antler pt. in thoracic cavity.
620	YA	F	23	F	L	O	4.7		
621	YA	F	24	F	L	X	3.9		
622	I	M?	3	F	B	O	4.8	22	Stone axe under left shoulder; pestle at right side; b s.
623	C	M?	5	F	L	X	2.3		b s.
624	C	F?	12	F	R	O	4.0		b s.
625	I	M?	7 Mo	P	B	X	1.7		b s.
626	I	M?	1	P	B	X	1.6		b s.
627	I	F?	1	P	B	X	1.7		b s.
628	I	F?	3 Mo	P	R	X	0.8		Red ochre.
629	YA	F	26	F	L	O	4.6		b s.
630	Nb	F?	—	P	R	X	2.2		
631	Nb	F?	—	P	L	X	2.3		b s.
632	I	M?	2	D		O	0.8		2 double drilled copper pendants under chin; tip of bone awl; red ochre stain on bones.
633	I	M?	8 Mo	P	R	O	4.4		
634	YA	F	21	F	B	O	3.8		6 d s b at left wrist; 1 cannel coal bd.
635	YA	M	24	F	F	O	4.3	12	
636	YA	M	23	F	R	X	2.2		
637	A	F	17	F	R	O	4.6		42 d s b at neck and around wrist; 1138 a s b; b s.
638	YA	F	22	P	L	O	3.4		55 d s b; at neck; 1 stone bd; graving tool; bone cylinder, 73 mm with incisor tooth in each end; skulless.
639	YA	M	23	P	R	X	1.7	14	a b 640; dismembered, arms and left leg missing.
640	YA	M	25		B	X	1.7	14	a b 639; dismembered, arms and right leg and lower left leg missing.
641	YA	M	25	F	R	X	0.9		Red ochre.
642	YA	F	22	F	S	O	4.8	13	b s.
643	YA	M	29	F	L	O	6.5	13	
644	YA	F	23	F	F	O	3.0		b s.
645	Nb	F	—	P	B	O	4.1		b s.
646	I	M	3	P	L	O	4.2		b s.
647	I	F?	2 Mo	P	B	O	3.6		2 large mussel shell halves.

Burial Number	Age Group	Sex Evaluation	Estimated Age	Burial Form	Burial Position	Burial Placement	Depth Below Surface	Illustration Figure No.	Remarks
648	YA	M	22	P	R	O	3.2		b s.
649	I	M?	3	P	R	O	4.7		14 d s b at neck; red ochre near right elbow.
650	A	M	15	F	R	O	4.7		121 d s b; a s b; 4 cut sections of jaw of Canis lupis (Wolf); b s.
651	I	F?	3	F	B	O	3.6		178 d s b at neck and pelvis; 1 stone bd; b s.
652	YA	F?	24	F	B	X	1.7		Dog Burial 18; b s.
653	YA	F	31	F	R	O	3.6		b s.
654	I	M	2	P	B	O	3.8	20	107 d s b at neck; 1 atlatl stone weight broken.
655	C	M	7	D		O	3.2	15	Dismembered; hole in skull; b s.
656	YA	F	24	P	R	X	1.9		
657	I	F?	2	P	R	X	2.2		Bone pin on right arm.
658	YA	F	23	F	R	X	2.4		
659	MA	M	40	P	R	O	4.1		b s.
660	I	?	9 Mo	P	L	O	4.9		Preservation poor; red ochre; skull only saved; b s.
661	YA	M	28	F	B	O	3.5		Residue of woven bark fabric both over and under pelvis; 2 curved, drilled shell ornaments at neck; b s.
662	I	F?	2 Mo	P	R	O	2.8		b s.
663	YA	F	24	F	R	O	2.6		
664	C	F?	8	P	L	O	3.3		b s.
665	YA	M	29	F	R	O	3.2		
666	A	F?	14	F	L	O	5.1		b s.
667	YA	F	22	F	B	O	5.1		b s.
668	YA	F	26	P	R	O	4.3		b s.
669	YA	F	22	F	R	O	3.5		Broken atlatl stone weight; b s.
670	YA	F	24	F	R	O	3.4		Double pointed bone pin.
671	Nb	F?	—	P	R	X	2.1		b s.
672	YA	F	22	F	R	O	2.4		b s.
673	Nb	F?	—	P	B	O	2.7		b s.
674	I	F?	5 Mo	P	B	X	1.8		
675	YA	M	25	D		X	2.1		Skulless; b s.
676	I	M?	1	D		X	2.1		b s.
677	YA	F?	22	D		O	3.2		Skull only saved.
678	—	—	—	D		X	0.6		No bones saved.
679	I	F?	9 Mo	P	L	X	1.5		115 d s b at neck; b s.
680	I	F?	4 Mo	P	R	X	1.5		A stain of red ochre near head; b s.
681	C	M?	1	F	L	X	1.6		11 d s b at neck; b s; red ochre.
682	Nb	F?		P	B	X	1.8		
683	C	M?	7	P	L	X	2.8		b s.

Burial Number	Age Group	Sex Evaluation	Estimated Age	Burial Form	Burial Position	Burial Placement	Depth Below Surface	Illustration Figure No.	Remarks
684	I	M?	3	P	R	O	4.3		b s.
685	YA	F	31	F	L	X	4.3		b s.
686	I	F?	2	P	L	O	4.3		Textile over and under burial, much decayed; b s.
687	YA	M	28	E	R	O	4.3	24	75 d s b; atlatl stone weight; antler hook in alignment; 1 carapace rattle; 21 pebbles; 3 conch shell pendants, 1 incised; bone pin; two mandibles (two pairs of jaws) and foot bones of a mustelid, probably weasel; 1 tone bd; 3 shell pendants.
688	A	M	13	F	R	O	5.4		
689	I	M?	3	P	R	X	4.3		
690	YA	M	33	P	B	O	7.5		a b 691, 692, 693, 694; flint pt. in spine at right scapula; b s.
691	C	F?	4	F	R	O	7.5		a b 690, 692, 693, 694; fl pt. which may have been in body at time of burial; b s.
692	C	M?	9	P	B	O	7.5		a b 690, 691, 693, 694; b s.
693	I	M?	3	D		O	7.5		
694	C	F?	6	P	L	O	7.5		b s.
695	MA	M	40	F	L	O	5.7	14	
696	YA	F	22	F	R	O	6.0		25 d s b; 2 shell pendants; b s.
697	YA	M	22	P	B	X	1.5		10 d s b and pendant made from end whorl.
698	YA	M	22	P	B	X	1.9		4 fl pts.; 4 antler pts.; 3 fl pieces; bird bone awl; bone pin; 2 ground hog jaws; deer jaw; cut beaver incisor and right ramus of raccoon.
699	Nb	F?	—	P	L	X	3.1		b s.
700	I	F?	3 Mo	P	B	X	3.4		b s.
701	YA	F	21	P	L	O	6.4		225 d s b at neck; b s.
702	MA	M	53	P	R	X	4.0		Bits of fibre twisted textile near right lower leg; b s.
703	YA	F	28	F	L	X	4.1		
704	I	?	3	P	B	X	3.7		22 d s b and 65 a s b at neck and side of burial; 1 coal bd; antler pt.; cloth fibres in earth; only teeth saved; b s.
705	MA	M	43	F	F	O	4.7		
706	A	F	16	F	R	X	4.1		Fl scraper, textile in earth under pelvis; b s.
707	Nb	F?	—	D		X	3.6		

Burial Number	Age Group	Sex Evaluation	Estimated Age	Burial Form	Burial Position	Burial Placement	Depth Below Surface	Illustration Figure No.	Remarks
708	YA	M	25	D		X	3.7	22	Fl scraper; 3 fl pts.; 5 pieces of fl, 1 worked; 3 antler tips; textile fragments; 20 bone pins, some broken; 5 pointed bone splinters; 5 bone splinters broken; 2 small animal vertebrae; 11 ground hog incisors; snake vertebrae; 3 tubular shell bds at neck; b s.
709	YA	M	25	F	L	X	1.0		2 d s b.
710	Nb	M?	—	D		X	0.9		
711	Nb	F?	—	P	R	X	1.7		6 d s b near neck; 1 barrel cannel coal bd; b s.
712	YA	F	26	P	R	X	1.3		
713	YA	M	27	F	R	X	1.6		
714	I	F	9 Mo	P	F	X	2.4		
715	SA	F	19	F	L	X	2.2		b s.
716	SA	F	20	F	B	X	2.5		b s.
717	YA	F	26	P	B	X	3.2		a b 718, 719.
718	A	F?	13	D		X	3.2		a b 717, 719; disturbed by ground hogs; b s.
719	I	M?	3	D		X	3.2		a b 717, 718; disturbed by ground hogs.
720	C	F	11	P	B	X	3.3		2 bone awls; 2 cut antler bases; b s.
721	Nb	F?	—	P	B	X	3.2		29 d s b; 1 tublar banded slate bd at neck; red ochre stains over burial; b s.
722	I	M?	2	P	R	X	3.5		b s.
723	C	F?	12	P	L	X	3.0		b s.
724	C	M	6	P	B	X	2.8		
725	YA	F	22	F	L	X	3.4		Feet gone; b s.
726	I	F?	3	P	L	X	3.7		11 d s b; 174 a s b back of skull; 1 coal bd at knee; b s.
727	YA	M	22	P	R	X	3.1		Textile fragments, visible in earth; b s.
728	I	F?	9 Mo	P	L	X	4.3		5 d s b; 1 stone bd at neck; b s.
729	Nb	M?	—	P	L	X	3.5		12 d s b; 1 red sandstone, 1 cannel coal and 1 red slate bd; 2 shell pendants at neck; b s.
730	Nb	F?	—	P	L	X	3.5		
731	YA	F	22	F	F	X	2.9		
732	YA	F	23	F	F	X	3.7		Dog Burial 19 lies across head of burial.
733	MA	M	40	F	B	X	4.2		b s.
734	Nb	M?	—	P	F	X	2.9		7 tubular shell and 1 tubular red sandstone bd.
735	YA	F	24	P	L	O	4.9		b s.

Burial Number	Age Group	Sex Evaluation	Estimated Age	Burial Form	Burial Position	Burial Placement	Depth Below Surface	Illustration Figure No.	Remarks
736	MA	M	50	F	L	O	4.7		11 d s b near left wrist.
737	YA	M	26	F	L	O	4.1		
738	YA	M	22	D		X	2.3		Aboriginal disturbance.
739	YA	F	22	F	L	O	4.1		b s.
740	C	M?	8	F	L	X	2.7		4 d s b at chin; 1 stone bd; bone pin back of skull.
741	I	M?	2 Mo	P	B	X	3.1		b s.
742	YA	M	27	F	R	X	3.4		b s.
743	I	M?	8 Mo	P	B	O	4.1	8 20	Atlatl stone weight and antler hook near face; 1 bone tube 135 mm; grave handle near feet; b s.
744	YA	M	24	F	R	O	4.3		9 canine teeth drilled; 2 curved shell pendants at back of neck.
745	YA	M	23	F	L	X	3.5		b s.
746	A	M?	13	F	L	X	3.3		Textile fragments at pelvis.
747	I	F?	3	P	B	O	5.0		9 slug pearls near wrist; b s.
748	YA	F	22	F	R	X	1.3		
749	Nb	F?	—	P	B	X	3.1		32 d s b; 16 tusk bds; shell bds; 1 coal bd; near neck.
750	Nb	F?	—	D		X	2.9		White clay pigment, left of head; red ochre; b s.
751	A	F	17	F	L	O	4.8		Red ochre under head; b s.
752	I	M?	5 Mo	D		O	3.7		b s.
753	—	—	—	D			3.6		No bones saved; dog Burial 19.
754	C	M	15	P	R	O	3.9	19	Atlatl stone weight and antler hook; atlatl weight ceremonially broken; antler handle; b s.
755	YA	M	28	P	L	X	2.4		5 d s b at left wrist; antler flaking tool; 2 bone awls; b s.
756	SA	M	19	F	R	O	4.0		60 d s b and 1 coal bd under neck; b s.
757	C	M?	5	D		X	2.9		4 fl points; 3 ground hog incisors; green pigment; b s.
758	SA	F	19	D		X	0.8		b s.
759	I	?	2 Mo	D			1.5		Dog ulna awl.
760	A	F?	17	D		X	1.7		166 d s b; 1 atlatl stone weight; a b 875; b .s
761	YA	F	21	F	L	X	2.1		841 d s b at neck; perforated shell disc 35 mm diameter; b s.
762	Nb	F?	—	P	R	X	2.9		
763	YA	M	35	F	R	O	3.7		
764	I	M?	1	F	R	X	3.3		b s.
765	YA	M	29	F	R	X	1.3		
766	YA	M	22	F	L	X	1.9	19	11 d s b; antler hook and handle near face; 1 coal bd at neck; bone hairpin; b s.

Burial Number	Age Group	Sex Evaluation	Estimated Age	Burial Form	Burial Position	Burial Placement	Depth Below Surface	Illustration Figure No.	Remarks
767	I	F?	1 Mo	P	L	X	2.2	24	a b 768; 4 restored conch pendants.
768	I	F?	1 Mo	P	F	X	2.2		a b 767; b s.
769	A	M	15	F	L	X	3.4	24	d s b; 68 a s b; 4 bone awls; 2 fl pts.; gray clay pigment at breast; fl pt. broken at neck; 1 coal bd; 4 conch shell pendants at right elbow; textile fragments near chin; red ochre; b s.
770	C	M	7	P	R	X	1.9		b s.
771	YA	F	22	D		X	3.3		
772	YA	F	22	P	L	X	2.2		201 d s b under head; b s.
773	I	F?	3	P	B	X	1.8		
774	YA	M	23	P	R	X	3.5		Textile and section of elk horn near right hand; 6 bird bone pins, charred.
775	YA	F	21	P	B	X	1.0		b s.
776	I	M?	2 Mo	D		X	0.8		Red ochre.
777	YA	F?	26	F	L	X	0.9		b s.
778	YA	F	22	F	R	X	1.7		
779	Nb	F?		P	B	X	1.0		2 d s b at right wrist.
780	YA	F	24	F	L	X	3.3		Scattered bones of Burial 876 overlaid Burial 780.
781	C	M?	5	P	L	X	2.7		28 d s b; 6 a s b; fl pt.; piece of bone pin; 2 pieces of worked stone; 3 antler tines; 2 bone awls; bone tube broken; 2 ground hog jaws; fl cores; a b 782; b s.
782	I	M?	3	P	R	X	2.7		10 d s b; 1 coal bd; a b 781; b s.
783	YA	F	29	P	B	X	0.8		b s.
784	I	F?	1	D		X	1.4		
785	C	M	7	P	L	X	3.1	17	1 antler hook; 1 carapace rattle; antler atlatl handle; textile under burial; b s.
786	YA	F	22	F	F	X	2.7		b s.
787	I	F?	1 Mo	D		X	0.9		Skull missing.
788	I	?	1 Mo	D		X	0.8		Bone awl.
789	YA	F	23	F	L	X	1.5		b s.
790	YA	F?	22	F	R	X	1.1		b s.
791	YA	F	21	P	B	X	1.3		b s.
792	YA	F	28	F	R	X	1.5		b s.
793	I	F?	3	P	B	X	2.0		3 d s b; 33 a s b around right arm; half jaw of raccoon; b s.
794	YA	F	23	P	R	X	2.1		b s.
795	I	M?	6 Mo	P	B	X	1.9		a b 877; b s.

Burial Number	Age Group	Sex Evaluation	Estimated Age	Burial Form	Burial Position	Burial Placement	Depth Below Surface	Illustration Figure No.	Remarks
796	SA	M	18	F	R	X	2.5	19	Antler atlatl handle and hook; b s.
797	MA	M	40	F	R	X	2.4		
798	A	M?	13	P	R	O	4.3	19	Atlatl stone weight; antler hook; b s. antler atlatl handle.
799	YA	F	27	P	R	X	2.1		Half of mussel shell perforated.
800	I	F?	1 Mo	D		X	3.0		
801	I	F?	2 Mo	P	L	O	5.6		3 d s b at sternum.
802	YA	F	21	D		O	6.2		69 d s b; a b 803; b s.
803	I	F?	4 Mo	P	L	O	6.1		a b 802; b s.
804	SA	M	19	F	E	O	7.4		
805	Nb	F?	—	P	B	O	4.9		Broken flint pt. at left wrist; b s.
806	I	F?	2 Mo	P	R	X	3.8		
807	C	—	—	D		X	6.2		1 carapace rattle; 2 fl scrapers; no bones saved.
808	MA	M	45	F	L	X	1.8		Bone pin.
809	C	F	12	F	R	X	1.8		a b 810; b s.
810	YA	M	23	F	L	X	2.1		a b 809; broken fl pt.; piece of bone awl; rough bone tube.
811	Nb	?	—	D		X	0.9		Atlatl stone weight; burial placed on mussel shell halves; shell shows no arrangement; headless.
812	YA	M	29	D		O	4.6		Part of skull and long bones gone; b s.
813	YA	M	22	D		O	4.6		b s.
814	SA	F	18	D		O	2.7		b s.
815	C	M?	5	P	F	X	1.7		Bone pin; perforated and etched; white shell bead near left hand; stone bd and piece of carapace at back of skull; b s.
816	YA	M	28	P	L	X	0.8		
817	YA	M	23	F	R	O	3.1		Dog Burial 21; b s.
818	I	F	1	D		X	2.2		Hole in skull.
819	YA	F	22	P	R	X	1.9		
820	I	M?	2 Mo	D		X	1.9		6 d s b at neck.
821	YA	F	22	P	L	O	5.8		a b 822, 823; b s.
822	C	F	11	P	R	O	5.8		a b 821, 823; 2 bone tubes; ear pendants; b s.
823	I	M?	3	P	L	O	5.7		a b 821, 822; b s.
824	A	F	15	P	B	O	6.9		1 carapace rattle; b s.
825	YA	F	30	F	R	O	6.7		b s.
826	C	M?	8	F	R	X	3.1		
827	YA	M	27	P	L	X	2.2	14	3 mussel shell halves; 3 cut antler pts.; 7 fl points; 3 fl scrapers; animal tusk shaped shell bd; yellow pigment; all near center of burial.

Burial Number	Age Group	Sex Evaluation	Estimated Age	Burial Form	Burial Position	Burial Placement	Depth Below Surface	Illustration Figure No.	Remarks
828	C	F?	6	D		O	2.5		
829	YA	F	22	P	B	O	3.7		b s.
830	Nb	?	—	P	B	X	2.4		
831	YA	M	26	F	L	O	3.6		Textile fragments under pelvis.
832	A	F?	15	P	F	O	5.7		b s.
833	I	F?	3 Mo	P	B	O	4.8		b s.
834	C	F?	9	P	L		7.5		
835	SA	F	20	E	B	X	1.0		b s.
836	SA	M	18	P	R	O	5.6		47 d s b; 1 carapace rattle; b s.
837	YA	F	23	P	B	O	5.4		b s.
838	I	M?	1	F	L	O	4.3		
839	A	M?	14	P	L	O	6.2		
840	YA	F	24	P	L	O	5.3		b s.
841	YA	F	22	P	B	O	4.2		
842	C	F?	7	F	L	O	5.8		14 d s b and 4 large drilled canine bds at neck; b·s.
843	YA	F	23	F	R	X	2.6		Skull is bent back over vertebrae.
844	I	F?	3	P	R	O	5.5		d s b at left arm and neck; bone chisel by arm; b s.
845	YA	M	28	F	R	O	5.4		d s b at neck.
846	I	F?	1	P	R	O	4.5		d s b at neck.
847	YA	F	22	F	R	O	6.7		b s.
848	YA	M	23	F	B	O	7.3		
849	YA	F	23	F	R	O	5.9		
850	YA	F	22	F	F	O	6.5		
851	YA	F	21	P	L	O	6.4		Fabric by pelvis; b s.
852	YA	M	28	F	R	X	0.9		Fabric over chest, under pelvis and left femur; bone hairpin at top of skull.
853	YA	M	23	P	L	O	7.6		43 d s b; segmented shell atlatl weight by left elbow back of head; beads between ulna and radius of right arm; long bone tube.
854	YA	M	26	F	R	O	8.7		b s.
855	C	M?	6	P	B	O	6.0		
856	Nb	F?	—	P	B	O	5.8		a b 857; scattered bones of Burial 878; b s.
857	I	?	8 Mo	D		O	5.8		a b 856; 10 distal phlanges of Lynx rufus; scattered bones of Burial 878; b s.
858	YA	M	24	F	L	X	1.5		b s.
859	YA	F	27	F	L	X	1.0		Lower part of legs cut off; apparently while burying 858; b s.
860	YA	M	28	P	L	O	7.9		d s b at right wrist; anculosa bds over pelvis were apparently sewn on belt or skirt.

Burial Number	Age Group	Sex Evaluation	Estimated Age	Burial Form	Burial Position	Burial Placement	Depth Below Surface	Illustration Figure No.	Remarks
861	I	F?	4 Mo	F	R	O	2.9		a b 862, 863; b s.
862	I	M?	5 Mo	P	B	O	3.2		a b 861, 863; above 863 and below 861; b s.
863	MA	M	42	P	L		3.4		a b 861, 862; b s.
864	YA	M	30	D		O	6.0		a b 865, 866; b s.
865	YA	M	24	P	B	O	6.0		a b 866, 864; headless; b s.
866	YA	F	24	F	R	O	5.2		a b 864, 865.
867	YA	F	24	F	L	X	2.4		
868	YA	M	28	P	L	X	1.5		1 carapace rattle; stone bar atlatl weight opposite right humerus; turtle shell fragments; Lepisosteus osseus (Garpike); b s.
869	SA	M	20	D		O	7.3		a b 59.
870	YA	M	25	D		O	5.8		a b 120.
871	I	F?	2 Mo	D		X	2.3		a b 388.
872	YA	F?	22	F	B	X	3.0		a b 581.
873	I	M?	3	D		X	1.7		a b 583.
874	YA	M	23	D		O	8.0		a b 598.
875	I	?	6 Mo	D		X	1.7		a b 760.
876	I	F	3	D		X	3.3		a b 780.
877	I	?	3 Mo	D		X	1.9		a b 795.
878	I	?	6 Mo	D		O	5.8		a b 856, 857; b s.
879	C	F?	11	D		O	7.4	10	a b 370.
880	YA	M?	22	D		X	2.9		a b 380; b s.

BURIAL STATISTICS

From the tabulation of these burial data it would be possible to derive a considerable mass of burial statistics. The publication of such statistical data is often of questionable value, for in general, it cannot be known in advance just what information is most desired by the reader. Having published the basic data on 880 burials, any serious student seeking information on a particular problem may be able to work out statistical relations as desired. Thus the statistical data furnished herein covers only the most obvious relations and the breakdown is not elaborate.

From the figures which follow, it is clear that more than half of the burials at Indian Knoll were in pits in the subsoil below the midden. Extended burials were so rare as to be almost negligible, full flexure was generally preferred, particularly for pit burials, and as has been pointed out, aboriginal disturbance of graves was frequent. There was clearly no preference indicated for position of the body in the grave, and many were even placed face downward at burial. Relatively few had artifacts placed with them at burial, (275 out of 879) and if one excludes burials having only beads (88 burials), which are worn as body decorations and in part attached to clothing, there remains only 187 burials having artifacts which might be considered as having been placed in the graves intentionally, from a desire to make a burial offering. This number might be still further reduced if one should exclude those burials which had evidence of textiles in the grave and nothing else, since textiles may be considered merely as clothing, the inclusion of which is not an indication of "burial offering." Further, as has been pointed out, no graves yielded any great number of flint, bone, or antler projectile points, which would have suggested any intention of depositing such a supply in a quiver. Generally, such projectile points as were found in grave association occurred singly, or in small number, and as stated, under such conditions as to indicate they may have been lodged in the body which they accompany at the time of burial and in some cases they surely were the cause of death. If such burials are eliminated from the list of *intentional* burial associations, the number of burials having true "burial offering" becomes still smaller.

However, there were burials showing positive evidence of intentional placement of artifacts with the dead. Certain artifact combinations are observed to recur more or less frequently. In the belief that association of artifacts with each other in the graves is an important consideration, many burial associations of artifacts are presented in Figures 23 to 30 inclusive. Each illustration is described in some detail. The occurrence of the various artifacts constituting the atlatl complex is discussed separately under the title "The Problem of the Atlatl."

Total burials in this excavation.. 880

Placement:

    Burials placed in subsoil pit 488

    Burials placed in midden 392   880

Burial Form:

    Fully flexed burials 524

Partially flexed burials	248	
Extended burials	11	
Disturbed burials, form indeterminate	97	880

Body Position:

Body on back	270	
Body on right side	237	
Body on left side	216	
Body on face	56	
Sitting position	4	
Disturbed, position indeterminate	97	880

Sex-Age Group:

Newborn, sex not determined		55

Infants: x–3 years

Males	92	
Females	103	
Sex undeterminable	14	209

Children: 4–12 years

Males	48	
Females	26	
Sex undeterminable	1	75

Adolescents: 13–17 years

Males	26	
Females	26	52

Sub Adults: 18–20 Years

Males	15	
Females	14	29

Young Adults: 21–35 Years

Males	203	
Females	185	388

Middle Aged: 36–55 Years

Males	34	
Females	2	36

Old Adults: 56–x Years

Males		3
Skeletons not available for study because of decay		33	880

Artifact Associations:

Burials with material associations		275	880

Burials with material associations (31.4%) ......　275　880

Bead Association:
Burials with beads only (anculosa, disk, shell, stone) ....　88
Burials with beads and other artifacts ....　69
Burials with other artifacts, no beads....................　118　275

Carapace Rattle:
18 graves had one carapace rattle each ....　18
1 grave had two carapace rattles......................　2
4 graves had three carapace rattles each ....　12

23 graves had carapace rattles total ....　　　　32
Atlatl and Association:
Burials having atlatl parts, carapace rattles and red ochre ....　1
Burials having atlatl parts, carapace rattles, but no red ochre ....　5
Burials having atlatl parts, red ochre, but no carapace rattles ....　2
Burials having atlatl parts, no red ochre, and no carapace rattles ....　36

Total burials with atlatl parts ....　44
Red Ochre:
Burials having red ochre and carapace rattles..　5
Burials having red ochre but no carapace rattles ....　29

Total burials having red ochre ....　34
Burials showing traces of textiles in grave..................　13
Burials containing flint or antler projectile points placed in manner suggesting cause of death............　23
Burials having perforated canine teeth ....　7
Rodent incisor teeth, total 31 were found in burials..　11
Animal jaws, total 31 were found in burials..............　11
Dismembered burials:
Headless ....　13
Limbs or other portions lost ....　12

Total dismembered burials ....　25

Multiple burial:　　　　　　　　　　　　　　　Indi-
　　　　　　　　　　　　　　　　　　　　　Graves vidual
2 in one grave ....　22　44

	Graves	Indi- vidual
3 in one grave	5	15
4 in one grave	1	4
5 in one grave	1	5
6 in one grave	2	12
Total multiple burials	31	80

ARTIFACTS FROM BURIAL ASSOCIATION

Artifacts from burial association represent a very minor portion of the total artifact assembly recovered at this site. It is important, however, to observe the association of arifacts as they were found to occur in burials.

SHELL ARTIFACTS

Figures 23 to 30 present illustrations of such associations. Each illustration is separately described in some detail.

Illustrations presented in Figure 23 may be described as follows:

A. This illustration presents a portion of the associated artifacts of Burial 610. This burial is interesting because of the suggestion it affords on the method of bead manufacture. The central group of Anculosa beads consists of part of the beads from what was evidently a beaded garment, see Figure 21 D. There were many fragments of large marine shell. It is apparent that in the manufacture of beads, the large shells were not broken irregularly, but were cut into strips, and these strips were then cut into squares; these squares were drilled and finally made into beads. The fragments of the shell lip, and the end of the central columella were also used to make pendants. The two long heavy curved segments are from the head of a large marine shell. They too were used for pendants. The only artifact in this photo not of shell is shown in the upper right hand corner. It is an antler drift.

B. In this illustration are shown many necklaces. They are generally made from large disk shell beads, but very often have one or more stone beads as a central decoration.

In the upper half of the photo the rectangle is made from a necklace from Burial 215, which has two large barrel shaped beads, one of cannel coal and one of stone. Inside this rectangle from top to bottom are three necklaces placed in straight lines from Burials

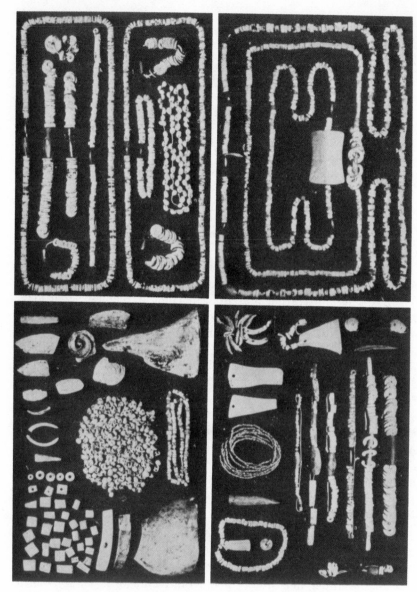

Fig. 23. Shell beads and pendants, stone beads and animal teeth from burial association.

756, 495, and 214. On the left side, within the rectangle is a necklace from Burial 652, and on the right, the small necklace is from
Burial 10. This is remarkable for the single large shell bead in it is
27 mm. in diameter and is 14 mm. thick. The large barrel shaped
bead with Burial 756 is 58 mm. long by 24 mm. diameter. The large
bead with Burial 495 is cylindrical. Its length is 47 mm. and
diameter 20 mm. The lower half of this photo is enclosed in a necklace from Burial 245. On the left are beads from Burial 704, in the
center from Burial 756, and on the right from Burial 198. The
Anculosa beads are typical of many burials where they were evidently used by sewing them on garments.

C. This photo shows in upper left corner shell beads and
pendant from Burial 512. At the left and under this necklace is
shown a small necklace of disk shell beads, two stone beads and
large central bead of cannel coal. This was from Burial 121 and
was accompanied by the bone projectile point shown in upper row.
In the center of the row is shown a portion of a necklace of about
2000 small shell disk beads. The average bead diameter is only 2.5
mm. and the hole is 1 mm. in diameter. These are from Burial 618.
The two shell pendants, 72 and 82 mm. long, respectively, are from
Burial 445. In the upper right is shown a necklace made of nine
drilled canine teeth from small carnivore, and two curved shell
pendants made to imitate teeth; these are from Burial 744. In the
central portion of the plate are shown six necklaces which from
top to bottom were taken from Burials 551, 734, 721, 637, 445,
and 740, respectively. The first of these has small disk beads and
a tubular red stone bead 19 mm. long. The necklace from Burial
734 consists of seven tubular shell beads and a barrel-shaped stone
bead 43 mm. long. The necklace from Burial 721 has disk shell
beads, 6 short tubular shell beads and a barrel-shaped bead of
banded slate, highly polished. Burial 638 had a necklace of 55 disk
shell beads and one barrel-shaped, cannel-coal bead, 30 mm. long.
The necklace from Burial 445 consisted of two tubular shell beads,
two tubular red stone beads, 23 and 29 mm. long, and three shell
rings so perforated that they slip over the stone beads. These rings
are 22 mm. in diameter and have a perforation of 11 mm. diameter.
In the lower row is shown a necklace from Burial 740 consisting
of 41 large shell disk beads with a relatively small perforation.
Diameter of beads is 20 mm. and of hole is 5 mm. The dark stone

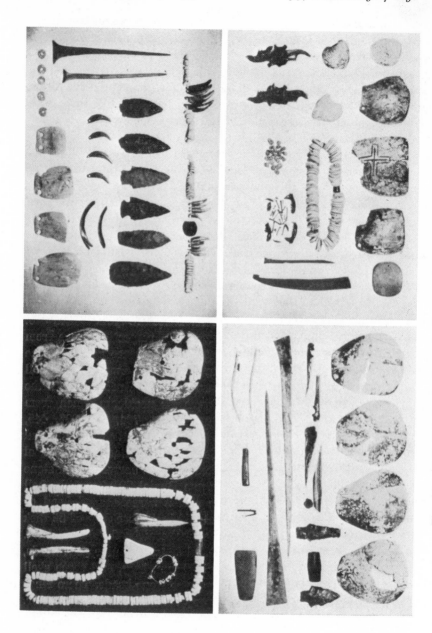

Fig. 24.　Shell gorgets, beads, and other associated artifacts from burials.

barrel-shaped bead is a very beautiful specimen, highly polished, and is 46 mm. long and 17 mm. in diameter. With this burial was a bone pin shown at the right. In the right hand corner a necklace consisting of 5 disk beads and a cannel-coal bead is shown; this was with Burial 711. The near triangular shell pendant, 70 mm. long and 52 mm. maximum width, with 12 disk shell beads, constituted a necklace found with Burial 512.

The long necklace bordering this illustration contains five barrel-shaped beads, one cannel coal, one jasper, and three silicious limestone, four shell tubular beads, one drilled canine tooth and 494 shell disk beads. It was with Burial 517. The inside rectangular necklace of beads, taken from Burial 571, consists of 107 disk shell beads, 51 short tubular beads, 12 large ring-like shell beads (not all shown in photograph), four tubular stone beads and one stone ring. They were originally strung as shown. Some of the shell rings have broken so that they could not be restored.

In the center of this photo is shown a necklace from Burial 544. It consists of two cannel-coal beads and some 225 disk shell beads. On this string of beads was found an atlatl weight strung as shown. This weight was a cream colored granite, with fine green markings. It is highly polished, prismatic in form, 81 mm. long, 56 mm. wide and has a hole 11 mm. in diameter through which the beads slip easily.

Illustrations presented in Figure 24 may be described as follows:

A. The left half of this photograph shows artifact from Burial 515. These consist of 264 disc shell beads, some quite small, two columella shell pins, the largest 98 mm. long, a triangular shell pendant, 38 x 47 mm., one stone bead and a bone awl made from the cannon bone of deer. The right half of this photograph shows four shell pendants from Burial 767. These pendants were found broken into many small fragments and are shown restored. They were made from the lips of large marine shells, and are in length about 120 mm. and in width 108 mm. They all show the natural curvature of the shell, and all have three perforations, two near the small proximal end, probably for suspension and a single hole near the center. The edges are very carefully rounded.

B. The upper three-fourths of this photograph shows artifacts from Burial 339. They consist of four shell pendants, five disc beads, four drilled canine teeth, two beaver *(Castor canadensis)* incisors, a flint knife, five projectile points, and two bone hair pins. With this burial beside these artifacts, there were antler projectile points, an antler atlatl hook and another beaver incisor. These last were all badly damaged by decay, and no more remained than was necessary to identify them. Also there was another large flint blade shown in Figure 21 E. The shell pendants had each two holes for suspension and two of them had single holes in the lower edge of the gorget as if something was to be suspended from them. The dimension of the two bone pins are as follows: larger pin, length 180 mm, diameter head 36 mm. and upper shaft diameter 9 mm; smaller pin, length 157 mm., upper shaft diameter 11 mm.

In the lower row, left, of this photograph is shown a necklace from Burial 749. This consists of disc shell beads, one cannel coal bead and nine drilled canine teeth. The original necklace had 42 shell beads, 16 teeth, some of which had so decayed they could not be strung. In lower row, right, is shown a necklace from Burial 842. This consisted of 14 cylindrical shell beads and four drilled bear canines.

C. The upper half of this photograph shows artifacts from Burial 55. These consist of an antler drift, a bone fish hook, a limestone bar atlatl weight, 73 x 32 x 12 mm., two drilled columella shell pendants, 11 mm. long, and two broad flat bone awls. These awls are hard bone of fine texture and seem to have been cut from human femora. They have maximum dimensions respectively of 324 x 28 x 5 mm., and 315 x 31 x 5 mm. The lower half of this photograph shows a portion of the artifacts from the Burial 769. These consist of four bone awls, two of which were made from the ulna of small mammals, a barrel-shaped cannel-coal bead 43 x 22 mm., four shell gorgets, and two flint points. The four shell gorgets show considerable curvature, having been cut from the lip of large marine shells. These have two perforations each in the smaller upper end for suspension and a single perforation in the center. Of the two flint points one has a broken tip. It was found at the neck of the burial. Its position suggests that it may have been the cause of death.

D.   Burial 357 had beside a quantity of disc shell beads, not shown, two pairs of ground hog jaws *(Marmota monax)*. The jaws of each pair were found lying together in the positions shown in the illustration. These jaws seem to have been intentionally placed and perhaps bound together in this position. Due to their form, the jaws of a pair make very substantial contacts and if bound together, they lock in such a way that there is no slip. It appears that there is a significance in the placement since these jaws show that the incisors which are exposed have been sharpened artifically, which suggests that a pair, when bound together, constituted a graver for cutting shell or wood. Incisor teeth are well seated in the jaw bone and thus admirably adapted for use as gravers. It has been found that incisors of other rodents were used as gravers by mounting them in hollow bone tubes.

All other artifacts shown in this photograph are from Burial 687. This burial had a stone atlatl weight and antler hook in alignment, a bone awl and three shell gorgets. They were restorable, as shown. At least two show that they were of the usual form with three perforations, two at the upper edge and one in the center. One of these gorgets, the largest of the group, was 80 x 85 mm. On the interior concave surface an equal-arms cross had been engraved as shown. The cross was outlined by an incised line, and a line also was incised along the center of each arm. Also three mussel shells were nested in the grave and some 75 disc shell beads with one stone bead, which constituted a necklace, had been scattered over the body. A carapace rattle had decayed beyond restoration, but the 21 pebbles from its interior were found in a cluster. Four jaws and the foot bones of a mustelid, probably a weasel, were found together, but no other parts of this animal, which suggests that these bones may have been part of the contents of a medicine bag.

A.   This photograph shows the burial associations of Burial 236. They consisted of 3400 small disc shell beads, some 95 disc beads in two larger sizes and a large cup made by cutting out the interior spiral of a large conch (Busycon perversum). There were also four shell pendants which lay inside the conch which was placed near the pelvis. These pendants had deteriorated considerably. They showed perforations only at the proximal end. There were in the grave three incisors of muskrat.

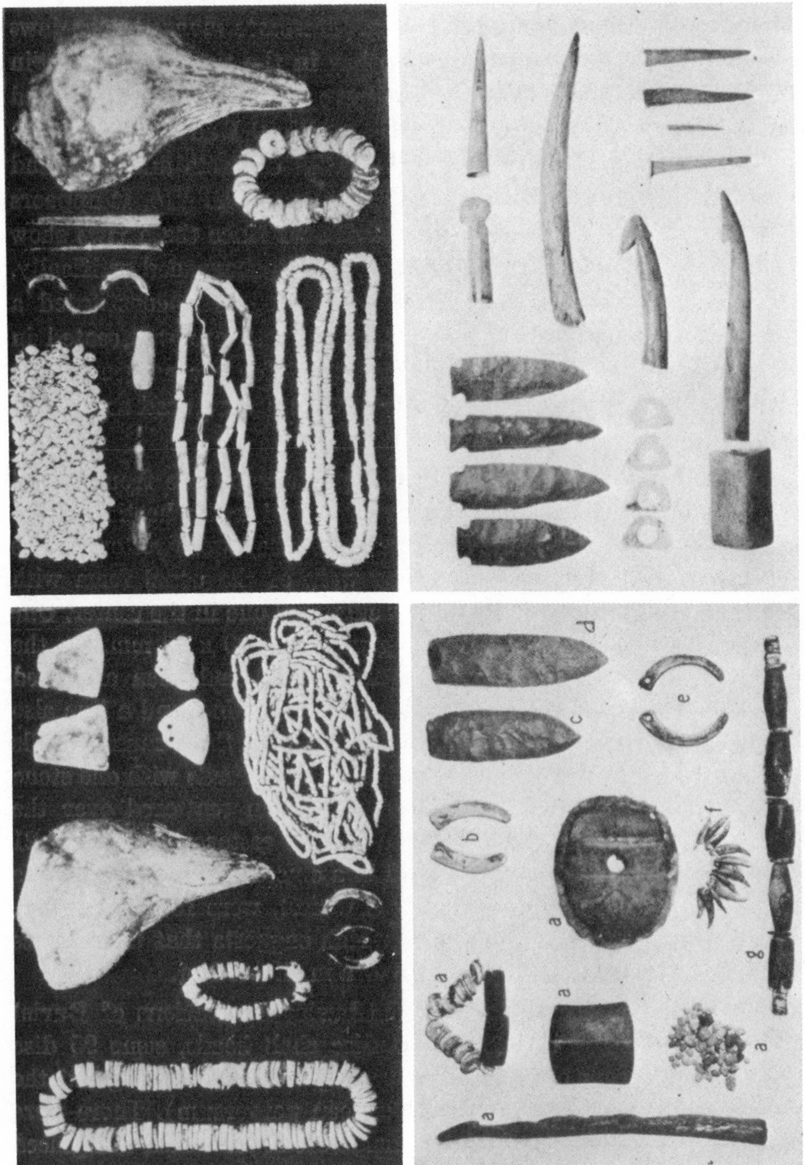

Fig. 25.   Shell artifacts with stone artifacts and antler atlatl hooks from burial association.

B. There is shown in this photograph most of the association of Burial 237. There were 36 large disc beads and about 1100 small disc beads, 38 tubular shell beads and about 500 Anculosa beads; with these were a conch shell cup and a large gastroped shell identified as Fasciolonia gigantea (kienen), together with two bone awls, three incisor teeth of muskrat and three barrel-shaped beads, one of cannel-coal, one of limestone, and one of fine grained sandstone. Beads and fragmentary shell about the neck indicated that some type of shell ornament, perhaps shell gorgets, had disintegrated.

C. Artifacts are from burial associations as indicated by letters.

(a) These are from Burial 217. The antler hook 238 mm. long was associated with the prismoid type of atlatl weight, made of reddish brown banded slate of high polish. It was 62 mm. long by 61 mm. wide and 26 mm. thick with hole 12 mm. in diameter. The shell disc beads and cylindrical coal beads are of usual form. The terrapin carapace rattle was well enough preserved to be restored. It was drilled through both bottom and top, suggested that a straight cylindrical handle of wood may have been attached. The 55 pebbles found in association were found inside the shell rattle.

(b) These were two curved shell pendants 60 mm. long from near the neck of Burial 661.

(c) Was a straight base flint knife 11.5 cm. long with Burial 409.

(d) Was a similar knife, 13.2 cm. long found with Burial 436.

(e) These were two curved shell pendants 67 mm. long cut from large marine shells. They appear to have been made to represent canine teeth of animals.

(f) This is a portion of a string of 19 perforated canine teeth, forming a necklace found with Burial 409.

(g) This string of beads consisted of 2 barrel-shaped beads of coal, two similar beads of brown stone and one cylindrical bone bead all about 43 mm. long and 18 mm. diameter. When found, they were strung with shell discs in between them.

D. The upper half of the photograph shows some of the artifacts from Burial 612. The four projectile points vary in length from 98 to 116 mm. and in breadth from 28 to 35 mm. The antler

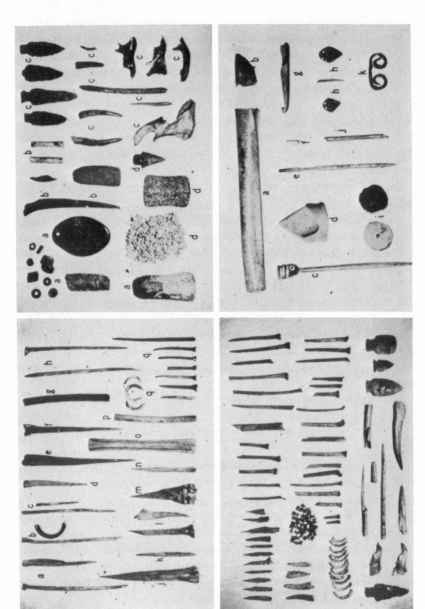

Fig. 26.   Miscellaneous artifacts from burial association.

atlatl hook, 77 mm. long, was found among the foot bones of this burial after the skeleton reached the laboratory. The cut antler seems to have been used as a flaking tool. The antler projectile point of usual form, well made and scraped to a sharp point, is 101 mm. long. The lower portion of the photograph shows artifacts from Burial 561. They consist of two antler atlatl hooks, one with large hook and transverse channel at the rear. The other hook was made from a tapering section of antler and has a small hook. It has suffered some disintegration and was fractured at proximal end. With these were an atlatl weight of white limestone of prismatic type, longitudinally broken, and eight sections of a shell composite atlatl weight. This had so decayed that only a few of the shell sectors could be recovered. Also there were two antler tines, a broken bone awl and a broken broad-headed bone "hairpin." A few shell disc beads and fragmentary shells about the neck indicated that some type of shell ornament, perhaps shell gorgets, had disintegrated.

MISCELLANEOUS BONE ARTIFACTS

A.   In Figure 26, burial associations are indicated by letter as follows:

(a)   A bird bone pin 172 mm. long and a splint bone awl 120 mm. long were found with Burial 487.

(b)   A perforated bird bone pin, point broken, 162 mm. long, and incisor of beaver, perforated, with Burial 434.

(c)   Two split bone pins, the largest 150 mm. long, were with Burial 413.

(d)   Hair pin, 103 mm. long, was at head of Burial 852.

(e)   Splinter bone awl was with Burial 788.

(f)   Bone pin, 158 mm. long, was with Burial 808.

(g)   Polished bird bone tube, 136 mm., was with Burial 743.

(h)   Double pointed bone pin, 185 mm., was with Burial 251. One end of this pin has stain of pitch which may indicate a shell or bone bead was once attached to it. It was probably used as a hair pin.

(i)   Bone pin, 165 mm. long, was with Burial 351.

(j)   Awl made from cannon bone of deer, 160 mm. long, was found with five shell beads and antler flaker with Burial 755.

(k)   Double pointed awl was with Burial 670.

(1)   Perforated bird bone awl and broken deer antler awl are from Burial 203.

(m)   Cannon bone awl was with Burial 135.

(n)   Bone splinter awl was at the head of Burial 414.

(o)   The bone gouge made from split deer bone had a chip broken from one end. It probably was used to hold incisor teeth of rodents, the combination forming a graver. The bone was 132 mm. long and was from Burial 359.

B.   Burial associations in this illustration are indicated by letter as follows:

(a)   Eight crinoid beads, a flint scraper, and an oval coal pendant with single perforation reamed from both sides, 94 x 64 x 7 mm. and an antler atlatl handle were with Burial 509.

(b)   Split bone awl, portion of beaver incisor, a fine-grained sandstone subrectangular bar, and two tubular shell beads 53 mm. long, were at the neck of Burial 503.

(c)   Four flint points, antler tines, bone awls, and jaws of deer, ground hog and wild cat were found with Burial 698.

(d)   Anculosa shell beads, a flint point, and a mottled granite atlatl weight, 77 x 49 x 27, were with Burial 518.

C.   In this illustration three flint points at lower right, some 42 bone awls, four antler tips, 11 incisor teeth of rodents and a group of snake vertebrae, all are from Burial 708. The flint point in the lower left corner, two ground hog jaws, four bone awls in lower section of photograph, a single antler tip and a broken bone tube are from Burial 781.

D.   This photograph contains artifacts in general not duplicated anywhere in the rest of the midden.

(a)   This bone is a worked right human femur. The proximal end is partly broken. Length of remaining bone 222 mm.

(b)   This broken antler atlatl hook of unusual form was taken from the general digging.

(c)   This hair pin was made of a sharpened bone shaft, 177 mm. long and 6 mm. in diameter. The hair pin head is made by a lump of asphaltum into which the bone pin is thrust. Four large disk beads, 18 mm. in diameter, are set on top of this lump of pitch, and four small shell beads are attached on the side.

(d) This is a basal portion of a broken stone jar, bowl or mortar, see Figure 41.

(e) This is a well formed bone hair pin, 152 mm. long; one end is pointed and the other which is cut squarely off, is stained with pitch suggesting it had a detached head perhaps similar to that shown in (c).

(f) This was a fish hook, 17 mm. long, from general excavation.

(g) A portion of an antler atlatl hook of unusual form was taken from the general excavation.

(h) With Burial 632 there were found a single bone awl and two thin oval copper pendants, each with two perforations, maximum dimensions of these pendants were 31 x 21 mm.

(i) There were two disk shell beads, 38 mm. in diameter, attached to the base of a cone of asphaltum. These possibly are the heads of hair pins.

(j) This most interesting artifact is believed to be a graving tool. It is made of a straight bone tube, 83 mm. long and 6 mm. in diameter. Into each end has been inserted an incisor tooth of a rodent, probably ground hog, with the distal end protruding. Because of curvature of the tooth, it could be driven into the hollow bone and made to hold firmly. The cutting end of the tooth was then sharpened on whet stones as needed to keep it sharp when used in carving. On one end this sharpening by grinding had proceeded to the point where the bone tube was also being slightly cut away. It must have been an efficient tool. It was taken from the pit of Burial 638.

(k) This copper ornament is of unusual form and its purpose is problematical. It appears to be formed from a nugget of native copper hammered into a sheet, folded and rolled into a rod, pointed at each end. It was then coiled into the form shown. It was found with Burial 248. Its over-all dimensions are 46 x 24 x 3 mm. It is shown in situ in Figure 20 D. It may have been used as a clasp to hold together two parallel portions of a string of disk shell beads.

HEAVY STONE ARTIFACTS

Figure 27 illustrates artifacts described in detail as follows:

A. (a) This is a rough gray hammer stone having dimension of 103 x 79 x 51, found in pit of Burial 464. In a postmold

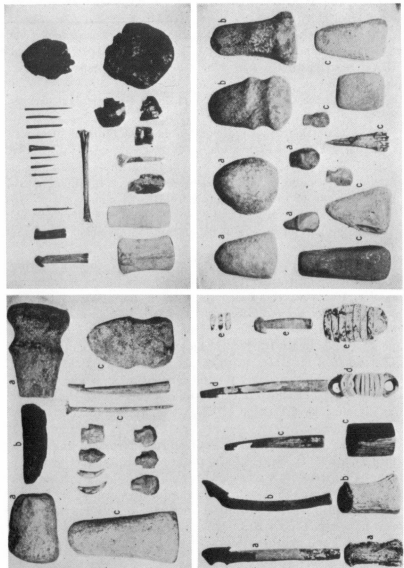

Fig. 27.   Heavy stone artifacts (grooved axes and pestles) from burial association.

near this burial was found the fully grooved limestone axe having maximum dimension of 136 x 98 x 50 mm. It is doubted if these artifacts were intentional associations.

(b)   This is a roughly chipped hematitic sandstone found in grave of Burial 463. This may be an unfinished subrectangular bar atlatl weight.

(c)   The remaining artifacts shown in this illustration are all from Burial 253. These include a pestle with maximum dimension of 158 x 78 mm., two drilled canine teeth, two flint points, one broken, three flint scrapers, a bone hairpin, 167 mm. long, an antler atlatl hook, 158 mm. long, and a fully-grooved limestone axe having maximum dimension of 120 x 78 x 42 mm.

B.   These artifacts are all from Burial 69. The two antler hooks were associated each with the weight immediately below it. The hook at the left which is 87 mm. long was associated with the prismatic atlatl weight of silicious limestone. This weight had dimension of 86 x 54 x 25 mm. with a hole of 13 mm. diameter.

The other atlatl hook is of quite unusual construction. It is made from a section of antler cut squarely off at both ends. It is only 50 mm. long. The subrectangular bar was made of limestone and had dimensions of 96 x 37 x 12 mm.

The flint scraper and drill were of the usual forms. The accompanying bone artifacts, awls and needles were not unusual. The fragments of a terrapin may indicate a rattle, but no pebbles accompanied the fragments. In the lower right is shown a large lump of red ochre which shows grinding on the concave inner surface. The object in upper right which shows no detail is a lump of pitch definitely placed in the grave. There is adhering to it a canine tooth unworked.

C.   In this illustration the associations are indicated by letter.

(a)   The heavy and well made, but decayed antler hook was 197 mm. long and had a shaft diameter of 17 mm. The accompanying handle, left rough on the exterior, was badly decayed, but was restorable. It was 90 x 41 x 30 mm. with drilled hole 17 mm. in diameter. These were with Burial 796.

(b)   The antler hook 191 mm. long was with Burial 785 and associated with the antler handle having dimensions of 90 x 57 x 35. The diameter of the perforation was 29 mm.

(c)   The antler hook, 146 mm. long and 21 mm. largest diameter, had drilled hole 14 mm. in diameter. It was badly decayed and a few fragments are missing. It was found in Burial 148 with the limestone atlatl weight, broken and repaired. It was 70 x 49 x 24 mm. with a drilled hole 14 mm. diameter.

(d)   The antler hook of simple pattern, broken and repaired was 150 mm. long and had a shaft of 19 mm. diameter. The hole was 14 mm. in diameter. This was with Burial 58 and was associated with a segmented atlatl weight. This was made of 8 shell segments and two segments of dark red stone. Unfortunately in this figure the stone segments are not shown in correct relative position. The stone segments were found, one between second and third segments and the other between seventh and eighth. With this burial there was a single large disk shell bead.

(e)   This atlatl hook, very simple in form, is 85 mm. long and 16 mm. in shaft diameter, with a hole diameter of 10 mm. It was with Burial 218. In association there were three shell bars and a composite shell atlatl weight of eight segments. This artifact was unusual because of the very great thickness of the shell segments. They were about 9 mm. thick, which would suggest that only a very large marine shell could attain that thickness.

D.   The associations of these objects are shown by letters.

(a)   The pestle and hammer stone, both of limestone, were with Burial 471, as also were the flint scraper and small hammer stone.

(b)   The fully grooved limestone axe was 140 x 82 x 65 mm. in dimension. It was with Burial 622 in association with the bell shaped limestone pestle 140 x 80 x 63 mm. maximum dimension.

(c)   The remaining artifacts were from Burial 465, these consisting of a subrectangular sandstone block for grinding, two limestone pestles, and a limestone hammer stone. There were two flint scrapers and a bone awl from the cannon bone of a deer.

ATLATL COMBINATIONS

A.   Figure 28 shows atlatl weights and associated antler hooks found in burial associations as indicated.

(a)   This antler hook, made from the tapering curved end of an antler tine, was broken and repaired. Its length was 222

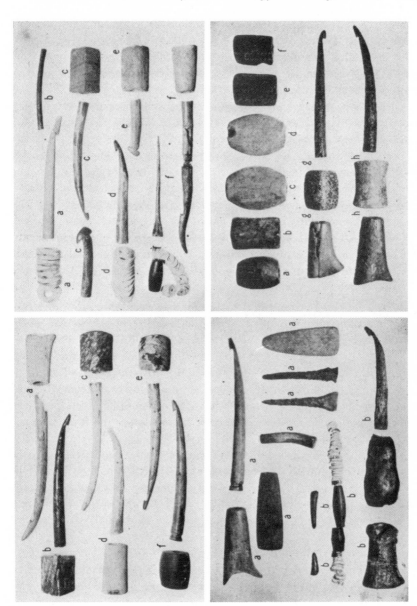

Fig. 28. Atlatl combination of hooks, weights, and handles from burial association.

mm. It was associated with an antler handle 76 mm. long, and was with Burial 124.

(b)   This green granite atlatl weight, found with Burial 92, was broken into many pieces and scattered in grave. The antler hook was 204 mm. long.

(c)   An antler hook 198 mm. long, and an atlatl weight of mottled granite, prismoid type 63 x 52 x 25 mm. in dimensions were with Burial 347.

(d)   A cylindrical atlatl antler handle and an antler hook were found with Burial 353.

(e)   An antler hook, broken and repaired, 192 mm. long, was found in alignment with a syenite atlatl weight, 55 x 49 x 27 mm. with Burial 396.

(f)   An antler hook, 215 mm. long, with circular groove at proximal end for attachment, and a brown, banded-slate atlatl weight with semicircular cross-section were found on the chest of Burial 579.

B.   In this photograph artifacts are designated by letters.

(a)   An eight-sectioned, shell, segmented atlatl weight and an antler hook, 197 mm. long were found with Burial 560.

(b)   A bone tube cut from a thin-walled bird bone from Burial 149 had a length of 106 mm. and a diameter of 11 mm.

(c)   On left, an antler hook 104 mm. long was from Burial 158. On the right, an atlatl weight of green and black banded slate, 69 x 49 x 23 mm., accompanied by an antler hook as shown, 182 mm. long. Both were with Burial 140.

(d)   With Burial 56 there was a shell, segmented, atlatl weight as shown with 11 segments, and an antler hook.

(e)   An antler hook of unusual form, only 87 mm. long, was associated with a prismatic type of atlatl weight of limestone with Burial 39. The limestone weight was encrusted with traventine.

(f)   With Burial 766 were found a cannel coal barrel-shaped bead 49 mm. long with 11 shell disk beads, all at the neck of skeleton. Also, there was a broken hairpin at the head, which was made from a bone splinter cut longitudinally from a cannon bone of deer. There was also in association an antler hook of unusual form. It was broken, partly decayed, and was 224 mm. long. With it was an antler handle, as shown.

C.   This photograph shows burial associations listed by letters as follows:

(a)   This illustration presents an antler hook, a subrectangular bar weight and antler handle found in association with Burial 452.   The handle is 103 mm. long and has a hole 14 mm. in diameter.   With this burial there were also an antler drift ground flat at both ends, two flint drills 112 mm. long, used as reamers, and a polished stone, 114 x 44 x 25 mm., which could have served as a small pestle, but which may have been an atlatl weight in process of manufacture.

(b)   Here are shown artifacts in association with the Burial 495.   These were two antler tines, a necklace of disk shell beads with two barrel-shaped beads, one of coal 34 x 19 mm., and an unusually highly polished stone specimen 60 x 20 mm.   With this burial were an antler handle, an antler hook, and a stone weight, all parts of the same atlatl.   The hook was 154 mm. in length of the usual form, and carefully finished, but the stone weight, a subrectangular bar was rough and unfinished.   However, its association leaves little doubt of the use to which it was put.

D.   This photograph presents in the top row six atlatl weights found with burials as indicated, from left to right.

(a)   This is a triangular stone atlatl weight found with Burial 158 in association with an antler hook, shown in C (c) above.

(b)   This is a prismatic atlatl weight of diorite found on the sacrum of Burial 160 without other associations.

(c)   This limestone atlatl weight with one flat side and convex edges was longitudinally fractured and recently reassembled. It was with Burial 669.

(d)   This limestone atlatl weight was with Burial 308.   It was flat on one side with convex edges.   It had been broken and one small fragment was not recovered.

(e)   This is a green granite prismoid type of atlatl weight found with Burial 811.

(f)   This atlatl weight of semi-circular cross-sections was broken (perhaps ceremonially).   A few fragments are missing.   It was with Burial 577.

(g)   With Burial 754 there was found an antler hook, a gray granite atlatl weight, and an antler handle.   These are be-

Univ.—8

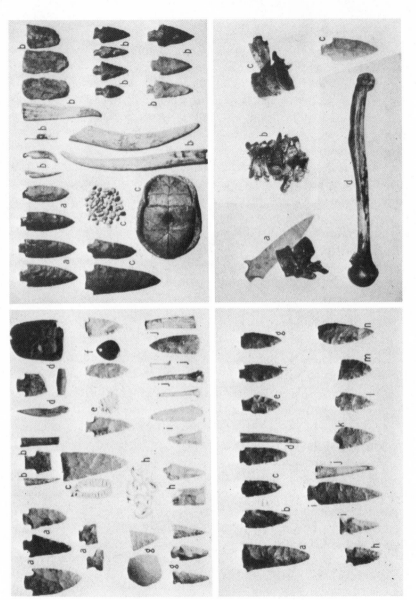

Fig. 29.   Flint artifacts in burial association.

lieved to be parts of the same atlatl. The weight and handle were found broken, but have been restored.

(h) This shows an antler handle, a prismoidal limestone atlatl weight and an antler hook found with Burial 798. They are doubtless parts of the same atlatl, the wooden portions of which have decayed.

FLINT

Flint artifacts from burial association are comparatively rare. Caches of flint knives have been found in the midden, but no large cache of flint was found with any burial. Flint points in burial association are so rare as to suggest in many cases the projectile point was not a burial offering made by friends of the deceased. Such flint occurrence in burial association is shown in Figure 31, described in detail as follows:

A. Artifacts from burial association are indicated by letters as follows:

(a) Five flint points, two broken, were with Burial 436.

(b) A bone awl, broken flint point, and a broken bone tube were with Burial 810.

(c) Disk shell beads and a triangular flint knife 10 cm. long were found with Burial 588.

(d) A bone awl, a flint point, broken, a barrel-shaped stone bead and a broken pestle of iron carbonate were with Burial 390.

(e) A flint point and shell disk beads from Burial 587.

(f) Two flint points and a slate pendant, perforated near the edge and reamed from both sides, were found with Burial 513.

(g) Four flint points and a scraper were with Burial 11.

(h) Flint point, scraper, and shell ring beads were with Burial 47.

(i) Two flint points were taken from Burial 183.

(j) An antler drift, a flint knife, a flint drill, a bone awl broken, and small bird bone were with Burial 614.

B. Illustrations are indicated by letters as follows:

(a) Four flint points were taken from Burial 757.

(b) Seven flint points, three scrapers, two antler tines, antler flaking tools, a bone awl and a carved canine tooth pendant, perforated for suspension and shaped in the form of a bird beak, highly polished, were all from Burial 827.

(c)   Two flint points, the largest 11.2 cm long and a carapace rattle with pebbles were taken from Burial 57.

C.   This illustration shows projectile points found with burials and without other associations, but in such condition as to indicate that the point may have been the cause of the death of the individual.   Associations are indicated by letter.

(a)   Flint point found with shell beads at neck of Burial 5.

(b)   Broken flint point was found among fragments of skull of Burial 70.

(c)   Broken flint point was found among the ribs of Burial 66.

(d)   Projectile point 72 mm. long between ribs of Burial 67 and bone awl found at foot of skeleton.

(e)   Flint point which was found in pelvic cavity of Burial 174.

(f)   Flint point which was found near spinal column of Burial 190.

(g)   This broken flint projectile point was found in pelvic cavity of Burial 185.

(h)   This flint point was found at right elbow of Burial 185.

(i)   Two flint points, the largest 113 mm. long, were found among the left ribs of Burial 254.

(j)   An antler projectile point 9.1 cm. long was found in right rib cavity of Burial 619.

(k)   This broken flint point was found at the center of spine, inside Burial 374.

(l)   This broken flint point was found in the thoracic cavity of Burial 691.

(m)   This broken flintpoint was found near left side of Burial 805.

(n)   A crude flint point 85 mm. long was with the neck bones of Burial 531.

D.   This photograph presents projectile points actually imbedded in portions of the skeleton, and probably indicate the cause of death of the individual.

(a)   Light colored flint spear point found thrust into the vertebral column of Burial 295, see Figure 22 F of burial in situ.

(b)   This shows an antler projected point lodged between the sixth and seventh cervical vertebrae pointing toward the ventral side inclined toward the right of the individual. There were no arms, legs or head with this Burial 537. It is shown in situ, Figure 15 B. The antler point was 76 mm. long, with outside diameter at base 21 mm. It had a hole diameter at the base of 14 mm.

(c)   This shows vertebrae from Burial 228 with flint point imbedded in it. In the right pelvis of the Burial, but not imbedded in the bone was another projectile point as shown. It was in form similar to the first and is 87 mm. long. It is probable both were in the body at the time of burial.

(d)   This illustration shows the right humerus of Burial 593. It has a flint projectile point imbedded in it beneath the caput, on posterior side.

UNUSUAL BONE AND SHELL ASSOCIATED WITH BURIAL

A.   In upper left, Figure 30, are shown the foot bones of a single foot of *Lynx rufus* (Bobcat) found with Burial 611.

In the upper row center are three nostrums cut from skulls of *Lynx rufus*, from left to right, taken from Burials 529, 158, and 492. These bobcat skulls were evidently cut to preserve the nostrum, showing both upper and lower canines. In the same row are shown portions of one upper and two lower jaws of *Martes pennanti* (Fisher) cut off like the bobcat jaws. The upper jaw shows the nostrum, upper canines and incisors.

At the lower left are shown two cut jaws of *Canis Lupis* (Wolf) taken from Burial 650, and in the center, canine teeth and an ulna awl taken from Burial 576. In the lower right, foot bones of dog are shown. They were found together but detached from any other portions of dog skeleton in association with Burial 228.

B.   In the upper corners are shown two bone awls of *Meleagris gallopavo* (Wild turkey) taken from Burial 614. At the top, center, is cut long bone of wild turkey. Its purpose is unknown. It was taken from Burial 588. The large bone 25 cm. long is evidentally an unfinished artifact. It is later described in detail and shown in comparison with a finished implement, in Figure 51-c. It was taken from Burial 59.

From Burial 203 the head and a quantity of the scales of *Lepisosteus osseus* (Garpike) were taken. Only this portion of this fish had been placed in the grave.

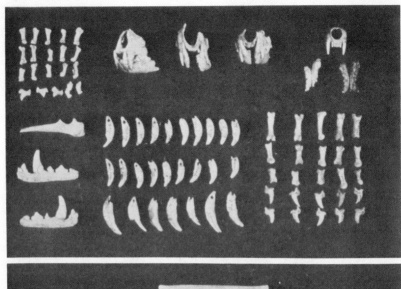

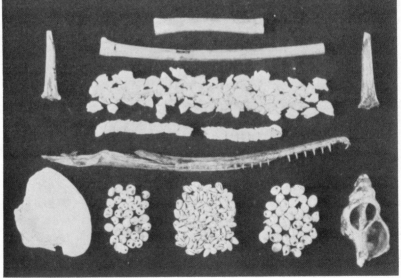

Fig. 30.   Unusual bone and shell associated with burials.

In the lower row are shown shell specimens which were not common and samples of three other species which were frequently found in burial association. From left to right they have been identified as follows:

Lampsilis ovata, Say. (rare) from Burial 612.
Sample of beads of *Anculosa praerosa,* Say. from Burial 613.
Sample of beads of *Marginella apicina* Menke from Burial 571.
Sample of beads of *Lithasia obovata* Say from Burial 380.
Fasciolonia gigantea Kienen (rare) from Burial 237.

LIST OF TOTAL ARTIFACTS FROM EXCAVATION

As a result of the careful excavation for a period of months by a large field crew at this important site, a total of 55,280 artifacts and field specimens have been recovered. This total may be subdivided into:

Flint	13,806
Ground Stone	3,270
Copper	3
Bone	8,427
Miscellaneous Bone	39
Antler	4,342
Shell	25,125
Miscellaneous Field Specimens	268
TOTAL	55,280

These all belonged to the people who built this midden and who buried their dead therein, of which 880 burials were excavated in this investigation, in addition to the some 298 burials reported by Moore. In addition to these artifacts, there were recovered artifacts from, on or near the surface, which do not belong to the period of occupancy of the shell mound people but to later prehistoric groups.

These artifacts may be classified as follows:

Ground and polished Celts (Adena)	4
Triangular projectile points (Middle Mississippi)	11
Broad bladed projectile points with pointed base (Adena?)	7
Potsherds, shell tempered	621
Potsherds, grit tempered	171

These artifacts show that Adena people and later Middle Mississipip peoples may have been transient visitors to this site. There is no evidence of their continued occupancy for any length of time.   At a distance of some 2,000 feet from Indian Knoll, on the same river terrace, surface excavation showed rectangular post-mold pattern houses of Middle Mississippi occupancy. There was no evidence of very long occupancy here, but from this site much of the surface material, not belonging to the shell mound people, could have come.

Besides these prehistoric artifacts, the excavation yielded broken china, crockery, glass bottles, iron nails, horse shoes, bits of iron chain, a railroad spike, and various other evidence of white occupancy in the historic period.   Some of this material due to recent digging of postholes for houses, barns, and fences had reached a depth of 3½ feet.

In the following tabulation of artifacts only those belonging to the shell mound people have been included in the primary list. Each type of artifact has been described in the Trait list, and where possible, illustrations showing range in form and size have been provided.   Much has been revealed as to the process of manufacture of these artifacts.   Such information is included in the description.

LIST OF ARTIFACTS, SITE Oh2

FLINT ARTIFACTS

	General Excava-tion	Burial Associ-ation
Projectile points:		
Stemmed		
Small (X to 6 cm)	459	15
Large (above 6 cm)	277	8
Corner notched		
Small	1,473	24
Large	444	4
Side notched		
Small	826	4
Large	170	
Short stem expanding from base		
Small	21	5
Large	6	1
Unique forms, unclassified	69	
Broken points	1,777	7
Broken fragments (unclassified)	3,261	8
Blades, blanks or knives		
Common (X to 11 cm)	549	12
Large (11 cm to X)	4	

	General Excavation	Burial Association
Drills		
Straight side	1,727	2
Flared base	96	1
Notched stem	65	1
Reamers	78	
Cores	22	
Gravers	20	
Abraiders, flint	51	
Balls, flint	20	
Scrapers		
Flake, chipped		
One edge, one side	467	10
One edge, two sides	72	
Two edges, one side	391	
Two edges, two sides	69	
Thumbnail scrapers	557	2
Notched for hafting	574	4
Disc scrapers	17	1
Concave edge	8	
Drawshave	4	
Choppers		
Bitted axes	13	
Stemmed cutters	4	
Notched cutters	6	
Chipped rectangles	81	1
"Hand axes"	11	
Hammerstones, flint	7	
TOTAL FLINT ARTIFACTS	13,696	110

GROUND STONE ARTIFACTS

	General Excavation	Burial Association
Atlatl weights		
Prismoidal, drilled, broken	75	26
Bar, subrectangular and fragmentary	173	6
Grooved axes		
Nearly complete	159	3
Bits, broken	17	
Mauls, grooved	11	
Hammerstones		
Igneous rock or sandstone, quartzite	602	3
Pitted	63	3
Abraiders, various stones (non-flint)	316	
Stone balls (non-flint)	37	1
Pestles		
Conical	1,379	21
Bell-shaped	13	1

	General Excavation	Burial Association
Cylindrical	22	1
Grooved	1	
Cupstones, or nutstones	56	1
Lapstones	36	2
Hoes		
Notched limestone	6	
Slabs of stone	13	
Stone fragments, worked	66	3
Stone beads		
Shale, slate, limestone	11	47
Coal	1	29
Pendants or gorgets		
Slate	3	1
Coal		1
Discs, slate		1
Whetstone		3
Grooved cylinders, hematite	1	
Pebbles, hematite, worked	42	1
Hematite worked fragments	12	1
TOTAL GROUND STONE ARTIFACTS	3,115	155

COPPER ARTIFACTS

	General Excavation	Burial Association
Pendants, thin sheets		2
Bent bar, ornament		1
TOTAL COPPER ARTIFACTS		3

BONE ARTIFACTS

	General Excavation	Burial Association
Awls		
Split bone fragments	6,413	26
Ulna, deer	141	1
Cannonbone, deer		
Part indeterminate	152	4
Fore leg, shaft	30	
Hind leg, shaft	32	
Upper end	99	
Lower end	1	
Ulna, other animals	24	3
Radius, deer	7	
Bird bone,		
Split shaft	20	
End	163	4
Mid-shaft	57	24
Perforated, made from flat bone fragments	50	1

	General Excavation	Burial Association
Tibia, deer		
Lower end	26	
Upper end	5	
Scapula fragments, pointed	27	1
Jaws of animals, some deer	7	
Bacculum, raccoon	8	
Scapula socket perforated	11	
Scapula worked blade	1	
Spatulae		
Ulna, deer	19	1
Long bone, split, unidentified	165	2
Bird bones	6	
Perforated	1	
Fish hooks		
Residues	10	3
Forked		
Long bones	207	
Bird bones	1	
Ulna	34	
Tibia	1	
Bone loops	10	
Hairpins		
Long cylinders	12	12
Flat expanded head	50	12
Projectile points		
Bipointed, large, 6 inches	8	
Bipointed, small	179	
Notched bone splinters	61	
Beads, bird bone sections	41	
Tubes, bird bone, (graver handles?)	6	11
Cut bird bones	14	
Rhombs, bone	2	
Engraved cylinder	3	
Painted bone hairpin	1	
Bone pendant	1	
Section cut large animal bone	1	1
Section cut human bone	1	1
Radius of small mammal perforated, longitudinally	1	
Chisels, large bone	3	
Toggle, bone	1	
Toe bone, deer, cut, perforated	3	
Fish vertebrae, large, perforated	2	
Cannon bone perforated between articular surfaces of epiphyses	1	
Rattles, carapace of box tortoise		32

	General Excavation	Burial Association
Rings cut from carapace	14	
Rectangles, flat sections cut from plastron	6	
Canine teeth, unperforated	12	4
Canine teeth, perforated		104
Graver, cut bone cylinder with rodent incisors		1
Incisors of beaver (part of gravers?)		10
Incisors of small rodent (for use in gravers?)		18
TOTAL BONE ARTIFACTS	8,151	276

MISCELLANEOUS BONE IN BURIAL ASSOCIATION

Jaws of wildcat (Lynx rufus)		9
Foot bones of single foot (Lynx rufus)		4
Cut section jaws of wolf (Canis lupis)		7
Foot bones of one dog foot		1
Jaws of weasel, four in one group		1
Jaws of ground hog, Marmota monax		10
Cut maxilla (nostrum) of fisher Martes pennati		4
Head of garpike		2
Tooth of Tapirus haysii Leidy		1
TOTAL MISCELLAEOUS BONE IN BURIAL ASSOCIATION		39

ANTLER ARTIFACTS

Cut bases	2,076	
Cut tips	1,399	25
Cut midshafts	44	1
Projectile points	541	7
Atlatl hooks	42	35
Atlatl handles	33	9
Drifts	116	5
Beads barrel shaped	1	1
Flat sections, worked	2	1
Chisels	3	
Cylinders, engraved	1	
TOTAL ANTLER ARTIFACTS	4,258	84

SHELL ARTIFACTS

Beads, disc, large		190
Beads		
Disc, small in 152 strings	24	15,620
Anculosa in 33 groups	122	7,338
Tubular, parts of 13 strings	2	133
Olivella, one group		38

	General Excava- tion	Burial Associ- ation
Marginella, four groups		1,462
Spherical		10
Rings, discs with large perforation		55
Conch		
Large marine		5
Cut into strips		6
Cut into squares		37
Gorgets, cut from large conch		20
Pendants		
Tooth shaped, long curved		7
Broad shell sections		21
Grooved		1
Bars, short, square, perforated	2	3
Atlatl weights, of matched shell segments		6
Pins, long cylindrical, expanded head		3
Disc, large circular		1
Conch columella		1
Conch fragments		2
Mussel shell, cut, worked		7
Slug pearl beads		9
TOTAL SHELL ARTIFACTS	150	24,975

MISCELLANEOUS ARTIFACTS

Concretions	13	1
Fossils, crinoids	19	8
Fossils	2	
Asphalt, chunks	1	3
Limonite (paint rock)	141	2
Hematite (paint rock)	55	18
Green pigment		1
White clay, chunks		3
Stone vessel fragment, flattened base	1	
TOTAL MISCELLANEOUS ARTIFACTS	231	36

THE TRAIT LIST

With all the limitations and difficulties inherent in a trait list, it still remains the most satisfactory way yet devised for describing the social activities and material possessions of a people as revealed by archaeological investigation. It is believed that Indian Knoll is one of the earliest sites in this region of Kentucky. It appears that this site represents a ''pure'' manifestation, uncontaminated by any other contemparary cultural manifestation. The trait list should, therefore, be of special interest because it probably represents the possessions of and the indigeneous development of a single people over a considerable time interval.

Trait No.	GENERAL TRAITS	No. of Occurrence
1.	Shell middens used as habitation sites	X
2.	Occupational levels marked by clay layers	2
3.	Fired areas on occupational levels	X
4.	Fire-cracked and burned stone scattered throughout midden	X
5.	Scattered post molds about fired areas	X
6.	Cache of flint chips, blades, knives	3
7.	Cache of heavy artifacts of utility	5
8.	Cache of gastropod shell about fireplace	2
9.	Charred nuts and hulls in debris about fire	2
10.	Domestication of dog	X
11.	Use of the dog as food	X
12.	Fossils brought onto midden	X

BURIAL TRAITS

13.	Round grave burials in pits	483
14.	Bodies laid on surface and covered with midden	385
15.	Fully flexed burials	523
16.	Partially flexed burials	248
17.	Extended burials	11
18.	Sitting posture burials (fully flexed)	4
19.	Graves unmarked during occupancy of site	X
20.	Bodies dismembered before burial	24
21.	Burial of separate skulls	3
22.	Projectile points lodged in skeleton and other evidence of violent death	23
23.	Multiple burials in single grave	31
24.	Use of red ochre in graves	24
25.	Dogs buried separately in graves	8
26.	Dogs buried in human graves	13
27.	Burials usually without artifacts	X
28.	Evidence of textiles	X
29.	Evidence of beaded garments (shell)	3
30.	Absence of pottery	X
31.	Absence of pipes for smoking	X
32.	Absence of ground stone celts	X

Trait No.	BURIAL TRAITS—Con't.	No. of Occurrence
33.	Intentional breaking of prismoidal atlatl weights	8–16
34.	Intentional breaking of complete atlatls	9–14
35.	Complete atlatls or broken parts placed in grave **before** placement of body	10
36.	Complete atlatls or broken parts placed in grave **after** placement of body	24

FLINT TRAITS

37.	Projectile points, stem with parallel sides	755
38.	Projectile points, corner notched	1,937
39.	Projectile points, side notched	1,001
40.	Projectile points, short stem expanding from base	33
41.	Blades or knives	565
42.	Drills, straight side	1,729
43.	Drills, flared base	96
44.	Drills, notched stem	66
45.	Reamers	78
46.	Gravers	20
47.	Quarry blanks	142
48.	Cores	22
49.	Scrapers, chipped flakes	1,027
50.	Scrapers, thumbnail	558
51.	Scrapers, notched for hafting	578
52.	Scrapers, concave edge	8
53.	Scrapers, drawshave	4
54.	Choppers	116

GROUND STONE TRAITS

55.	Atlatl weights, prismoidal, drilled	101
56.	Atlatl weights, subrectangular bar	179
57.	Axes, fully grooved	179
58.	Mauls, grooved	11
59.	Hoes, slabs of stone, some notched	19
60.	Hammerstones, not pitted	605
61.	Hammerstones, pitted	66
62.	Pestles, conical	1,400
63.	Pestles, bell-shaped	14
64.	Pestles, cylindrical	23
65.	Cup-stones, nutstones, anvils	6
66.	Lapstones, concave depression	38
67.	Abraiders	316
68.	Balls, spherical, polished	38
69.	Beads, barrel-shaped, shale, slate, coal, lime	88

Trait No.	GROUND STONE TRAITS—Con't.	No. of Occurrence
70.	Whetstones	3
71.	Pendants or gorgets	5
72.	Stone vessel, siltstone	1

COPPER TRAITS

73.	Pendant, thin sheets	2
74.	Bent cylinder, ornament	1
75.	Pendants, flat bar expanded center	1

BONE TRAITS

76.	Awls, splinters of unidentifiable bone	6,424
77.	Awls, deer ulna	142
78.	Awls, deer cannon bone shaft	218
79.	Awls, deer cannon bone ends	99
80.	Awls, deer radius	7
81.	Awls, deer tibia	29
82.	Awls, deer scapula fragments	28
83.	Awls, deer lower jaw	7
84.	Awls, bird bone, midshaft	100
85.	Awls, bird bone, ends	167
86.	Awls, ulna of small mammals	27
87.	Awls, flat bone fragments, perforated	51
88.	Awls, flat bone fragments perforated, engraved	1
89.	Awls, raccoon bacculum	8
90.	Awls, fish spines	17
91.	Pins, short uniform cylindrical	11
92.	Head of deer scapula, detached, glenoid cavity perforated	11
93.	Spatula, ulna of deer	20
94.	Spatula, split longbones, flakers	167
95.	Spatula, bird bones	6
96.	Fishhooks from bone loops	12
97.	Forked long bone spatula	209
98.	Forked, deer ulna and tibia	34
99.	Loops of bone, fishhook manufacture	10
100.	Gorges, rohmbs, pointed bone	2
101.	Beads, cylindrical, cut bird bone section	41
102.	Toe bone of deer, cut, perforated at end	3
103.	Hair pins, long cylindrical, plain	30
104.	Hair pins, long, expanded flat head	62
105.	Hair pins, long cylindrical, head asphalt and beads	4
106.	Hair pins, long cylindrical, engraved	3

Trait No.	BONE TRAITS—Con't.	No. of Occurrence
107.	Hair pins, painted, red stripes	1
108.	Projectile points, pointed at both ends	186
109.	Projectile points, notched bone splinters	61
110.	Tubes, bird bone sections, graver handles	17
111.	Graver, bone tube, rodent incisors mounted in ends	1
112.	Incisors of beaver, and small rodents for use in gravers	28
113.	Gravers, made by crossed pair of jaws of groundhog	10
114.	Engraved cylinder, bone	1
115.	Chisels, large bone	3
116.	Rattles, carapace and plastron, box tortoise	30
117.	Rings, cut from carapace of tortoise	14
118.	Sections from turtle carapace, flat rectangles	6
119.	Canine teeth, small mammals, perforated at base	104
120.	Canine teeth, mammals, unperforated	16
121.	Scraper from deer scapula or pendant	1
122.	Artifacts cut from human bone	4
123.	Long bone tube, lateral perforation	1
124.	"Medicine bags" shown by contents	18

ANTLER TRAITS

125.	Antler tines broken off, for transportation	X
126.	Antler tips cut from base	1,421
127.	Cut midshaft, antler	45
128.	Cut antler bases, discarded	2,068
129.	Antler drifts	100
130.	Projectile points base conically reamed	547
131.	Atlatl handles	42
132.	Atlatl hooks	76
133.	Antler flakers or awls	21
134.	Chisels	3
135.	Beads, barrel-shaped	1
136.	Engraved antler cylinder	1

SHELL TRAITS

137.	Beads, small disc, less than 2 cm. diameter	15,620
138.	Beads, large disc, 2 cm. diameter or more	190
139.	Beads, tubular	135
140.	Beads, spherical from large conch columella	10
141.	Beads, Anculosa	7,453
142.	Beads, Pearl	9
143.	Beads, Olivella	38
144.	Beads, Marginella	1,462
145.	Rings, discs with large perforation	55
146.	Conch container, large marine	5
147.	Gorgets, perforated conch sections	20

Trait No.	SHELL TRAITS—Con't.	No. of Occurrence
148.	Pendants, broad strips, perforated or notched	21
149.	Pendants, long curved sections, tooth shaped	7
150.	Pendants, tooth shaped occur in pairs in graves	3
151.	Bars, section square, perforated, toggles	5
152.	Atlatl weights, matched shell segments	6
153.	Pins, long cylindrical, expanded head	3
154.	Gorgets, with burials, in groups of four	5
155.	Gorgets, engraved to represent carapace	1
156.	Gorgets, incised with equal-arm cross	1

DESCRIPTION OF INDIVIDUAL TRAITS

GENERAL TRAITS

1. *Shell Middens used as habitation sites.* This trait is the outstanding one in the manifestation of this complex. The seeming dependence of these people on the river for food caused them to choose a location on the river bank where shell fish were abundant. Here, because of the quantities of shell fish consumed, and as a result of long occupancy, huge middens accumulated. A considerable portion of the refuse was the discarded shells of many species of pelecypods and gastropods. One fact contributing to the use of such piles of debris as habitation sites is the simple consequence that the cast off shell helped to raise the level of the occupation site slightly above that of the surrounding terrain. This had a very distinct advantage in time of high water. In most localities, which would be chosen by these people along river banks, floods were always a potential menace to continued occupancy. While it has been shown that occasionally these people built small villages (Ward and Kirkland sites)[1] on hill tops some what removed from large river banks, and did not accumulate at such sites large shell middens, yet the fact remains that the largest sites and by far the greatest number of sites are to be found as shell mounds on the immediate banks of large streams.

2. *Occupation levels marked by clay layers.* It appears that sometimes the occupants of these middens brought in clean clay and spread it in a thin layer possibly two inches thick over an area roughly circular, perhaps twenty-five feet in diameter. In the center of this layer a fire was built and occupation seems to have continued with the accumulation of debris until the clay layer was submerged.

This was by no means a universal custom, as most occupational levels which can be recognized as such in shell mounds are simply made on what was once the surface of the midden.

3. *Fired areas on occupational levels.* These occupational levels are marked by accumulation of ashes, charcoal, burned stone, burned bone and other evidences of life about a central fire. One

---

[1] Webb, Wm. S. and Haag, Wm. G., 1940, p. 68.

would expect ashes and charcoal to accumulate about any fire, and burned bones might be expected to be the result of the cooking of animals for food and the discarding of the bones in the fire. However, the outstanding marker of these occupational levels is the quantity of burned and broken rock, usually sandstone, which occurs in the firebed. This could be the result only of the intentional placing of stones in the fire, and points to some utilitarian purpose for them, possibly hot-rock cooking.

4. *Fire cracked and burned stone, scattered throughout the midden.* The quantity of such stone seems to demonstrate the use of hot-rock cooking. Seemingly river pebbles of a wide variety of stone, and blocks of sandstone were placed in the fire for heating. When hot, these stones have been dropped into containers holding water. The water was boiled and the food cooked, perhaps by repeated operations. Such sudden cooling of stones used for such purpose would eventually cause them to be broken and the fragments would then be cast out in the debris. By some such process one may explain the considerable accumulation in the midden of broken sandstone and river pebbles showing fire action. This burned rock debris is scattered throughout the midden.

5. *Scattered postmolds about fired areas.* These are not numerous on any limited area and never suggest any definite pattern. However, they were frequent enough to show that posts were intentionally set in the midden, about occupational levels. Possibly such scattered postmolds are the remains of only simple shelters, perhaps only "wind brakes" partially to shelter the fire. It is to be doubted that these people had any form of wooden structure which might properly be regarded as a house. It is quite possible that a simple shelter of poles covered by animal skins served their needs.

6. *Cache of flint chips, blades and knives.* These are found in the midden, usually about an occupational level and probably represent a storage of surplus knives or quarry products, later to be specialized into artifacts.

7. *Cache of heavy artifacts of utility.* These caches or groups of heavy artifacts consist of lapstones, pestles, hammerstones, nutstones, and grooved axes. They usually occur as a group of artifacts in a small area on an occupational level, and probably

represent kitchen utensils used about the fireplace for the preparation of food. While such heavy artifacts may occur singly in the midden, and very rarely in grave association, they often occur in groups which suggest that when that particular area was last occupied, they were left together near the fire for possible future used. If the area was deserted, and occupation changed to a new area, these groups of artifacts would be covered over in time and remain together as a group.

8. *Cache of gastropod shells.* These occur about fire places. There are hundreds of small gastropods in a cache. They are thought to be merely the result of emptying a container in which the shell fish had been cooked. The cooking, perhaps, was no more than an aid in removing the fish from the shell or extracting its food value. Such shells were usually small and the food value would not be easily available otherwise as in the case of the larger species.

9. *Charred nuts and hulls in debris about fire.* This trait easily observed in shell mounds, suggests that large quantities of walnuts, hickory nuts, acorns, were brought on the site and consumed as food. It is probable that nut shells and hulls cast out in the debris would soon decay and leave no record of their presence except as an increment in the dark soil of the shell mound. Only those shells and hulls which by accident had been charred, would be preserved. These charred remains naturally would be found most abundant about fire places. The considerable bulk of such remains seems to indicate that the shell mound dweller at Indian Knoll consumed tons of nuts and acorns and may even have gathered and held in reserve against a time of scarcity a supply of such valuable food.

10. *Domestication of the dog.* The shell mound dwellers seem to have had only a single variety of dog, but this they had in abundance. The animal is a true dog and shows evidence of long domestication. The burial of dogs in carefully prepared graves and their inclusion in the graves with the human burials, discussed elsewhere in this report, seems to indicate a high veneration for the dog as a companion to his human owner.

11. *Use of the dog as food.* There seems to be abundant evidence that the dog was eaten as well as other animals. In the midden debris scattered animal bones in great quantity occur. These

are of bird, fish, deer and small mammals. Many show charring as if burned in the process of cooking. Among these bones, seemingly the discarded bones of food animals, the bones of the dog occur frequently. Some are burned. The conclusion seems inevitable that the dog was eaten for food, even though certain individual dogs were so highly respected as to be buried in the manner of, and sometimes with, their human masters.

12. *Fossils brought onto midden.* Fossils occur in considerable numbers in the general debris and occasionally in grave association. They are not artifacts in any sense since they show no evidence of any working or modification by man. Their presence demonstrates the Indian's powers of observation and his interest in the unusual and potentially useful. Fossils must, therefore, have been brought on the midden because of man's curiosity. What he thought of them and what he did with most of them must remain largely a secret. Some of them he included as burial furniture along with other objects which suggests the use by the shell mound dwellers of "medicine bags". See Trait No. 118. In Figure 52, in the upper row are shown a number of crinoids of possibly four or more species. In the lower left is shown a fossil pelecypod, probably Allorisma. In the lower right is a specimen of calamites. In the center of the lower row is a fragment of a fossil tooth found in association with Burial No. 492. This has been identified by the National Museum as tapirus haysii, Leidy.

BURIAL TRAITS

13. *Round grave burials in pits.* These usually occur in the sandy subsoil below the midden. They have been described in chapter on burials and are illustrated in Figures 8 and 10. The round grave was usually only large enough to contain the body tightly compressed. This leads to the assumption that at burial the body was rolled into a bundle and tied in that position with cordage or textiles. It may have been made into a "bundle", covered with textiles or possibly animal skins. The grave pit was then made just large enough to contain the bundle. In such a bundle the orientation of the body would be lost. This might explain the lack of any definite orientations of the skeletons in the pits.

14. *Bodies laid on the surface and covered with midden debris.*
In the case of burials within the midden, there were many which
showed no visible pit. The body may have been laid on the surface of the midden or in a shallow depression and covered with
loose shell. Such burials would show no pit walls, but they have
otherwise the same wide variation in orientation as the pit burials.
This suggests that here too the body was bound into a "bundle"
before being covered over with midden earth. As the midden grew
in depth it became very difficult to excavate a pit sufficiently deep
to reach the underlying sand. It must be supposed that these
burials in the midden, showing no pit walls represent the later
burials at the site and thus in a very crude way, present stati-
graphy. This is marred by very considerable digging on a limited
area and the very considerable intrusion of later burials into
earlier ones.

15. *Fully flexed burials.* The great majority of burials were
fully flexed. As pointed out, this was not accomplished by an
orderly and regular arrangement of the body as such in a grave,
as seems to have been the case in some later prehistoric peoples,
but the "complete" flexure seems to be the result of tying a body
into a "bundle" before burial.

16. *Partially flexed burials.* This type designates burials
with legs bent at the hip, where the flexure of the thighs may vary
from very little to as much as a right angle with the body. Such
burials are not a dominant type in shell mounds, but they do occur
in considerable numbers. They represent the burial of bodies not
rolled into a bundle, but laid on the midden surface and covered
with shell debris.

17. *Extended burials.* These are so rare in shell mounds as
to be altogether remarkable and usually represent considerably
less than two percent of the total at any site, provided the site
shows only the shell mound component. Frequently the shell
mounds of Alabama, particularly along the Tennessee River, were
used as the burial places of later peoples. In such cases these later
peoples of Middle Mississippi times used the extended burial almost
universally. So rare is the extended burial used by the shell mound
builders that when found, it immediately suggests the intrusive

burials of later people. However, it is certain that shell mound dwellers did but rarely use the extended form of burial.

18. *Sitting posture burials.*   This type of burial seems to be the result of placing in a small burial pit, a body which had been rolled into a bundle.   Such "bundles" were probably ellipsoidal in form, and if the burial pit was small, they could be placed in the grave "on end.".   This supposition seems to be justified by finding a very few burials which show the head downward. Usually in "sitting burials" the head was placed upward. With the passage of the flesh the skeleton would slump in the grave. The knees, resting against the pit wall, would usually remain in position, but the head would fall forward and usually would be found face down in the pelvic cavity.

19. *Graves unmarked during occupancy of site.*   This lead to the disturbance of many burials by the intrusion of later into earlier graves.   This trait seems to indicate not only that no care was taken to mark graves and thus avoid disturbance, but even when in excavation for a new grave, an earlier one was discovered, this fact seemed not to be deemed important.   The new pit was often continued right through the earlier grave to the desired depth.   The portion of the disturbed skeletons are often missing, suggesting that they were removed and discarded.   Sometimes they are found buried in a pile in the newly made grave.   Sometimes they were thrown in promiscuously in the fill of the new grave. This would seem to indicate in the shell mound people a complete lack of veneration for the dead or interest in the deposition of their remains, which seems quite at contrast with the attitudes of later peoples.

20. *Bodies dismembered before burial.*   This dismemberment sometimes is indicated by the removal of the head, arms, legs, any or all of them, and their complete absence from the grave. This is illustrated in Figure 15. Sometimes the body is cut into portions involving the cutting of the trunk in two. Such portions are buried in nonanatomical order. It is difficult to imagine a motive for such dismemberment unless it be assumed that it is the result of violent combat, after which the remains of the body, or so much of them as could be recovered, were buried in the usual way.

21. *Burial of separate skulls.*   This is a rare trait but does

occur. It may be that individual heads, removed in the process of dismemberment were later buried separately. However, in any site the number of separate skull burials is far less than the number of dismembered burials showing the loss of heads.

22. *Projectile points lodged in skeleton.* This observation, often repeated, is associated with other evidences of violent death. Projectile points of both flint and antler are frequently found lodged in the spinal column or in the larger bones of the skeleton in such condition as to indicate that they were propelled with great force. Frequently flint projectile points are found within the thoracic or pelvic cavities in such positions and under such conditions as to certainly indicate they were imbedded in the flesh.

23. *Multiple burials in single graves.* This type of burial is not uncommon in shell mounds. Often only two bodies are in a grave together, but frequently there may be three or more. Cases are noted where as many as six have been found. The evidence shows that these bodies were all buried simultaneously. Some of these multiple burials show signs of violent death, i.e. have projectile points associated with them.

24. *Use of red ochre in graves.* This trait while definitely intentional, seems to take no special form. Ochre in small quantities seems to have been spread over the body at time of burial. Often this appears in the grave of children. In this excavation of Indian Knoll there were 34 occurrences of ochre. Moore reported it from his excavation as found in 11 graves. In such cases as those reported, the ochre used was in such quantity that it remained as a red stain on the bones, and often the grave pit, and the earth surrounding the skeleton were stained red. However, many well preserved skeletons at this site were found to have scattered areas of bone stained black. The amount of the area stained varied greatly from burial to burial, and the density of the stain varied from bone to bone.

It was suspected that this black stain was also an evidence of the use of red ochre at the time of burial,[5] but in limited quantities so that due to chemical change incident to the passage of the flesh, the bone became stained black. This problem was submitted to Mr. Joseph H. Gardner, who made analyses of scrapings from stained areas of bone, comparing them with analyses of scrapings from

[5] Maxson, R. N., 1943, p. 618.

unstained portions of the same bone, and from soil samples in the vicinity.

From Mr. Gardner's analyses, (see his report published herein) it seems demonstrated that these black stains were produced by an abnormal amount of iron, more than could be found in the natural soil of the grave pit, and more than could be found on unstained bone. It is believed that this points to the fact that the use of red ochre as a burial accompaniment was very common at this site, maybe almost universal, but it is today observable as a red stain only where excessive amounts were used. Smaller amounts are to be noted only as black stains on the bones.

25. *Dogs buried separately in graves.* This trait would seem to indicate a certain veneration for the dog. Sometimes the dog is found buried in the midden in graves much like those of humans. This is discussed in the chapter on Burials.

26. *Dogs buried in human graves.* This trait is illustrated in Figure 16, and is discussed in the chapter on Burials under ''Dog Burials.''

27. *Burials usually without artifacts.* This is generally true of all shell mound sites. At Indian Knoll 68.6% of the burials had no artifacts of any kind, not even shell beads. This would seem to suggest that the custom of placing varied objects with the death at burial was quite rare, and that in most cases the clothing and personal adornments of the deceased were such that nothing was preserved. Artifacts of utility were placed with the dead, however. At Indian Knoll 21.5% of the burials had artifacts other than beads.

28. *Evidence of textiles.* In many graves at Indian Knoll there was evidence of the form of textiles about the body. The textiles had decayed quite beyond recovery, but the imprint of woven textile of large mesh was visible in the earth. This usually occurred in the region of the hips and clearly indicated that these people had coarsely woven textiles and used them as garments.

29. *Evidence of beaded garments.* This trait is illustrated in Figure 21. Shell beads (Anculosa) were found in patterns, in rows and layers, having a top and bottom side. This would seem to be the result of sewing shells in the pattern desired upon some medium capable of holding them in place in the pattern. This most

probably was leather from the skin of deer or other animals. These garments in many cases show that they were wrapped about the body, the pattern of the shells being found both above and below the bones of the skeleton.

30. *Absence of pottery.* Negative traits are always of questionable value, but the absence of pottery not only in the graves but throughout much of the midden is important as indicating that these people had not yet developed the ceramic arts.

As indicated elsewhere in this report, there was a small Middle Mississippi site on the same side of the river bank as Indian Knoll and distanced about 1500 feet from it. This site showed some shell tempered potsherds and a few rectangular post mold patterns. At Indian Knoll a few of these shell tempered potsherds were to be found on the surface clearly the result of chance visitation of Middle Mississippi people of later time. Of this prehistoric pottery, there was not as much on the surface as there was of broken China, the result of white occupancy of the site for the past century. Certain it is that the people of Indian Knoll made and used no pottery of any kind.

31. *Absence of pipes for smoking.* The absence of pipes and all other evidence of the smoking custom is an outstanding fact. Moore excavated 298 burials and reported no pipes at Indian Knoll. The recent excavation of an additional 880 discovered none, not even a broken fragment that might remotely be an indication of the use of pipes. One must conclude that if the practice of smoking was in vogue, the means of its accomplishment were in no way connected with the manufacture of imperishable artifacts which have remained to the present time. The author is of the opinion that smoking had not been introduced into this region when Indian Knoll was occupied.

In the shell mounds of Alabama, on the Tennessee River, there have been reported[6] a few conical stone tubes in burial associations and a few fragments of such tubes have been found in the middens. The number is much too small to indicate any general or widespread custom of smoking even assuming these stone tubes to be, in fact, pipes. The circumstances of their occurrence and the artifacts themselves would seem to indicate that they are the "blowing" or

---

[6] Webb, Wm. S. and De Jarnette, David L., 1942, p. 75.

"sucking" tubes of "medicine men" as suggested by Willoughby[7] in discussing the "Old Algonquian Stock." Such tubes have not so far been found in the shell middens of Kentucky.

32. *Absence of ground stone celts.* The shell mound dwellers seem to have produced full grooved axes in many forms, large and small. They left no evidence that they ever used ungrooved ground or polished stones of comparable size. Among later peoples, the celt was a very important artifact of general utility and it was made both by chipping and grinding. In this cultural complex these artifacts seem nonexistent. Occasionally single celts have been reported from shell mounds, but investigation shows that they were fragmentary blades and show in most cases that they are fragments of grooved axes. No complete, polished or ground stone celt has as yet been found in a shell mound in Kentucky, which could with certainty be attributed to this people. This fact was observed by Moore[8] when he excavated Indian Knoll and is expressed as follows:

> "No celts were found by us in the Knoll, with the sole exception of a diminutive one but 2.1 inches in length, though fifteen grooved axes were unearthed none more than 6.5 inches in length, two distinctly with burials, the others badly battered as a rule, scattered in the midden deposit. There axes, most of limestone though one at least is of sandstone, evidently took the place of celts in the aboriginal life on the Knoll."

33. *Intentional breaking of prismoidal atlatl weights.* The breaking of atlatl weights is clearly intentional and was regarded by Moore as a ceremonial destruction. The parts are usually scattered in the grave and sometime not all of the parts of a particular specimen are found. However, in many cases recovery of all parts of the artifact permit the prismoidal weight to be completely restored. This would seem to indicate that the breaking took place at the grave and probably at the time of burial. The fragments often show that the weight was struck a single heavy blow with a blunt instrument which shattered the weight often into four nearly equal pieces.

34. *Intentional breaking of complete atlatls.* The reasons for believing that this trait was of frequent occurrence are ex-

---

[7] Willoughby, Charles C., 1935, p. 93.
[8] Moore, C. B., 1916, p. 449.

plained in the chapter on "The Atlatl", page 326. After breaking, the parts of the atlatl were usually deposited in the grave in a small pile with their long dimensions parallel. This trait is illustrated in Figures 17-20. Evidence of it was also reported by Moore.

35. *Complete atlatls or broken parts were placed in the grave before placement of body.* This is definitely demonstrated by finding skeleton on top of such deposits in round graves. It is conceivable that this previous placement of artifacts in the grave may have been part of a "ceremonial preparation" of the grave for the receipt of the body.

36. *Complete atlatls or broken parts placed in the grave after placement of body.* This is readily demonstrated by an inspection of Figures 17-20. The deposit of artifacts in the grave after the placement of the body seems a natural procedure, in the view of the custom of other prehistoric peoples. It is recorded here as a trait only because it is not the only manner of depositing artifacts used by the people of the shell mounds.

FLINT TRAITS

Flint was used in great quantity at this site. The source of most artifacts of flint was a concretion, yielding dark blue to gray blue flakes, and breaking with the usual concoidal fracture. These concretions weathered to a light color on the outside and often had a heavy coating of "country rock" surrounding the deep blue flint. Much of the flint working was done by percussion and in the manufacture of many scrapers this may have been the only technique used. This flint, which seemed to be in abundant supply, worked by percussion very readily, and when resort was had to pressure fracture, exquisite examples of fine chipping were possible.

The flint projectile points, while numerous, tend to larger sizes, the number less than 40 mm. in length being a negligible percentage of the total. In the preceding list, even those classed as "small" are fairly heavy, and most are in length close to the maximum of 60 mm., the maximum allowed for that class. This general robustness of the flint projectile point may suggest the use of the atlatl rather than the bow; however, it proves nothing conclusively since many light projectile points were used which were made of bone and antler.

A very simple classification employing three major groups seemed all that was necessary to describe the vast majority of flint points at this site. These types were designated as "straight-stemmed", "corner-notched", and "side-notched". In the List of Artifacts, each group was divided into "small", (6 cm. or less) and large (more than 6 cm.). These types are illustrated in Figure 31, which shows typical examples. Since only the base of the projectile point was considered no account was taken of other features, save length, and that only by designations "small" and "large". Obviously there was thus considerable latitude in size in any form and the individuals in any type differed considerably one from another.

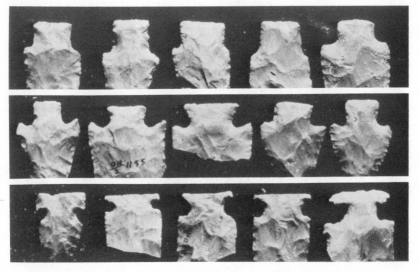

Fig. 31. Three dominant forms of projectile points, "straight-stemmed", "corner-notched", and "side-notched".

37. *Projectile points, stemmed.* In this type (small, up to 6 cm., large, more than 6 cm.) the stem has a straight base and parallel sides. The shoulders are usually weak, giving the impression of a slender projectile, see illustration in Figure 32 A. The smallest, in the top row, left, has maximum dimension of 28 x 49

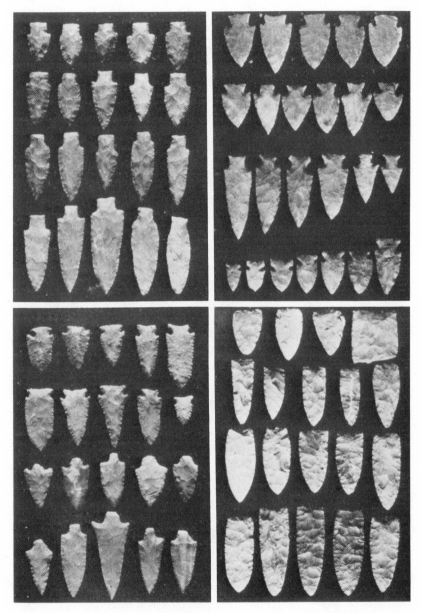

Fig. 32. A. Straight stemmed projectile points. B. Corner and side notched types. C. Serrated and "weak stemmed" types. D. Flint blades, possibly knives.

mm. The largest specimen, lower row, center, has maximum dimensions of 38 x 110 mm. In some of these the flaking is large, as if done only by precussion, while in others the chipping is small, and may represent very delicate retouching by pressure.

38. *Projectile points, corner-notched.* These were divided into "small" and "large" depending on whether or not they were 6 cm. long or longer. In the "corner-notch", a relatively short stem is formed, having a straight, concave or convex base with sides of the stem non-parallel, the stem contracting from the base. This makes the shoulders usually pronounced, often sharp, and sometime barb-like. Since the stem next to the blade is thus narrower than the base, the blade can be broad and often is twice as wide as the stem. This produces a point which is massive, robust and doubtless efficient. They are illustrated in Figure 32 B. Rarely these blades are serrated. The specimen in top row right has maximum dimensions of 37 x 60 mm. and the specimen on left in the third row is 32 x 95 mm. As the tabulation shows, this was the dominant type in use at this site.

39. *Projectile points, side-notched.* Most of these are of the small size, less than 6 cm. The larger size usually appear as broken and incomplete specimens. The notch in this type is chipped into the side of the blade and forms a base usually as broad as the blade itself. The range in size for complete specimens is shown in the lower row of Figure 32 B. The small specimen on the left has dimensions of 18 x 31 mm. while the largest specimen on the right has dimensions of 30 x 64 mm.

In the top two rows of Figure 32 C there are shown specimens of the corner-notched type which have been serrated. Some of these are very well chipped and quite sharp. The number of serrated points is quite small.

40. *Projectile points, short stem, expanding from base.* In the lower half of Figure 32 C a stemmed type is illustrated which differs somewhat from the usual stemmed form. Here the stem is crudely made, the shoulders are often weak, and the stem "expands" from the base. This form of point is not numerous. One would suspect that it was particularly difficult to attach firmly to a shaft. Perhaps it was intended to be easily detached. The large specimen in the bottom row has maximum dimensions

of 44 x 102 mm. and the one on its right has dimensions of 30 x 76 mm. This form, although insignificant in number, is interesting because, while it is less than one per cent of the total, it appears often in burial association in such situations as to suggest that instead of being a burial offering, such specimens may have been imbedded in the flesh of the body at burial and may have been the cause of death.

The large specimen referred to above is almost an exact duplicate of the specimen found in the Burial 295, illustrated in Figure 22 F, which surely must have taken the life of the individual with which it was found associated.

While the flint work of this site is broadly quite similar to that of the shell mounds of the Tennessee River in Alabama, it is interesting to note that this type of point particularly the sharp robust type, illustrated in the third row from the top, Figure 32 C, has been previously reported imbedded in the skeletal parts,[9] and within the body cavity of burials in shell mounds in Pickwick Basin in Alabama. It is clear that this type of point, insignificant in total number on a site, seems to occur in significant burial association out of all proportion to its importance numerically.

41. *Blades or knives.* Under this term is included many very carefully chipped blades, often quite thin, with nearly parallel or slightly convex sides, as illustrated in Figure 32 D. The smaller blanks tend to a broad triangular form. The base of most of them is straight. Fragments of such blades show that many were of considerable length. They could have been easily converted into other forms of artifact by very specialized chipping; however, they could have served as knives without further modification. In Figure 33 D the specimen, central position, lower row, had dimensions of 31 x 103 mm. The width of the base of large broken specimen, right, top row, was 49 mm.

In the general excavation, two caches of blades were found. One cache contained 5 and the other 10 blades. These are shown in Figure 6. Such caches seem to suggest that these blades were blocked out and kept in quantity to be later converted into any type of artifact desired.

In the cache of 5 blades, shown in Figure 6 F, they are very

---

[9] Webb, Wm. S., and De Jarnette, David L., 1942. Plates 289-2 and 290-1.

uniform in size, 90 mm. long by 37 mm. broad with straight bases, and are finely chipped.

In the cache of 10 blades, the points are blunt and the bases convex. The largest specimen is 165 x 48 mm. in dimensions. The others are about 100 mm. long and 42 mm. wide. In the cache they were placed on edge as shown in Figure 6 D.

42. *Drills, straight sided.* These artifacts are called drills on the assumption that they were used to perforate by rotation. This implies that they were probably attached longitudinally to a shaft which by a bow or other device could be caused to rotate, and thus drill a hole in wood or stone. These drills are very numerous, indicating much need for such tools. The number and variety of artifacts which show perforations of diameters such as would be produced by these drills, is relatively large. Shell beads are perforated by holes much smaller (1 to 3 mm.) than the average diameter of these drills, the smallest of which have stem diameters of 7 mm. Many are large enough to drill the large holes in atlatl prismoidal stone weights. They seem not to have always been used for that purpose since holes in some cases show the marks of reed drills of uniform diameter. However, they were used in making some atlatl weights as the broken fragments of the weights show, and they would have served admirably to produce the deep conical holes in antler projectile points.

This type is illustrated in the top row, Figure 33 A. The flint here is chipped into a bar nearly circular in cross-section, and only slightly tapering to a blunt point. Extreme dimensions are shown in top row, the largest, left, is 16 x 93 mm. and the smallest, right, is 11 x 37 mm.

43. *Drills, flared base.* These, as illustrated in Figure 33 A, have the same form of body as the straight sided drills, but at one end there may be a more or less disc-like base (second row), or a gradual swelling into a straight base (third row), which in extreme cases may stretch into a slender cross-arm (fourth row). It is assumed that these enlarged ends, expanded bases, and cross-arms rendered the drill somewhat easier of attachment to a spindle. Maximum dimensions of specimen on right, third row, are 27 x 81 mm., for drill on left, fourth row, 29 x 56 mm. with

diameter of shaft 8 mm. The drill on right fourth row, had a shaft diameter of 7 mm. and maximum dimensions of 29 x 36 mm.

44. *Drills, notched stemmed.* Figure 33 B shows a variety of these notched stems. The notch is presumptively an advantage in attachment. In the top row, the expanded shoulders must have had some advantage. The first and third specimens from the left in this row have maximum dimensions of 22 x 53 mm. and 30 x 69 mm., respectively. Some of these drills might perhaps be used as projectile points, particularly the type shown in the third row. These are sharp pointed and not wholly unlike "gravers". They, as well as the larger forms illustrated in fourth row, show wear on their sides, which seems to be the result of grinding against a hard surface. This type of wear could hardly be produced by percussion fracture, and it is doubtful if any process except actual use as a drill would so effect the flint edge. It is to be noted that in many cases, the effect of this wear has been to make the drill nonsymetric in form. The specimen in the lower row, left, has maximum dimensions of 33 x 105 mm., and the specimen immediately above it was 20 x 28 mm. The specimen in lower right has a maximum breadth of 39 mm. and a base width of 25 mm. Since it was broken, its original length cannot be known, but even though broken, it shows the effect of wear due to use for the full length of the remaining stem.

45. *Reamers.* Reamers may be distinguished from drills generally by their larger size, their increased diameter and crudeness in their chiping. Many have flared bases, presumptively to aid in holding them and in twisting them in the perforation when in use. Many are broken and show abrasion on the sloping edges of the shaft which indicates use. The conical shaft of these reamers and their rather blunt points would seem to indicate that they served to enlarge perforations already made by smaller drills. They could have produced conical cavities such as are found in the base of antler projectile points. Figure 33 C illustrates various types of reamers. The specimen, second from the left in the top row, has maximum dimensions of 33 x 67 mm. The specimen, second from the left in second row, is much more massive, producing a larger diameter of perforation. Its dimensions are 31 x 65 mm. The longest specimen, extreme right, second row, is 114 mm. long. The crudest

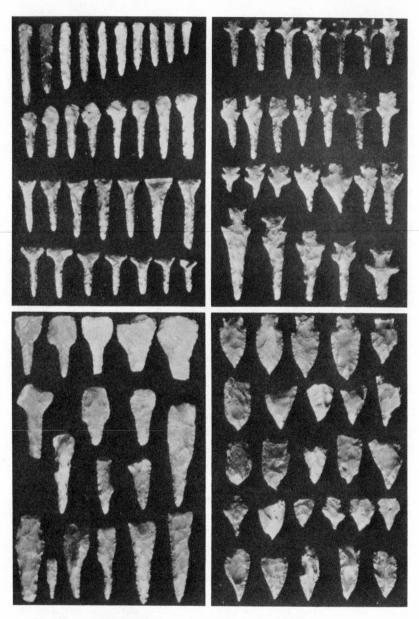

Fig. 33.   A. Flint drills, straight, round base, and expanded base form.
B. Drills notched for hafting.   C. Reamers.   D. Flint gravers.   (Note hooked
points of some.)

specimen, left on third row, is 25 x 88 mm., and immediately under it the small specimen is 45 mm. long with maximum width of 12 mm., and a small shaft diameter of 5 mm.

46. *Gravers.* These are sharp pointed flint blades which seem designed to "cut" only at a point. Many illustrated in the top row Figure 33 D, are hardly to be distinguished from very sharp projectile points. Some of them, stemmed or notched, as in top row, may have been designed for hafting and indeed may have been projectile points; but other unfinished blades, without stems, very rough, with no evidence of hafting, also have identically formed sharp points. Some of these show "resharpening" as if "retouched," and a number of them as illustrated have "bent" or hooked points. It could hardly be supposed that people so skillful in the working of flint as were these people, would make a projectile point with a "hook" at the point. In a graver, such a hook may have served a useful purpose. In a few specimen of gravers, the blade is very heavy, and the point very sharp while the base is worked to a scrapping edge. This would produce a combination graver and thumbnail scraper, see lower row, Figure 33 D. Such implements generally are so well made, so sharp and so carefully designed as to indicate that the one common characteristic in each, the sharp point, was the one important element.

47. *Quarry blanks.* These were struck out of large blocks of flint, many showing that they were the residue of concretions which had all of the original surface removed by percussion. In general, they show no use as tools, and many of them were too crude to have served as knives or scrapers. Figure 34 A illustrates the range in form and size. The largest (center lower row) is 68 x 150 mm. and 20 mm. thick, while the smallest (center top row) is 51 x 68 mm.

48. *Cores.* Flint cores in the site were not very numerous, but they were found as discarded interior sections of concretions, from which flakes had been struck off.

49. *Scrapers, chipped flakes.* Flint scrapers in many forms were used at this site. The scraper was an outstanding artifact as suggested by the large number found in the midden, and its extensive use as shown on the artifacts of bone and antler. It undoubtedly was extensively used in many processes as working wood and dressing skins. There was a marked absence in this shell mound complex of the general utility artifact commonly called a "celt."

Fig. 34. A. Quarry blanks. B. Non-flint hammerstones. C. Abrading stones. D. Stone balls, possibly abraders.

The scraper at this site seems to have been in a measure a substitute for the celt so often used by other peoples. While many of the scrapers were well formed, carefully chipped, and had sharp cutting edges, it is believed that many were made entirely by percussion fracture.

The chipped flake type of scraper is illustrated in Figure 35 A. Many are long, narrow flakes showing conchoidal fracture. From their smooth concave surfaces, small edge flakes were struck off to give the curved flake a fine cutting edge. The flake at right in center row is flaked on two edges, from one side only. It is 122 mm. long. In the center of the third row from the top, the curved flake is 19 mm. wide and 96 mm. long, similarly flaked from both edges. In the lower row, left, a large flat chip, 5 x 54 x 74 mm. is flaked from one side on one edge only. Sometimes flakes were used, which when struck off from its concretion still retained part of the outer surface of the concretion or "country rock." This crude rough surface seemed to be no bar to the use of such a flake as a scraper.

50. *Scrapers, thumbnail form.* These scrapers, illustrated in Figure 35 B all have one oval end, chipped to a sharp scraping edge. They are made from long curved flakes, struck off from flint concretions. They vary in thickness from 3 mm. to 16 mm. at the scraping edge, and are usually thinner at the handle end. Some may have been hafted, but there is no notch cut in this type. The flake was long enough to have been held in the hand without a handle and to have been used effectively.

In the top row, the specimen fourth from the left was 34 mm. wide and 90 mm. long. In the second row from top on right, the specimen had dimensions of 41 x 78 mm. In bottom row, three scrapers on the left are "double ended," that is, they were worked to a scraping edge on each end. They are especially excellent illustrations of the thumbnail type. On the extreme right, lower row, this flake scraper is 3 x 24 x 66 mm. in dimensions.

51. *Scrapers, notched for hafting.* Hafted scrapers have a definite stem, or notches as if made for attachment to a handle. The scraping edge is similar to the thumbnail scraper. This gives some of them the appearance that they were once projectile points from which the tip was broken off, and the basal portion of which was later converted into a scraper. Indeed, this may have been the case

in some specimens. However, there can be little doubt that many specimens were made originally as scrapers in this form. The reason for this opinion lies in the fact that in many specimens where this basal end looks like a projectile point, the scraping edge is very thick—too thick to have ever been part of a projectile point. Further, so skilled were the workers in flint at this site that it is reasonable to assume that they could very quickly make any type of flint tool desired. That is, they could have produced a scraper from a new flake as quickly as they could have found a broken point and converted it into a scraper. Figure 35 C shows something of the range in size and form of this very abundant tool. In some specimens (top row) the scraping edge is very short, nearly the entire instrument is in the shaft. This must have been a very efficient cutting tool for when hafted, the leverage was great. Two specimens, left second row, have double notched for hafting. They have, from left to right, dimensions respectively of 29 x 41 mm. and 31 x 38 mm. The specimen on the left, fourth row, is typical of a subclass of hafted scrapers which have a long stem, contracting toward the base. They are all made from flakes showing conchoidal fractures and the handle probably was laid against the flat side of the flake, and then bound tightly about this rugged stem. The handle probably extended along this flat surface of the flake on the reverse side nearly to the scraping edge. This would have made this type of scraper very efficient. This specimen, left fourth row, had dimensions of 32 x 61 mm. The largest of this type is shown in lower row, right. Its dimensions are 33 x 68 mm.

52. *Scrapers, concave edge.* These were relatively rare, but did occur, evidently made by intention. They are interesting because of the evidence that Folsom man used this type of scraper. In the top row, Figure 35 A, there is shown a series of concave edged scrapers. The three on the right show the rough surface of the concretion. The specimen in the top row at left is a double concave scraper, having two concave edges showing use and some evidence of retouching or sharpening.

53. *Scrapers, drawshaves.* This name is suggested for a type of flint artifact, seemingly a scraper of some sort, not because its function is fully understood, but because it has the form of the blade of a drawshave, sometimes used by modern carpenters and

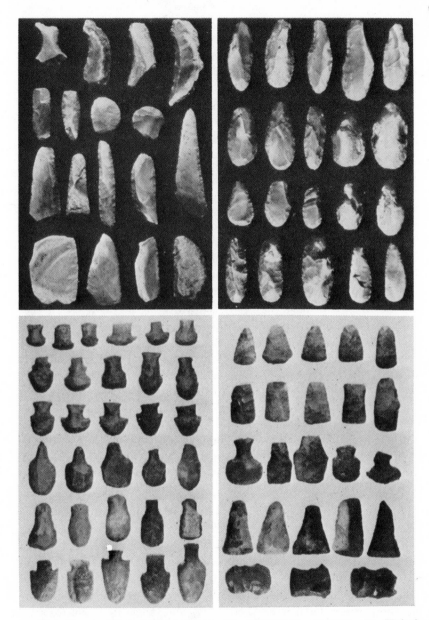

Fig. 35. A. Flint flake scrapers. B. Thumbnail scrapers. C. Hafted scrapers. D. Flint "choppers".

in particular by wheelwrights. This artifact is not numerous, only four were found, two of which were fragmentary, and the other two are somewhat damaged. These appear to have been notched at each end so as to form a stem for hafting. These specimens are illustrated in Figure 36. The two specimens on the left have dimensions of, top 27 x 65 mm., and bottom 26 x 63 mm. One edge is usually somewhat convex, and the other edge nearly straight. Such a tool hafted at both ends would have made a very effective scraper. It may be noted that at a superficial inspection these artifacts look like broken projectile points, especially when in two of the specimens one end has been broken. It is doubtful if the ends which were removed, assuming they too were stemmed, could have been distinguished from fragments of projectile points. The character which distinguishes these drawshave scrapers is very fine chipping of the scraping edge, its obvious use which has dulled it, an evidence of rechipping to sharpen it. This chipping is accomplished originally in some specimens by the removal of very long narrow flakes which run more than half the width of the blade. A further distinguishing characteristic is that the stem is often not set symmetrically in the center of the end of the blade as it would be in most projectile points, but is often displaced to one side, usually away from the most important scraping edge, and sometimes the axis of this stem is not parallel to the axis of the blade. That is, it is "bent" in an oblique position. While these implements are believed to be "drawshave scrapers" which were doubly hafted, it is unfortunate that due to damage, not one of the four possesses all the properties of a complete instrument. A complete specimen has been reported from Alabama.[10]

54. *Choppers.* This term is introduced to describe a class of flint artifacts illustrated in Figure 35 D, which seemingly were used to "chop", having one sharp edge which sometimes shows battering and wear, and occasionally shows some polish on the side of the blade. These instruments are not "celts". They show no attempt at intentional grinding, are made entirely of flint, and while a few show a suggestion of a central groove possibly for hafting, others have a notched stem, and some are contracting toward the base. The majority might be properly described as

---

[10] Webb, Wm. S. and De Jarnette, David L., 1942, plate 183-1.

Fig. 36. Flint "drawshave" scrapers.

"chipped rectangles". It is believed that these artifacts were used when hafted as small hand-hatchets. In the case of the rectangles and particularly those with the flared blades, it may be their bases were set in holes cut in wooden clubs, leaving the blade protruding. Such a mounting would have accounted for the side polish observed. The top row, Figure 35 D, shows "choppers" contracting at the base, but with very thin blades. Maximum dimensions of specimens on the left is 29 x 43 mm. This seems much too small to have been used as a "celt" unless hafted. The second row, by far the most common form, are somewhat more exactly described as chipped rectangles; the center specimen having dimensions of 31 x 48 mm. The third row from the top shows hafted choppers. These are not hafted scrapers. The cutting edge is flaked from *both* sides, and they show battering. The specimen on the right, third row, has the appearance of having been many times resharpened. The unique specimen on the left, third row, is very beautifully made by careful and symetric chipping. Maximum dimensions are 43 x 54 mm. The stem has a minimum width of 7 mm. The fourth row shows a very robust type of chopper, contracting toward the base and relatively thick

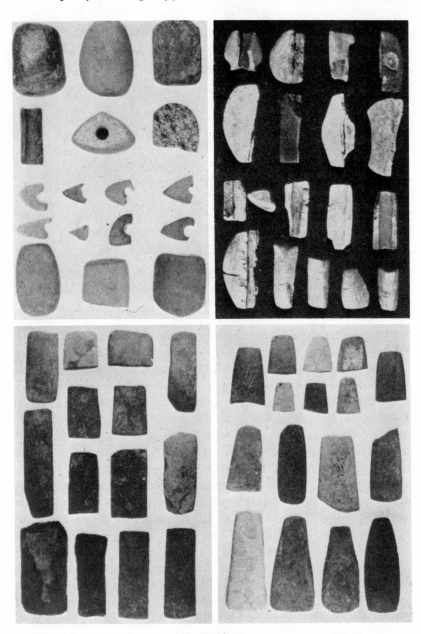

Fig. 37. A. Unfinished and fragmentary prismoidal atlatl weights. B. Fragmentary weights showing evidence of repair, and the use of asphaltum. C. Straight bar atlatl weights. D. Tapering bar atlatl weights.

in body. The center specimen of this row has maximum dimensions of 44 x 58 and it is 8 mm. thick. In the fifth row these "choppers" seem to be double bitted. That is, they appear to be miniature double bitted flint axes, which have only a suggestion of a central groove. They all show battering on the blades, and the central specimen shows some polish on the sides, probably the result of slipping in the haft. Its dimensions are 39 x 47 mm.

GROUND STONE TRAITS

55. *Atlatl weights, prismoidal.* One of the most interesting types of ground stone artifacts at this site is the atlatl weight, which was made in many forms. The manner of its use and its occurrence in burial association are discussed elsewhere in this report. From the general excavation, broken atlatl weights of many forms, fragments showing attempts at repair, and unfinished specimens partially completed have been found. Such broken and unfinished specimens lead to a very complete understanding of the method of manufacture of the weights and the manner of their attachment to the atlatl, and furnishes evidence of their relative abundance.

The various materials used for the manufacture of these artifacts as determined from an analysis of 75 broken specimens may be listed as:

Limestone	44
Marble	1
Sandstone	6
Dark igneous rock	5
Light igneous rock	4
Slate	7
Quartzite	8
Total	75

The form of the prismoidal weight is quite varied. It has usually one broad flat side, which may be slightly convex, *never* concave. The near prism is formed by two other intersecting surfaces, plane, convex or concave. This produces at the intersections of the surfaces a wide variety of edge form, straight, concave or convex. Thus with one flat face, the prismoidal weight may have concave edges, i.e., have a waist at the center; or it may have convex edges, i.e., be greatly expanded at the center; or if its edges are straight, it may have almost a uniform triangular cross-section. Moore went to considerable pains in his report on this site not only to furnish excellent colored illustrations of these artifacts, but to show drawings of their cross-sections. The serious student would do well to study Moore's illustration as to the form of these weights. Figure 37 A illustrates seven unfinished weights found in the village debris. Why they were not finished is not clear in all cases. One is broken transversely, and one seems to have developed a slight crack, which may account for their being discarded; but the others seem to have been capable of completion, had the process been continued. In the top row, in order from left to right, the specimens are a fine grained igneous rock, a sandstone, and a limestone. Their maximum dimensions are respectively, 47 x 56 x 75 mm.; 40 x 60 x 67 mm.; and 36 x 50 x 68 mm. Had they been completed the finished artifacts would have not been greatly different in size. The process of manufacture seems to have been to select a pebble or block of material of approximate size and shape, and by rough pecking, to dress it to the shape desired. This probably was a fairly simple task. If the specimen failed to stand up under these operations, it was, of course, discarded.

The central specimen in the top row shows that before drilling began cavities were pecked into the end of the prism, probably as an aid to seating the drill. It appears that drilling was the most crucial step in manufacture. No polishing was done till after the hole was drilled. This may have been to save the chance of wasted labor if the stone should fail while being drilled. Drillings seem to have been both conical (probably by means of a flint drill), and also cylindrical (by means of a reed and possibly sand).

The bore of some of the broken fragments show conical holes drilled from both ends of the weights. In some cases these holes did not meet "on center." This probably could be corrected by reaming out the channel. However, if the stone split in the process, the conical holes remained. This is illustrated in Figure 37 B, third row from top, fourth specimen from the left. Here the conical holes were considerably off center. Some fragments show a very uniform bore from one end to the other, indicating that the drill was a cylinder. However, a close inspection of these channels in the broken fragments will show annular grooves cut into the wall of the bore at very regular intervals of about one mm. The interior surface of some bores have the appearance of a negative impression of a crinoid—so uniform is the spacing of these grooves. This condition could have been attained if a reed drill was used with water in the hole and sand was used as the cutting agent. This would, for the best operation, require periodic cleaning out of the hole and the introduction of fresh sand having a sharp cutting edge. When the sand was fresh and sharp, it would not only cut ahead of the reed as desired, but would also cut into the wall of the bore. As the sand became less sharp, the cutting continued, only under the reed, where there was sufficient pressure. If this be a reasonable interpretation, the number of these rings may indicate how many times the workman cleaned out the hole and introduced new sand. In some of the broken specimens, nearly 80 mm. long, one may count 65 to 70 of these rings. It may also be observed that in some stones the rings are wider than in others, perhaps due to the relative softness of the stone. In some very hard stones, these rings are very obscure and in some places in the bore non-existant. In the second row, center, of Figure 37 A, there is shown an end view of what would have been if completed, a typical prismoidal weight. This is a limestone, rough pecked into form, having maximum dimensions of 40 x 60 x 67 mm. The hole is 12 mm. in diameter and is only 30 mm. deep, not yet half way through. In the bottom row, the three stones are from left to right, quartzite, limestone and sandstone. The quartzite on the left has a surface almost ready for polishing, and drilling was ready to begin as small depressions had been pecked in each flat end. This might suggest that, at first a conical flint drill was used, and then the reaming was done by a reed. Figure 37 A shows a number of end views of fragments illustrating size of bores which range from 11 to 14 mm. in diameter. The specimen on the left in the second row, which is split longitudinally, is of banded slate and has a hole diameter of 13 mm. In the second row, on the right, is shown what appears to be about one fourth of a so-called ''winged banner stone.'' It is a gabbro, highly polished, and quite thin. It was enlarged in the central zone to a thickness permitting the usual perforation. A portion of the perforation shows on the vertical edge, not enough to determine its diameter.

Figure 37 B illustrates some 18 fragments of prismoidal atlatl weights. In the top row at the extreme right is an igneous rock, and next to it a felsite. In the second row, the second specimen from the left, is hematite. All other specimens are limestone.

The felsite specimen with hole 13 mm. in diameter is unusual because while it has the general form of the prismoidal weight, there is an added hook at one end. This is the only specimen showing this form found at this site. Moorehead[11] figures a very beautiful and perfect specimen of this type from Indiana. It is to be noted that in the specimen shown, the hook is on one end and a lug on the other, both of which might have been useful if this stone had served both as an atlatl weight and also as a hook.

The igneous rock, upper row right, Figure 37 B., seems to have been subjected to drilling after it was broken. There is a shallow circular abrasion of its polished surface on both sides of this fragment. The specimen on the left, top row, seems to suggest a unique form. Its maximum width was 42 mm. and at its waist was only 28 mm. The hole diameter was 13 mm. The second row of fragments well illustrates the straight, convex and concave edge types. The over-all lengths of these specimens are in order, from left to right, 87, 80, 82, 88 mm. The bottom row shows many specimens grooved transversely as if binding was necessary to hold the split fragments together. All five specimens in the lower row show evidence of this type of repair. In the third row, the specimen on the left shows circular grooves in the wall of the central hole. The second specimen is an end view of a fragment which was grooved transversely and which broke along this groove. The third and central specimen of this row shows a considerable amount of asphalt clinging to the interior wall of the bore. The fourth specimen shows conical drilling from the opposite ends, in which the cones are off center, and the specimen on the right has very prominent rings in the bore wall.

56. *Atlatl weights, subrectangular stone bars.* Stone bars seem to fall into three general types: flat rectangular bars with parallel sides and nearly square ends, flat bars with sides sloping, and bars nearly cylindrical except for one flat side. The specimen on the left in the bottom row is of quartzite and has dimensions

---

[11] Moorehead, W. K., 1917, Figure 186, p. 236.

of 14 x 53 x 105 mm. It is unfinished and not yet polished, having been chipped to its present form. Just above it is a polished quartzite bar and to its right, in lower row, is a bar of iron carbonate. All the other are of sandstone. The third from the left, lower row is 10 x 33 x 96 mm. The specimen in the top row, left, is 10 x 37 x 80 mm. Stone bars with sloping sides are illustrated in Figure 37 D. They are made of limestone, sandstone, banded slate, hematite and shale. In the lower row, counting from the left, specimens 1, 2 and 4 have dimensions respectively of 22 x (30-45) x 112; 18 x (25-51) x 107; and 14 x (20-35) x 107 mm, Some stone bars, as shown in Figure 38 A, have an almost cylindrical section except they have one flat side. They are of various forms as illustrated. The specimen shown in the second row from the bottom, on the right, is of banded slate. It is nearly triangular in section and appears to have been made from a fragment of a prismoidal stone which was broken longitudinally. In the lower row, on the right, the two specimens have maximum dimensions of 34 x 74 mm. and 33 x 85 mm. respectively from right to left.

57. *Axes, fully grooved.* The type of grooved axe used at this site is illustrated in Figure 38 B. It was fully grooved and the blade contracted toward the bit. Not a single specimen of flared bitted axe was found on this site. Of the some 159 specimens from the general digging, only three could possibly have been considered as other than fully grooved. These specimens superficially looked like three quarter grooved axes, but a careful inspection shows that on the nearly straight side, the surface had been slightly rough pecked and a shallow groove was in process of formation. One of these specimens is shown in the top row, left. This specimen is of limestone, having dimensions of 45 x 80 x 116 mm. In this row, the next two specimens are also limestone, and the one at the right is sandstone. In the second row, left, this axe is of hematite and has been slightly damaged. The other two in that row are limestone. In the bottom row the specimen on the left is sandstone and the other two are limestone, having maximum dimensions respectively of 56 x 95 x 178 mm. and 53 x 82 x 138 mm. Very rarely axes were found in burial association.

58. *Mauls, grooved.* These artifacts were blocks of sandstone, limestone, or hematite, which were grooved quite like the axes, but

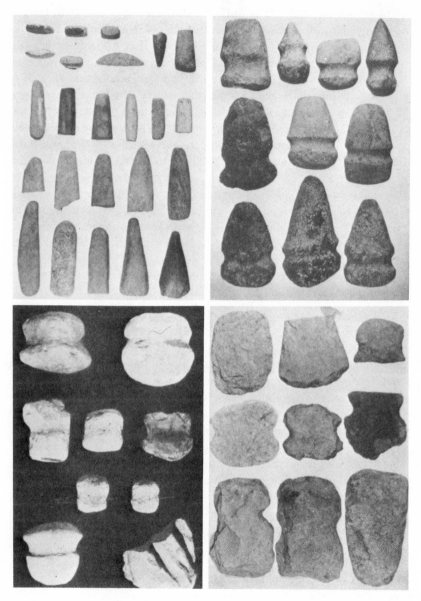

Fig. 38.   A. Stone bar weights.   B. Grooved Axes.   C. Stone mauls and whetstone.   D. Notched limestone hoes.

they had no bit. They appear to have been hafted and both ends were used for pounding. In Figure 38 C, the upper left specimen is a hematite concretion having maximum dimensions of 72 x 85 x 100 mm.

59. *Hoes.* These were usually made of limestone slabs, although sandstone, chert, and quartzite were used. All were crudely chipped, and few were notched as illustrated in Figure 38 D. In the bottom row, on left, specimen had maximum dimensions of 20 x 105 x 160 mm, and specimen in center of bottom row had dimensions of 23 x 112 x 170 mm. It is very doubtful if these hoes should be regarded as agricultural tools, or an evidence of agriculture. It is believed they were made primarily for purposes of excavation of pits, such as the burial pits in the sand below the midden, or storage pits.

60. *Hammerstones, not pitted.* These were of two kinds. Quartzite pebbles, flint concretions, igneous rocks, and blocks of sandstone or limestone were battered into near spherical form. They definitely show abrasion by percussion. They are illustrated in Figure 34 B. In the center top row this sandstone block has a fairly smooth surface, the result of battering, and is 39 x 90 x 96 mm. in dimensions. At the right, a quartzite pebble, which still retains a portion of its original polished surface, has dimensions of 46 x 73 x 75 mm. The specimen in the lower left, a quartzite pebble, has only been slightly used, but obviously had the process been continued, it would have been reduced to a heavy disc form.

61. *Hammerstones, pitted.* Another type of hammerstone is illustrated in Figure 39 A. These are blocks of sandstone, limestone, or quartzite, which have nearly parallel sides, and nearly rectangular faces. In the center of at least four faces, there is a deep circular depression. All of these stones show battering, and it may be that the depressions have been made by pounding on some blunt instrument, like a chisel, gouge or drift. It is possible that some of these circular cavities were made by the use of these stones as drill sockets. In the illustration all are sandstone save two. In the top row, right, the stone is limestone, and in the bottom row, right, the stone is quartzite. Its dimensions are 50 x 81 x 85 mm. The depressions on its faces seem to have been made by rough pecking, and they are thus not very deep. The stone shows that

Fig. 39. A. Sandstone block hammerstones. B. Conical pestles. C. Bell-shaped pestles. D. Cylindrical pestles.

it has not been greatly used as the other in this group. The stone in bottom row, left, has dimensions of 49 x 70 x 83 mm., and the specimen in third row, from top right, has dimensions of 49 x 52 x 103 mm.

62. *Pestles, conical.* These were made from a variety of stones. Many were hard limestone, but sandstones, fine grained igneous rocks, quartzite, and hematite were used. Many were approximately conical as shown in Figure 39 B. Where the bases are right sections, they are almost circular. The smallest specimen, a limestone, shown in top row, third from right, had basal diameter of 38 to 42 mm. and a height of 60 mm. Two of the best executed specimens of average size are shown in third row, left and right. Specimen on the left had diameter of 70-70, and height of 87 mm. The largest specimen, a limestone, center bottom row, is rough pecked over entire surface. It has basal diameter of 96 to 101 and a height of 152 mm.

63. *Pestles, bell-shaped.* Bell-shaped pestles were rare at this site, but there were a few. They are all of limestone. Seven are shown in Figure 39 C. Central specimen is 72 x 72 x 110 mm. The specimen on lower left has an elliptical base, 68 x 91 mm. and a height of 149, while the specimen on the right, lower row, has an almost circular base, diameter 70 x 76, and a height of 147 mm. Many of these pestles are non-symmetric, the plane of the base is not at right angles to the major axis, as is easily observed in specimens in lower row.

64. *Cylindrical pestles.* These were made from limestone or sandstone, carefully worked and highly polished. They do not, in general, show battering by percussion as do the conical or bell-shaped pestles, which suggests that they may have been used as rollers to crush grain, nuts, or seeds as desired. There have been no "mortars" found at this site in which they could work by percussion, which does not prove, however, that they might not have been used end down in a hollow wooden mortar. If the high polish suggests use as a roller, one might hope to find some kind of grinding surface upon which these pestles could roll. So far, none have been found at this site. The limestone pestle on its side in the top row has a diameter of 63 mm. and a length of 175 mm. The broken pestle section on end presents a diameter

varying from 58 mm. to 63 mm. The exceptionally well-polished specimen in center is limestone and is 60 x 271 mm. The sandstone cylinder on the right is slightly pointed at the ends and is somewhat roughened by weathering. It has an average diameter of 57 mm. and a length of 302 mm.

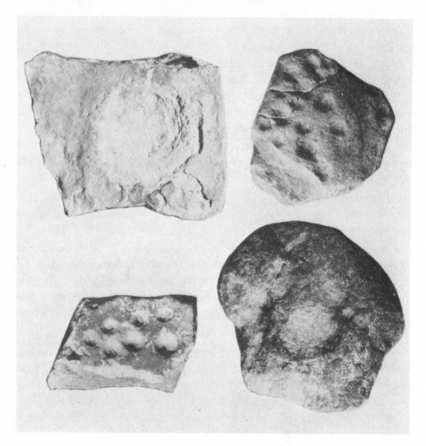

Fig. 40. Lapstones and cupstones.

65. *Cupstones, nutstones, anvil stones.* There were irregular blocks of sandstone of which 56 were found in the midden and only one associated with a burial.

This stone, shown in the lower left of Figure 40, is typical. It has dimensions of approximately 20 x 17 x 9 cm. It shows on one face 13 well defined pits about 25 mm. in diameter and about 12 mm. deep. These cup stones have been called nutstones, and also anvils. Their purpose is unknown. The cups in them vary from one or two to sometimes as many as 14. The term anvil stone suggests that they were used as a sort of anvil or ground rest upon which objects were held when being drilled. It is assumed by this terminology that the cups were made by the drill points penetrating the object being manufactured. The specimen in lower left, Figure 40, was found in association with Feature 19, a fire place. It had been damaged by fire action. Surrounding it were many charred nut hulls, which suggest that the term nutstone may be appropriate, if it was used about the fire as a means of holding nuts when they were being cracked. Cupstones are usually found in the midden on or about an occupational level.

66. *Lapstones.* These are illustrated in Feature 40. There were some 36 found in the midden, and two were found associated with burials. The specimen shown in the upper left of Figure 40 is typical. It is an irregular block of sandstone, some 37 x 30 x 9 cm. It was associated with Feature 21, a fire place. It shows much battering and has a concave depression on each face. Such cavities are about 11 cm. in diameter and about 1 cm. deep. They seem to have served as mortars, used in grinding and are frequently found about a fireplace, or on a definite occupational level.

67. *Abraders.* These artifacts were made of blocks of sandstone and quartzite pebbles, as well as sections of bedded flint, but flint concretions were often used. They may have once been rough pecked into form, or in some cases used as hammers, but all are characterized by rough surfaces showing abrasion as the result of "scouring." They distinctly constitute a type of artifact intentionally produced, which presumptively served a useful purpose, which was not percussion. In form, many have slightly flat faces, which may suggest that at first they were roughly subcubical. By use, corners and sharp edges are worn off and they came to show abrasion over the entire surface. Of those illustrated in Figure 34 C, two are sandstone, two are quartzite, and eight are flint. The largest specimen, bottom row, right, has dimensions of 62 x 65 x 70 mm.

68. *Balls, stone, spherical, polished.* It is not easy to distinguish stone balls from abraiders, except that in size the balls

are somewhat smaller and as the name suggests, they are nearly spherical. In many, the uniformity of curvature is so obvious that one is forced to speculate on the possibility that sphericity was intentionally produced by the workman for a purpose. Perhaps they may have been gaming stones. Their general appearance is like the abraiders, and they may have been so used. Many are made of flint, but they are also made of quartzite, sandstone, fine grained igneous rocks, and rarely of hard limestone. Eighteen are illustrated in Figure 34 D. The smallest, top row, right, has a diameter of 33 mm., while the specimen on the left in the fourth row from the top, the largest, has a diameter of 68 mm. Of those illustrated, four are sandstone, three are flint, seven are quartzite, two are chert, one is limestone, and one is of fine grained igneous rock.

69. *Beads, barrel-shaped.* These beads were made of cannel coal, sandstone, and sometimes of banded slate. They were worn on a necklace, usually a single stone bead at the center of a string of disc shell beads. Rarely, there were several stone beads on the same necklace. In Burial No. 233 a string about the waist had five large beads, two of stone, two of coal and one of shell. The range in dimensions of these beads are as follows: length, from 18 to 60 mm.; maximum diameter, from 10 to 20 mm.; minimum diameter, from 10 to 12 mm.; bore, from 5 to 7 mm. The great majority of these beads were found in burial association.

70. *Whetstones.* These were made of sandstone and usually show long grooves, probably made by sharpening bone and antler tools. They were not abundant at this site. One, broken, is illustrated at lower right, Figure 38 C.

71. *Pendants, or gorgets.* The pendants or gorgets were made from flat thin plates of slate or cannel coal, cut in elliptical form, and have a single perforation for suspension near one end of the long diameter. This hole was reamed from both faces. Five pendants were found in this excavation, three in burial association.

72. *Stone vessels.* Figure 41 shows two views of a broken stone vessel found at a depth of 4.1 feet in the midden. Its nearly circular flat base is 48.3 mm. in maximum diameter. The base is not perfectly circular, and seems certainly not to have been "turned" on a wheel or lathe. At the constriction above the base, the diameter is 45.5 mm. Its other dimensions cannot be determined.

It is a very fine grain sandstone, commonly called a siltstone. It was not associated with any burial or feature and was unique at this site. Although this trait manifestation is rare, it is not unique in the complex, two other sites having yielded three other broken specimens, one of steatite and two of limestone, all quite similar in form and size.

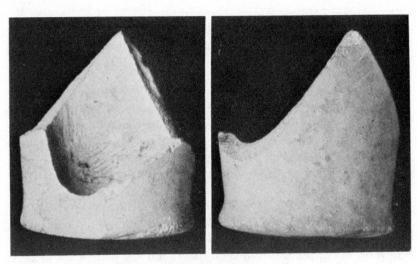

Fig. 41. Two views of fragment of siltstone vessel.

USE OF COPPER

Moore reported on copper found by him as follows:

"While the makers of "The Indian Knoll" knew of the use of copper in the manufacture of ornaments, they possessed but little of it, as will be noted in the detailed list of objects found with burials."

He reported copper artifacts found with three burials, which he described as follows:

"Bu 64 (a child) had a string of shell beads "and terminally an ornament of copper about 4 inches in length somewhat resembling a small ceremonial blade. At the cutting edge, however, is a perforation for suspension."

Bu 103. "At the face was an ornament of copper 6 inches long, centrally perforated and somewhat resembling a bar amulet in outline."

Bu 185 (a child) "Against the lower jaw has a small ornament of sheet-copper somewhat broken."

In this last excavation of Indian Knoll only three artifacts of copper were found, all in burial association in two graves. It is to be noted that both these burials were male infants from two to three years old.

Of the three burials reported by Moore, two were designated as children and of one the age is unknown.* It seems certain, therefore, that while copper was available to the dweller of Indian Knoll, it was quite scarce and seemed to be used chiefly as ornaments worn by children. A total of five graves yielded only six small pieces.

COPPER TRAITS

73. *Pendants.* With Burial 632, a male infant about two years of age, were two small thin oval copper pendants, each drilled with two holes. These are illustrated in Figure 26 D (h). They have maximum dimensions of length 31 mm., width 21 mm., and thickness 1 mm. They each appear to have been beaten into shape from a single nugget.

74. *Bent cylindrical rod (ornament).* Only a single specimen was found with Burial 248, a male infant, about three years old. It is illustrated in Figure 26 D (k). To make the artifact, a thin sheet of copper was folded on itself, and about the edge of this fold, the sheet was rolled into a long cylinder The ends were then coiled on themselves. Overall dimensions are: length 46 mm., width 24 mm., thickness 3 mm. The diameter of the end coils are 17 mm.

75. *Pendant, flat bar expanded center.* This is a rare trait in the shell mound complex, but has been found in two sites. Figure 53 shows a thin flat bar of copper having maximum dimensions of length 153 mm., breadth 31 mm., and thickness 2 mm. This bar was taken from Burial No. 1 at Site McL 4 at a depth of 1 foot. No such object has been found at the Knoll in this recent excavation, but Moore reports from Burial 103 of his excavation a copper ornament 6 inches long "resembling a bar amulet in outline." Mr. E. K. Burnett, curator of the Museum of the American Indian, Heye Foundation, present custodian of the Moore Collection, has kindly furnished an outline of this copper ornament. This outline presented in Figure 53 shows that Moore found at Indian Knoll, a copper pendant very similar to the specimen from Site McL 4.

---

* Later evidence indicates this individual to be 24 years of age.

This outline drawing shows maximum dimensions of length 151 mm., breadth 51 mm., and thickness 2 mm. The slot is 21 mm. by 3 mm. Of this specimen Mr. Burnett says:

> "Moore terms the slot a perforation. Whether or not it should be so considered is a matter of opinion. The entire outer edge of this specimen has been hammered to a tapering thinness, but it is not in any sense a sharp surface."[12]

It is to be noted that in both specimens the two ends of each specimen are not identical. One end, (the lower end if the bar was to hang as a pendant) is an expanded spatulate form of gradually rounded "corners," which form could well have been attained by simple hammering of the bar. The other end, however, has a convex edge extending the full width of the bar, and beyond, finally terminating in sharp angular corners. In the photograph of the specimen from Site Oh 2, there is shown at this end, the impression of a band encircling the bar just below the angular corners. This seems to indicate the means of suspension, and suggests that this band encircled the "neck" of the pendant.

BONE ARTIFACTS

Bone artifacts were numerous at this site. These people used bone and antler for many purposes, and had developed many elaborate techniques for working such material. The preservation of bone material was exceptionally good due to the considerable lime content of the soil. Thus many artifacts were seemingly as sound as when they were first made. The midden yielded a great mass of deer bones, indicating that deer was an important item in the food supply. Such bones are rarely found complete. The type of breakage observed is not one of simple shear, which might cause a bone to break into two parts. The broken bones generally seem to have been subjected to a torque, which not only caused the bone to break, but split as well. This produced many long pointed rough splinters, often with the end of the bone remaining attached. Some have thought that this breakage of bones was due to the desire of the inhabitants to obtain the bone marrow. Whatever the reason, the cylindrical bones show definitely that the rupture was due to a torque rather than to a simple shear. This resulted in many long

---

[12] Burnett, E. K., 1946, Personal Communication.

splinters, which with very little work could be made into needles, awls, pins, for any purpose desired.

BONE TRAITS

76. *Awls, bone splinters.* These are bone splinters which have lost their identity as individual bones, since the ends of the bones and all distinguishing marks have been removed. Such awls, showing evidence to torque, are illustrated in Figure 42, B and D. They are of two general types. Figure 42, B, shows the bone worked to a long cylindrical point as if for deep penetration. The longest of these awls is 95 mm. in length.

In Figure 42 D, the points shown are very sharp, but the shaft is blunt. They were used, seemingly, for shallow penetration when making a small hole. The shortest of these awls is 48 mm. in length.

77. *Awls, deer ulna.* Deer ulna were well adapted to the manufacture of awls and frequently used, and were cut in a variety of ways as illustrated in Figure 44 C.

78. *Awls, deer cannon bone shafts.* In many cases, the awl was made from a bone fragment which still retained diagnostic characters. The cannon bone was often thus used. When split longitudinally, long flat heavy bone awls were made, as illustrated in Figure 42 A. These show the characteristic longitudinal channel and foramen of the cannon bone, and often one can tell whether it was a fore or hind leg bone that was used. The longest of these awls, lower left, Figure 42 A, was 174 mm. in length.

79. *Awls, cannon bone ends.* Sometimes the cannon bone was cut obliquely leaving the epiphysis attached. Such awls appear as short, blunt perforators, as illustrated in Figure 44. In the lower row the method of cutting is shown. The specimen in this row on the right is from a hind leg, the other three from a fore leg, the one on the extreme left from a young animal where complete ankylosis of the epiphysis had not taken place, so that after slight decay the epiphysis had become detached. In the top row of the same illustration is shown the result of cutting the cannon bone obliquely and splitting the end longitudinally. The specimen on the left and the two on the right are distal ends, the other three in this row are proximal ends.

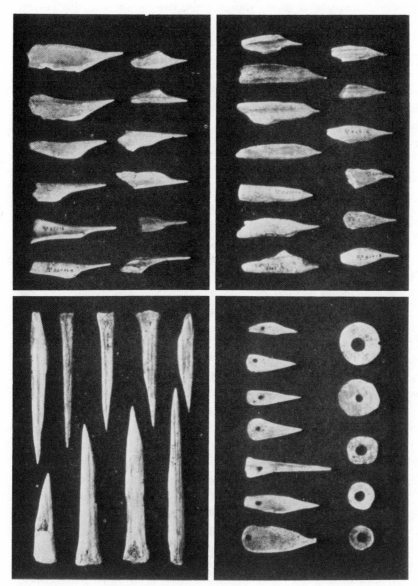

Fig. 42. A. Split cannon bone awls. B. Awls with long points from bone fragments broken by torque. C. Perforated discs of terrapin carapace. D. Blunt pointed awls from split bone fragments.

80.   *Awls, deer radius.*   This bone was not often used for this purpose. Figure 44 B shows radius awls, the upper row illustrates the proximal end and the lower row the distal end of the radius.

81.   *Awls, deer tibia.*   This was a heavy bone, well adapted to the making of awls. Both ends were used as illustrated in Figure 44 A. The lower row shows the distal ends, which made blunt awls not too easy to use or handle. The proximal end of the tibia has a heavy curved ridge, easily recognized, and when split off from the bone makes a substantial and very efficient awl. In the center of the top row this awl is 125 mm. in length. On the left in Figure 48 C, there is shown a tibia awl 185 mm. long. This is the largest of this type so far found at this site.

82.   *Awls, scapulae.*   The large blade of the scapula was cut from the socket, and fragments of this "blade" were ground down to show a good point as illustrated in Figure 46 C. Such awls are easily recognized by the porous structure or cancelluous tissue which always appears near any point, since it lies between the two surfaces of the scapula blade. Of these awls, the longest is 98 mm. and the shortest is 59 mm.

83.   *Awls from deer jaws.*   The mandible of deer is a very hard compact bone and well suited to make a satisfactory awl. Some mandibles were so used, leaving the teeth in place. The large specimen shown in Figure 48 D was 14.2 cm. long. The more common type is the smaller form which is about 67 mm. long. A very fine specimen of this awl is shown on the right, in Figure 49.

84.   *Awls, bird bone, midshafts.*   These were made by cutting the shaft obliquely and grinding the severed end to a sharp, oblique point. Both the wing and leg bones of large birds were used, and many bones after the ends have been removed show a considerable length of hollow shaft. Many of these awls cannot be identified as to species of its origin, since all identifying characters have been removed. Such awls are illustrated in Figure 43 A.

85.   *Awls, bird bone ends.*   In Figure 43 B are illustrated many awls with ends of the bone remaining. Many of these show clearly their source, and wild turkey bones seem to be the most widely used bird bones for awl manufacture. Many bird bone awls, while sharp, were relatively fragile because of the thin wall of bird bones. One wonders if these thin-walled, pointed, hollow cylinders

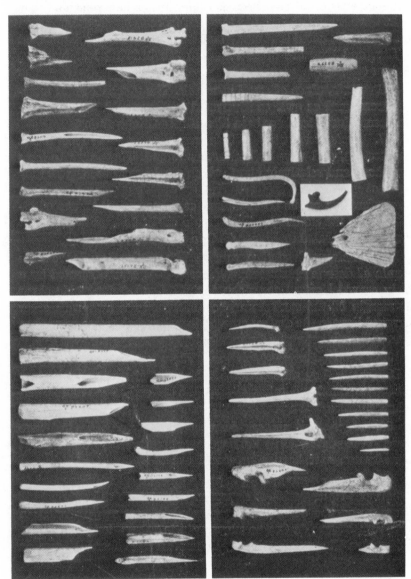

Fig. 43. A and B. Bird bone awls. C. Awls from small mammal ulna fish spines, and bone pins. D. Bone tubes, awls, pins, and bone pendant, and bear claw.

were awls in the sense that they were used as perforators. These bird bone awls could have been clothing pins or hair pins, and they might have served as forks or skewers, in cooking about the camp fire. It is to be noted that many bird bone awls are found damaged by fire, and they are often found in ash beds where fires were used for cooking.

86. *Awls, ulnae of small mammals.* The ulnae of small mammals were used as awls as illustrated in Figure 43. Some of the specimens illustrated have been identified as ulnae of dog.

87. *Awls, perforated.* These were usually made from a flat bone section, and were drilled near one end. They seem to have been short, and relatively blunt, which would seem to suggest they were not used as perforators. If they were used as clothes pins, the perforation might be explained as a convenient means of attachment to the clothing so that the pin might be readily available. They are illustrated in Figure 42 C in top row.

88. *Awls, perforated engraved.* The specimen made from the scapula of deer is illustrated in Figure 54 A. It is decorated by a finely carved zigzag line, which forms a band 4 mm. wide along the margin of the surfaces on both sides of the awl, with other engraved lines in the central area. This awl probably was more than 8 cm. in length before its tip was broken off.

89. *Awls, raccoon bacculum.* These are shown in Figure 43 D. Usually they were cut off at the point of greatest curvature and the proximal end only was used, the cut end of the shaft being resharpened.

90. *Awls, fish spines.* Many spines from fish fins were found in the midden. Only those were counted as awls which showed polish by use, or resharpening, see Figure 43 B.

91. *Pins.* Bone pins were made of bone splinters worked to a small and rather uniform diameter. Usually one end was cut off squarely and the other sharply pointed. They are illustrated in lower row, Figure 43 C. The longest pin is 84 mm. long and 5 mm. in diameter. The smallest is only 30 mm. in length and 2.5 mm. in diameter.

92. *Heads of deer scapulae, glenoid cavity perforated, detached.* The purpose of these artifacts is not clear. They seem not to have been beads. They are never found in burial association. The

socket of the scapula, naturally round and having a very smooth concave surface, the glenoid cavity, are about 35 mm. outside diameter. They were drilled with a perforation about 7 mm. in diameter. The socket was then broken off from the blade of the scapula. No attempt seems to have been made to polish this broken surface, which would have been very easy to do if these objects had been used as beads. The interior surface of the perforations is often highly polished, which may indicate they were used as drill sockets to hold the drill shaft steady when in operation. These drilled sockets are illustrated in Figure 46 C.

It is quite possible that these scapula heads were used as drill sockets while still attached to the body of the scapula, and that due to use or accident as drill sockets, the heads of the scapula were broken off. They were thus useless and so were discarded in the midden. This may explain why the broken surface was never worked or polished, and the fact that such perforated bones are never found in burial association as one might expect if they were beads.

93. *Spatulae, ulnae of deer.* This bone was frequently selected for the manufacture of spatulae being fine grained, dense bone. These qualities were much to be desired either in a flaker or in a fish hook. These spatula are illustrated in Figure 45 C.

94. *Spatulae, split long bones, flakers.* These are formed by splitting a long bone of deer or other large animal and grinding it to a flat broad section usually with rounded end. Usually the grinding is continued till the original identity of the bone was lost. These are illustrated in Figure 45 A. Such spatula might have served many purposes. They have been, by some, called "flakers" on the assumption that they were used in flaking flint by pressure fracture. Many may have been so used. It now seems certain that at this site many were used in the manufacture of fish hooks by a process to be described later. A spatula 145 mm. long made from the distal end of deer cannon bone, foreleg, is shown in Figure 48 C.

95. *Spatulae, bird bones.* The long bones of birds were worked into spatulae possibly for making fish hooks of smaller size.

96. *Fishhook.* The first step in the manufacture of a fish hook seems to be to produce a broad strong spatula of bone such as are shown in Figure 45 A. The spatula then had an elongated slot

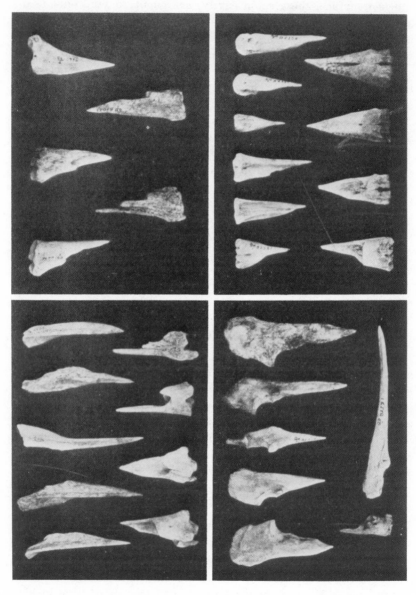

Fig. 44.   A. Deer tibia awls.   B. Deer radius awls.   C. Deer ulna awls.   D. Deer cannon bone awls.

worked in it, which when it had perforated the bone, was further developed to form a bone loop. This loop was subrectangular in form as illustrated in the top row of Figure 45 D by a series of spatulae with perforations in various stages. After the loop had been developed, the hook form was scraped, polished, and finally the distal end of the loop was cut off to form the hook. In doing this, one side of the loop was left much longer than the other side. Such hooks required further finishing by polishing, scraping, and pointing. Some fish hooks had a small knob worked on the stem as an aid in attachment, see Figure 45 D, lower row.

97. *Forked spatulae.* After a fish hook was cut from a bone loop, the remaining portion of the spatula was cast aside, thus producing the forked implements, which occur in great numbers in the middens. These constitute evidence of the importance of the bone fish hook at shell mound sites. There are thus forked spatulae of split bone fragments as illustrated in Figure 45 B. Sometimes a split bone spatula had a fishhook loop cut from each end, thus leaving a "fork" at each end as illustrated in Figure 45 D. There are also illustrated some flat bone spatulae which show that two "loops" were cut in the spatula side by side. This seems to indicate that fish hooks were made with two points on one shaft, i.e., a hook on each side of a shaft. No such hooks have been found, but the forked implement having three forks, i.e., the remnants of two parallel loops are numerous. In Figure 45 D, there is shown the series of operations from a grooved spatula to the finished loop. The stem of most hooks, like their points, were sharp which causes one to wonder how they could have been attached to a line. The finished hook on the left, bottom row, has a stem terminating in a knob.

98. *Forked deer ulnae and tibiae.* These forked bones show that these bones were frequently chosen in the manufacture of fish hooks. They are illustrated in Figure 45 C.

99. *Loops of bone.* These, made in the process of the fish hook manufacture, were not very numerous since if many were produced, they would have been cut into hooks. However, a few were found in various stages of manufacture, but many fragments of them, showing that many near perfect loops failed in construc-

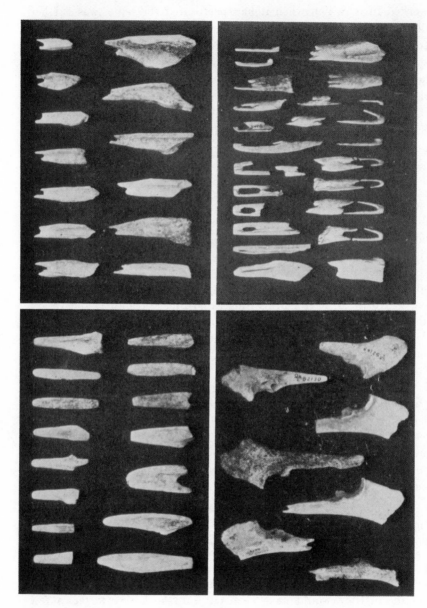

Fig. 45.   A. Bone spatulae.   B. Forked spatulae.   C. Spatulae from deer ulna.   D. Steps in the manufacture of fish hooks.

tion and the split and broken fragments were discarded in the midden.

100. *Gorges.* These are elongated sharply pointed bone rhombs, supposed to have been used in catching fish. Two are illustrated in Figure 48 C. The largest is 50 mm. long. There is some evidence that the fish line was tied about the center of the gorge, one end of which was held against the line by the "bait." After the fish had swallowed the bait both ends of gorge became free and since it was attached to the line at its center, it could not easily be withdrawn by a pull on the line. They were not numerous at this site, although also found by Moore[13] and illustrated by him. They are much more numerous at the Lamoka[14] site, in the Archaic of New York.

101. *Beads, cylindrical.* Beads of bone were made by cutting bird long bones into lengths of from 20 to 40 mm., and carefully grinding the ends. A few are illustrated in central column, Figure 43 D. The smallest bead which has an engraved ring near each end is 24 mm. long and is 5 mm. in outside diameter.

102. *Toe bones of deer, cut, perforated at end.* These artifacts were made by cutting off the proximal end, and grinding the cut surface. The remaining major portion of the bone is hollow, and could serve as a bead or pendant if perforated. This was done by drilling the distal end longitudinally as shown by specimen presented end on in Figure 48 C. Willoughby[15] in discussing types of bone implements in common use among the Algonquians, illustrates perforated and cut deer toe bones and says they were used to play games. He also indicates by diagram how they were strung on a string like beads.

103. *Hairpins, long cylindrical, plain.* Hairpins are usually found in burial association, and are usually about the head, hence their assumed function. Splinters of bone some 155 mm. long were worked into cylindrical form about 4 mm. in diameter and sharply pointed at one end. They are highly polished as if by use.

104. *Hairpins, long, expanded flat head.* These are usually cylindrical, but may be flat. They show much grinding and polishing. They are illustrated in Figure 51 A. From the right in order

---

[13] Moore, C. B., 1916, Figure 8.
[14] Ritchie, Wm. A., 1932, Plate IX.
[15] Willoughby, Charles C., 1935, p. 217.

the four pins illustrated have lengths of 155, 165, 162, and 180 mm., respectively.

105. *Hairpins, asphalt and bead head.* These are usually the long cylindrical pins which have had shell beads attached in various ways by a ball of asphalt. Four are shown in Figure 51 A. To the left of the longest specimen are illustrated three pins which have heads made of asphaltum, to which have been added shell beads. Two pins had disk shell beads 37 and 38 mm. in diameter attached to bone shafts by a cover of asphaltum. The bone shafts were from right to left, 150 and 185 mm. long, respectively. The specimen illustrated third from the left was made by a shaft 175 mm. long. To this a lump of asphaltum had been attached and on top of this lump, four disk shell beads 18 mm. in diameter had been added, one on top of the other, all held together by asphalt. On the sloping sides of this lump of asphat, four smaller disk beads had been imbedded in the asphalt which caused the asphalt to push up through the perforation in the beads, making their attachment very secure. Moore[16] reported two hair pins of similar design, one having five disk shell beads, forming the head of the pin, held on by a lump of asphalt, and a second pin in which the lump of asphaltum was used to seal a cylindrical shell bead to the end of a bone pin. In the surface of this lump of asphaltum, small disk shell beads were set in after the manner illustrated in Figure 51 A.

106. *Hair pins, engraved.* These were not numerous, but it seems to be significant that bone carving was beginning to be observed at this site. Since hair pins were presumptively ornamental as well as useful, one would expect to find bone carving on hair pins if the art was known. The longest pin, illustrated in Figure 51 A, is a solid bone 10 mm. maximum diameter and 225 mm. long. It has a cylindrical bead of shell attached at the head, and it has been drilled transversely. The surface is carved in a spiral band which circles the pin three times. This pin has suffered some decay and portions of the surface near the point have been lost.

107. *Hairpins, painted, oblique red stripes.* This trait is represented by only a single specimen and that one broken. It is shown in the center of the lower row, Figure 48 C. This slim evidence of this trait is quite important, however, in view of the fre-

---

[16] Moore, C. B., 1916, Plate XII.

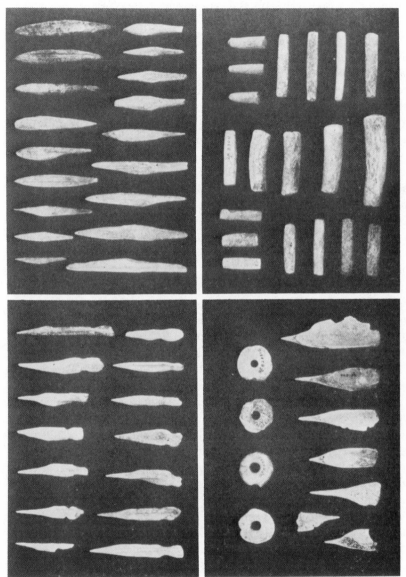

Fig. 46.   A. Notched bone projectile points.   B. Pointed base projectile point.   C. Scapula awls and drilled scapula sockets.   D. Drifts of antler.

quency of its occurrence in the Archaic of New York as reported by Ritchie.[17]

108. *Projectile points, pointed at both ends.* Projectile points of bone were made from long heavy bone splinters. Many show the groove, and foramen of the cannon bone of deer. Even when the specific bone is not identifiable, it usually shows a longitudinal ridge or extra heavy portion, indicating that such bone splinters were specially selected for projectile points. The splinter was then ground to a heavy blunt end, the tip of which was made sharp. This was the piercing end, the effective point of the projectile. This end was scraped, polished, and no work was spared to make it smooth and fairly symmetric. Often these ends are found shattered, showing the result of impact with some hard object. The other end is tapered to a slender stem, not nearly so well worked. This is the end which was attached to the projectile shaft. It is believed that this type of point was used with a hollow shaft, perhaps made of a cane stalk. Some of these stems show annular scratches as if they had been set in some form of socket, and a few have been found showing asphalt covering their entire stem end. Two very well made specimens, one showing asphalt on the stem, are illustrated full size in Figure 49. If a cane shaft was used and the stem of the bone projectile point inserted into a hollow cane and held by asphalt and wrappings, a very efficient union could have been made. It is just possibe that such points were never intended to be firmly attached to a shaft, but if inserted in a hollow cane shaft when projected, they might on impact with the target penetrate it and remain imbedded in it. This would allow the shaft to fall off, making the removal of the point more difficult. Figure 46 B illustrates this type of projectile point. In the top row, fourth from the right, the specimen has, instead of a point, a very sharp well worked chisel-like blade. Some of these specimens show slight discoloration at the point which may be the result of heating in the fire in an attempt to harden the point. This condition is too generally noticeable to be due to accident. Of the specimens shown, the longest is 123 mm. and the shortest is 52 mm. long. The average length is about 83 mm. The two specimens shown in left in Figure 49 have dimensions, from left to right, width 13 mm., length 76 mm., and width 11 mm., length 92 mm. The stem of this specimen is 35 mm. long.

---

[17] Ritchie, Wm. A., 1932, Plate VIII and XI.

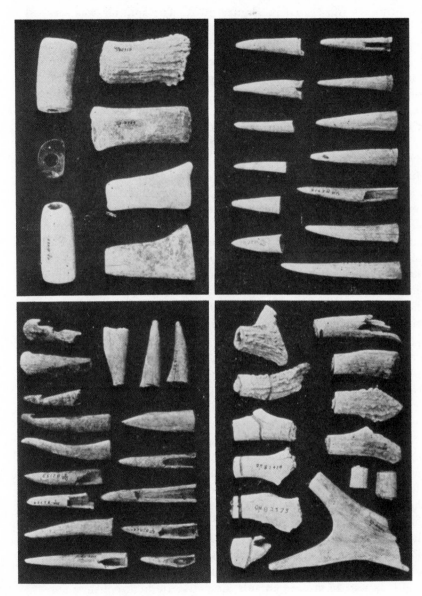

Fig 47. A. Method of working antler. B. Atlatl antler handles. C. Cut antler. D. Antler projectile points.

109.   *Projectile points, notched.*   These were made from bone splinters, as illustrated in Figure 46 A. The splinter was scraped and ground to a long delicate point, quite sharp but generally lacking the robustness of the double pointed type. They were definitely notched at the base, probably for hafting to a shaft. If such a point was tied to one side of a shaft, it could hardly have been a symmetrical arrangement, unless the shaft was split as was probably the case in most flint points. The notching of these bone points is definitely *non symmetric.* The groove extends on one, two or three sides of the bone, always leaving one flat side at the base. This suggests that the shaft also had a flat side, to which the point was bound. Since such a combination was quite non symmetric at best, there was no need to make the projectile point symmetric. This may account for the very obvious non-symmetry in this type of point. This non-symmetry even went so far as to include points of considerable curvature. The plane of the groove is not always at right angles to the principal axis of the point. The basal end, except for the groove, is poorly finished and such points give one the impression of hasty and make-shift construction of a poor workman. Of the points illustrated, the longest is 98 mm. and the shortest, 59 mm., which fairly represents the range in length.

110.   *Tubes, bird bone section, graver handle.*   Bone tubes were made by cutting off the ends of large bird bones. Such bone tubes were highly polished as if they had been much handled. They were not always perfectly straight, but slightly curved bones had been selected for such working. Two are illustrated in Figure 43 D, lower row, center. The largest of these tubes is 119 mm. long and is 16 mm. in outside diameter. These complete bone tubes were found infrequently in the midden. If they had had one end broken off, they would not have been recognized as tubes, and would have been classified as end sections, or mid-section of bird bone awls. Thus the number of complete bird bone tubes reported does not necessarily indicate the total use of such tubes. The tabulation shows that there were more complete bird bone tubes found in grave association, a total of 11, than were reported from the midden, a total of 6. A typical tube of bird bone is shown in Figure 49. It was 137 mm. long and 13 mm. in outside diameter. Its high polish is observable in the illustration. Its ends were not squarely cut off, but appear to have been ground off obliquely. It is this circumstance

which suggests they were used as graver handles to hold incisors of rodents. As these teeth became dull due to use as cutting tools, the teeth could be sharpened by grinding and as the tooth was worn down, the grinding finally cut into the bone handle.

Moore[18] reported finding five such bone tubes in burial association. He was much impressed by their high polish, and gives the dimensions of some of them. He says of Bu. 114 (a young child):

> "About 6 inches from the feet of the skeleton was a bone tube 5.25 inches in length, apparently polished by use, as are the other four tubes from this place."

Of Burial 173 (an infant):

> "At the face was a tube of bone 6.7 inches in length and .8 inch in maximum diameter, highly polished, like all similar tubes in this mound, as already stated."

Of Burial 189 (a young child):

> "At the pelvis a tube of bone slightly smaller than the one described in connection with Burial No. 173."

Of Burial 244 (an infant):

> "At the head was a tube of bone, while another lay at the feet. These tubes, as stated in the introduction, are highly polished, each about 4.5 inches in length, and with three others found singly were with infants or young children."

111. *Gravers, bone tube, rodent incisors.* In one burial, a bird bone tube, 83 mm. long and 6 mm. in diameter, shown in Figure 49, had attached in each end an incisor tooth of a rodent. Because of a curvature of such incisor teeth, it was easy to force the root end of the tooth into a hollow bone tube and by pressure to firmly seat it therein. The distal end of rodent incisors are by shape and hardness well adapted for cutting wood, shell, or other moderately hard substances. It is believed this composite implement was a graver. This opinion rests upon the fact that the distal ends of these teeth had been sharpened by grinding, and that, seemingly many times. Their surfaces show they have been ground down past the point where they would have been worn down by their animal users, for in the animal as tooth wear occurs, the tooth grows outward. Further, in sharpening these teeth, at one end of the graver the tooth became so worn down that the grinding stone cut into the

---

[18] Moore, C. B., 1916, p. 474.

bone handle and removed an oblique sector of the end of the tube. This left a notch in the end of the tube which shows clearly that it was cut out as the tooth was sharpened. Ritchie[19] has reported an incisor of porcupine held in a hollow bone handle, from the Lamoka Lake Site, the ''Archaic'' of New York.

112. *Incisors of beaver and other smaller rodents, in graves.* There are often found in grave association incisor teeth of the beaver, and other smaller rodents. These teeth are not drilled for suspension, and except for having a sharp cutting edge show no evidence of having been worked. As pointed out above, large bird bone tubes are also found in graves, and as shown by the large specimen in Figure 49, sometimes the ends of these tubes, once square cut as shown by a portion of the remaining end surface, has been partially cut off obliquely, leaving exactly the appearance noted in the graver which has been sharpened. This leads to the suggestion that such bone tubes, especially those with secondary oblique cuts on the ends, may have been the handles of gravers used to hold larger rodent incisors. This may account for the placement of rodent incisor teeth in graves. Moore[20] reported incisors of the beaver (Castor canadensis) in graves investigated by him.

113. *Gravers of crossed ground hog jaws.* The use of bone handles for gravers finds circumstancial evidence of confirmation in the occurrence of separate lower mandibles of ground hog Marmota monax) in grave association. These jaws are unaccompanied by any other parts of the animal skeleton, and were presumptively placed with the dead for some purpose. They have been found so placed, in pairs, that if bound together they would form a handle with a single incisor tooth protruding from each end, see Figure 49. Such use as gravers may partially account for the inclusion of separate rodent incisor teeth and jaws of ground hog, in burial association. This finds confirmation in the recent report by Tyzzer.[21] Moore[22] also reported ground hog jaws in burial association.

114. *Cylingers, engraved bone.* These are rare artifacts made from the mid section of a bird bone. The single specimen

---

[19] Ritchie, William A., 1932, Plate X-5, page 102.
[20] Moore, C. B., 1916, pp. 462 and 472.
[21] Tyzzer, E. E., 1943, p. 354.
[22] Moore, C. B., 1916, p. 474, Bu. 242.

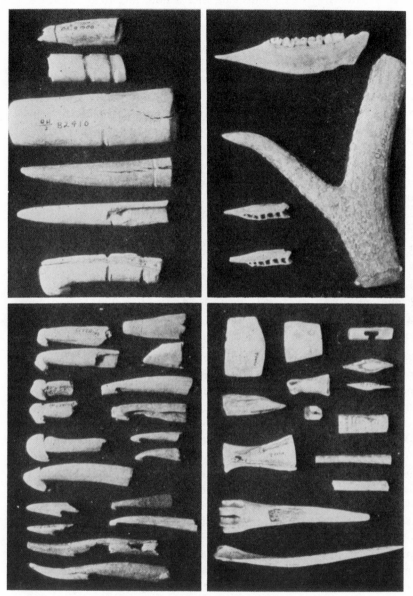

Fig. 48. A. Types of antler atlatl hooks. B. Illustrating cause of failure. C. Rare bone artifacts. D. Antler chisel and awls from deer jaws.

found at this site is 54.5 mm. long and 9 mm. in outside diameter. It was engraved in a 4 or 5 concentric diamond pattern. The design is shown in Figure 54 C, right. It was found unassociated at a depth of 3 feet in the midden. This is not a unique artifact, however, for they have been found in other shell mound sites. Another specimen found at site McL 11 is of similar length and size, and is engraved by a similar technique, the pattern being shown for comparison in Figure 54 C, left. It is possible these bone tubes may be beads, but they are *not* found in burial association or with other beads. Their use remains conjectural.

It may be noted that the concentric diamond pattern as an art motif is suggestive of this type of decoration on some Adena pottery.

Further, the interlocking rectangular scrolls on the bone tube from Site McL 11, suggests the curvilinear interlocking scroll cut in antler found at Indian Knoll.

115. *Chisels, large bone.* These are heavy sections of deer cannon bone split longitudinally, and ground to a sharp broad edge on one end. They are too heavy to be designated spatula and may have been used as chisels or wedges. They are not numerous, only three being found in this excavation.

116. *Rattles, carapace and plastron, box-tortoise.* These are made by placing from 20 to 50 small pebbles in a terrapin carapace and placing the plastron in position. How these parts were bound together is not known. Such rattles are usually found in grave association. Always the group of pebbles appears with the shells. In cases where bone decay has been relatively great, pebbles alone are found which may indicate the body of the rattle has disappeared. Sometimes the plastron has a central perforation about 14 mm. in diameter, which, it is assumed, indicates the presence of a handle. Often the carapace is also perforated in the center with the same size hole. When both carapace and plastron are perforated, the holes are symmetrically placed, one above the other when the two portions are put in anatomical order. If a handle had been thrust completely through both portions of the terrapin shell, it would have been easy to have bound all together. A rattle is presented dismembered in Figure 50. Maximum dimensions over all are 56 x 96 x 128 mm. The hole in the plastron is 13 mm. in diameter, and

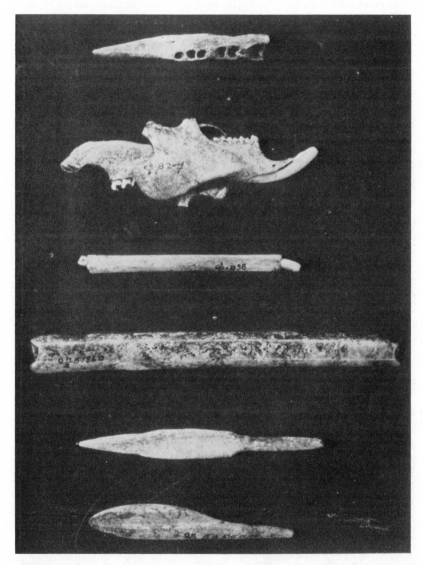

Fig. 49.   Projectile points (bone), bone tube, gravers, and deer jaw awl.

that in the carapace is 12.5 mm. in diameter. There were 22 pebbles in this rattle. In this excavation, 23 graves yielded 32 carapace rattles. Rattles were also reported by Moore as found in his excavation in 8 graves.

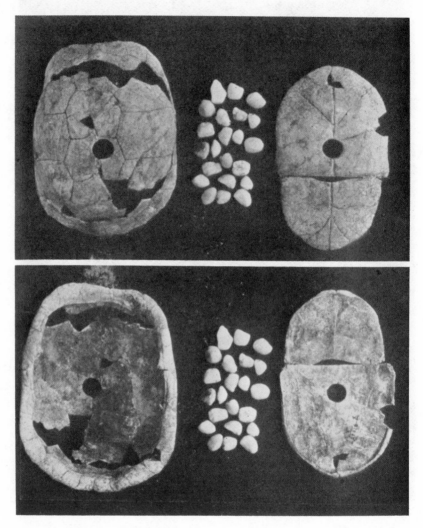

Fig. 50.   Rattles made from the carapace of terrapin.

Graves having rattles were often found to have also ochre in association. Moore reported this combination of traits in two of his 8 graves.

117. *Rings.* These were cut from the carapace of terrapin. None have been found in burial association which leads one to wonder if they were "beads," and if not, what purpose they could have served. They vary somewhat in size, the range being well illustrated in the lower row of Figure 42. From left to right, the external and internal diameter in mm. are, in order, 25-10, 26.5-10, 27-10.5, 37-7.5, 42-14. The sutures remaining seem to indicate they were all cut from the carapace of the terrapins, and thus have the slight curvature of that portion of the carapace from which they came.

118. *Sections of turtle carapace.* These were cut and ground with straight edges to forms more or less rectangular. Their purpose is unknown. These are illustrated in Figure 48 C. They were found in the midden only, not in burial association.

119. *Canine teeth, small mammals, perforated.* These were occasionally found in the midden, but were most frequently found in burial association and were strung as beads. The teeth were small, usually of raccoon, opossum, and dog. These are illustrated in Figures 24 B and 25 C. Bear canines seemingly were not used as pendants by these people. Only one bear canine was found on the site. It was not drilled or worked in any way, and may well have been brought to the site by others than shell mound people.

120. *Canine teeth, small mammals, unperforated.* These teeth were unworked and technically were not artifacts, but some were found in burial association which seems to suggest that they were considered as having potential value, probably as pendants.

121. *Scrapers, deer scapula, pendant.* Only one such artifact was found at the Indian Knoll site, and alone it might be regarded as unique and not evidence of a trait. However, scapula scrapers are numerous in the Lamoka Site of New York, which seems to indicate this single specimen from Indian Knoll may be significant as indicating a crosstie with the Eastern Archaic. This specimen cut from proximal end of a scapula is 70 x 35 mm. and is illustrated in Figure 48 C.

Univ.—13

122.   *Artifacts cut from human bone.*   This seems to be a trait relatively rare at any one site, but wide spread among the shell mound people. In Figure 51 B are shown four artifacts from worked human bone, from top to bottom described as follows:

1.   A well worked awl 12.2 cm. long by 1.5 cm. in diameter, from human fibula, possibly distal third of shaft of right bone. Rasp marks are visible on the edges.

2.   A squarely cut and polished lower shaft section 22.2 cm. long of right femur, possibly that of a female.

3, 4.   Two flat sharp pointed awls 31.5 and 32.4 cm. long, from shaft section of human long bone, possibly tibia or femur. These two artifacts have the same bone texture, color, and weight. The bone was diseased and it is possible that these two pieces came from the same pair of leg bones, if not from the same bone.

From the Pickwick Basin Site Ct⁰27,[23] there was reported a bowl made from the top of a human skull and two carved bone spatulae from fibulae. From Site Lu⁰59 there was reported five bone awls, one from a human radius and four from human fibulae.

123.   *Long bone tubes lateral perforation.*   Figure 51 C, lower half, illustrates a very interesting cut section of long bird bone, perforated as shown. Its use is unknown. It is made of a long bone of some large bird. Positive identification of the species is rendered difficult by the removal of both ends, and almost all identifying characteristics. However, Dr. A. Whetmore* had tentatively identified them as Ulnae of the Whooping Crane, Grus americanus. The largest bone section is 250 mm. long and 14 mm. in diameter at the larger end. This specimen (lower), the only one found at this site might appear to be a finished specimen except for the fact that excavation at Site Bt 5, a shell mound of Butler County, Kentucky, has yielded another specimen, shown in same figure just above it. This Bt 5 specimen is 212 mm. long and 15 mm. in diameter and as shown is engraved at both ends and perforated in a manner quite similar to the specimen from this site. This is a complete specimen, and by comparison it is obvious that the specimen from Site Oh 2 was not finished. The end section at the left is only partly cut off, and it remains undecorated. The purpose of

---

[23] Webb, Wm. S. and De Jarnett, David, 1942, Plates 287-b and 298-a; and Plate 129-a, and page 124.
* A.   Whetmore, personal communication Sept. 26, 1941.

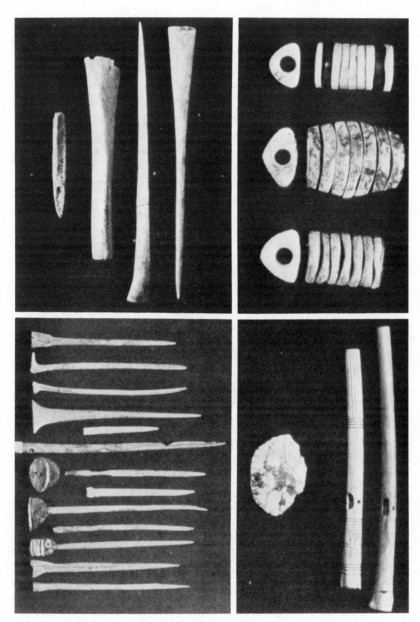

Fig. 51. A. Hairpins. B. Worked human bone. C. Rare implement from bone tube. D. Shell atlatl weights.

these implements is quite unknown. The perforations are nearly rectangular in each case. In the unfinished specimen, the hole is 8 x 15 mm., and in the engraved specimen the hole is 6 x 13 mm. On each of these rectangular perforations, which in the cylindrical surface of the bone represents a notch cut in the bone, there is a circular transverse hole 2 mm. in diameter. This suggests that some shaft with perforated end might have been thrust into this notch, and if a bone pin could have been thrust through the side holes, the shaft might have been held in position. What could have been the purpose of such construction is quite problematical. The bones are hollow from end to end, which has lead to the suggestion that this tube may be a musical instrument, the side hole being used to attach a mouth piece. Such an explanation remains quite unverified.

124. *Medicine bags.* The probable use of medicine bags seems to be suggested by the grave associations of many dismembered parts of animal skeletons, which show in themselves no evidence of workmanship. These grave associations are not strictly artifacts; they certainly are not chance inclusions, and while some of them might have been ornaments of dress, some clearly are not, and their position in the grave would suggest merely inclusion at the time of burial, not necessarily attachments to the clothing of the deceased. The peculiar nature of these inclusions seems to suggest they were the varied contents of, or the parts of medicine bags. Hoffman[24] describes the medicine bags of the Menomini as follows:

> "The members of the Mitawit employ for medicine bags the skins of small animals, birds, snakes, also panther and bear paws, and similar objects of animals origin, but at no time have bags been seen or even heard of, made of any part of a fish. The reason for this could not be ascertained from the Indians themselves, but an explanation of tabu will perhaps be found in the mythology relating to the totems.
>
> When an animal is to be skinned for the purpose of making a medicine bag, an incision is made in the breast, and through this the carcass is removed leaving the skin on the head, feet and tail entire."

The peculiar burial inclusions which may indicate the use of medicine bags may be listed as follows:

---

[24] Hoffman, Walter James, 1896, p. 261.

Burial No.

158   With each burial, the lower jaw and cut maxillae (nos-
305   trum portion) with canine incisor teeth remaining, of
      the fisher (Martes pennati), see **Figure 30 A.**

203   Head of gar-pike (Lepisosteus osseus) and 160 scales
      in one group, see Figure 30 B.

808   Head of gar-pike.

 59   Many bones of the whooping crane (Grus ameri-
      canus).

492   Three lower jaws and three cut maxillae, nostrum por-
      tion, of bob cat (Lynx rufus), see Figure 30 A, and a
      fragmentary fossil tooth (next to the last upper left
      molar of Tapirus haysii, Leidy)*, see **Figure 52.**

529   Nostrum portion of maxilla and lower jaw of Lynx rufus.

606   Bones of three feet of bobcat (**Lynx rufus**).

611   Three groups of complete foot bones of Lynx rufus,
      see Figure 30 A.

650   Four cut sections of jaws of wolf (Canis lupis), see
      Figure 30 A.

687   Two mandibles of a mustelid, probably a weasel, in one
      group with foot bones of one foot.

698   One right ramus of raccoon, one cut beaver incisor, and
      one unworked deer jaw.

708   Two vertebrae of small mammal and pile of snake ver-
      tebra.

857. Ten distal phalanges of bob cat (Lynx rufus).

ANTLER ARTIFACTS

125. *Antler tines broken off, for transportation.* Deer antler
was extensively used on this site for the manufacture of a variety
of artifacts. The midden has yielded very few deer skulls, but
evidence that thousands of deer were eaten at this site. In view
of the large number of artifacts made from antler, and the very
large number of antler fragments taken from the midden, it seems
very certain that as deer were killed, probably at some distance
from the actual habitation site, only such parts of the animals
as were useful were brought to the site. Instead of complete antlers, it appears that some large sections of antlers and many tips
of tines were broken off at the kill for convenience in transportation, and were brought upon the site for later working. Since

---

* A. Wetmore, personal communication March 11, 1943.

antlers were shed accordng to season, it is very possible that deer antlers were picked up in the woods and the tines broken off as the most useful parts, and were saved for later use.

126. *Antler tips cut from base.* The tip was really the valuable portion of the antler. Since it was already pointed it could be converted into a projectile point very easily by scraping. Abundant evidence is apparent that in this scraping, care was used to render the point quite symmetric, even curved points were very considerably straightened by this process. From antler tips there were made projectile points, atlatl hooks, antler flakers, and sometimes awls.

127. *Antler, cut midsections.* Where midsections were to be used, the tips cut off by incising and breaking were also discarded. Many of these occurred in the midden. From these midsections flakers, drifts, handles and chisels were made.

128. *Antler bases.* After the tines were brought to the site, it seems that such of them as were to be used were encircled by a deep transverse groove, the position of which determined the length of the useful portion. This tine was then broken at the groove and the basal portion discarded as worthless. These discarded, cut and broken bases of antler tines occurred in the midden by the hundreds. They are illustrated in Figure 47 C. These specimens show how the basal portion presents a ragged appearance, the result of breaking off the tine. The distal end of the tine shows each tine had one or more grooves—cut completely around it. These grooves were cut almost through the hard outside wall of the antler, which made the severance of the tip from the base easy. Sometime the tine had a midsection removed in the same way, but there was a basal portion to be discarded in the midden. These fragments show one end cut, and the other end broken, generally without cutting.

129. *Drifts.* Because antler could be easily worked, but was strong and tough, sections of it were used as "drifts" in indirect percussion fracture. It was well adapted to such use. Some of the smaller sections of antler may have been used as flakers in pressure fracture. Drifts are illustrated in Figure 46 D. Many are cylindrical with ends cut and ground off squarely. Some are reduced to heavy flat spatula with rounded ends.

Occasionally the section of the drift is sharply conical, indicating they were cut from antler tips. In the illustration, the largest specimen in the central row was 88 mm. long and 20 mm. in diameter. The smallest specimen in the same row is 63 mm. long and 7 mm. in diameter. The cut tips are only 31 mm. long.

130. *Projectile points.* Aside from antler fragments, cut bases and tips discarded in the midden, the antler projectile points were the most numerous of all antler artifacts. They are illustrated in Figure 47 D. The antler projectile point was made by cutting a flat base on an antler tine of the desired length, and drilling in its base a conical hole. It appears from an inspection of broken and unfinished specimens which are numerous in the midden that the outside surface was not worked until the hole was completed. This seemed to be the critical operation for many tines split longitudinally during this operation, and were discarded, never having had their surfaces worked. After drilling the tine was scraped to a fairly sharp point, the shavings being removed in such manner as to leave the point symmetric relative to the conical drilling. This required ofttimes the removal of more material from one side than from the others, and even a tine which was slightly curved could thus be straightened. This procedure is obvious on many specimens, and the tool marks of the scrapers remain apparent. The outer surface of the projectile point thus became conical in form. In the most accurately made projectiles, this cone was not allowed to terminate in a delicate point, but a blunt conical point was made by grinding. In Fgure 47 D, the longest point, lower row left, was 120 mm. long and 18 mm. maximum outside diameter. The bore at the base was 12 mm. in diameter, and the hole was drilled 40 mm. deep. The shortest specimen, top row second from the left, was 48 mm. long, with external diameter at the base of 16.5 mm. and a bore of 12 mm. diameter. A considerable percentage, nearly half, of these projectile points had at the base a groove cut transversely around the base. The purpose of this groove is believed to be to permit the base of the point to be wrapped tightly and thus as far as possible prevent the natural tendency of the antler tip to split longitudinally. This tendency of the antler to split was doubtless increased by the conical drilling, for in order to "seat" the point on the shaft,

the shaft must be thrust tightly into the bore. Such outside binding at the base was thus a seeming necessity, to prevent splitting,
and in some cases, it may have been applied after splitting had
started as a measure of repair. Some points have been found in
which the groove seems to be in a later cutting than the original
surface of the point. It is not believed that this grooving of the
base served in any way as an aid in attaching the point to the shaft
since that seems to have been accomplished in most cases by the
use of asphaltum. Even with basal binding, these points, when
they ''failed,'' show that the damage was the result of the point
splitting longitudinally, which often permitted a portion of the
conical surface to be broken off. Thus damaged points nearly all
have a section of the base removed, as illustrated in Figure 47 A,
lower row. Those on the left in this row show asphalt still clinging
to the interior wall of the bore. The removal of such basal sections
of these points leaves the bore exposed which permits a study of
the interior surface. Most of these bores show transverse grooves
cut into the wall of the bore, suggesting that its conical surface
was worked out by flint reamers of appropriate size. The specimen
on the left, top row, Figure 47 A, shows these interior grooves,
the specimen next illustrates the long longitudinal tool marks
made by scraping the outside surface of this as yet unfinished
specimen, and the next specimen on the right (broken) reveals the
typical ''blunt point'' in many of the better projectiles. The term
projectile implies that these points were ''cast'' or ''propelled''
when in use. It is assumed that they were used in conjunction with
the atlatl, and were thus points on the fore shaft. It seems certain
that many, perhaps most, were so used. If so, asphaltum in the
socket is believed to have been a sufficient means of attachment
of such a point to a shaft if the shaft was properly pointed, and
carefully ''seated'' before the asphaltum was applied. Such use,
however, does not preclude the possibility that these points may
have served as the heads of spears to be used by hand. In fact, so
frequently have some of the larger antler points been found firmly imbedded in skeletons under such circumstances as to indicate
the use of great force that it now appears that some of these larger
antler points may have served as spear points.

131. *Antler atlatl handles.* The use of antler handles for
atlatls has been discussed elsewhere. The form and manner of con-

struction is illustrated in Figure 47 B. In the top row, left to right, the two specimens shown broadside on, have length of 79 mm. and 75 mm., respectively. The diameters of perforations of these three specimens, left to right, are respectively 14.5, 14 and 13 mm. The central specimen injured by fire was broken. In the bottom row from the left, the first and third specimens had length of 92 and 94 mm., respectively. The diameters of the bores of these four specimens, left to right, in order, are 18.5, 14.5, 15.5, and 19 mm. These dimensions are important as they indicate the size of the atlatl shaft upon which they were thrust, and thus indicates something of its strength. The specimen on the right was not quite finished, but when completed, its outside surface would still have been rough. These seem to have been preferred in some cases. The roughness or smoothness of the surface was a matter of choice, since the surface of the antler was to some extent determined by the season of the year in which the deer was taken.

132. *Antler atlatl hooks.* The use of the antler hook as an important part of the atlatl has been fully discussed elsewhere. As a burial association, it is illustrated with other such artifacts. However, there were more antler hooks found "floating" in the midden than were taken from the burials. This seems to prove beyond question that the atlatl was a utility implement and not merely an artifact designed for burial association as some have suggested.

The midden yielded many unfinished specimens, and also others which were worn out by use and had been discarded. Some had been discarded only after attempts to repair them had been made. Observations on such specimens are of interest since they show the method of construction and the usual forms of failure in the implement, incident to its construction, or due to long usage. In the manufacture of such a hook, an antler tine of the desired length, size, and curvature was selected and after a preliminary attempt at reshaping, it, like all antler projectile points, was conically drilled at its base. Figure 47-A shows tines on which this preliminary work had been done, seeminly to fashion them into a form similar to the hooks shown by their side. Before going too far, attempts were made to drill them, and if the specimens failed under the drill, it was discarded. Enough work had been done on some specimens, however, to show clearly that they were antler hooks in the process of manufacture. The actual form of the hook seems to have varied widely, yet there were certain types, within which individuals differed from one another very little. Figure 48-A shows several types, each illustrated by two hooks to show how nearly duplicates were made within the type. It is difficult to describe these different forms adequately. The basal portions were all drilled with a conical bore about 13 mm. in diameter at the base. Use was made of the natural curvature of the antler tine to elevate the hook somewhat above the surface of the atlatl shaft, which made seating of the projectile easy. Figure 48-B shows an antler atlatl handle, two projectile points and an atlatl hook, all of which had begun to split. Grooves had been cut in them for wrapping by way of repair. For the handle and one of the points, it seems to have been effective, but for the other two, breakage finally caused them to be discarded.

133. *Antler flakers or awls.* There are found many antler tips cut squarely from the base, which have been scraped to a sharp point, but not otherwise worked. They would have made suitable flint flaking tools if the point was not too sharp. The sharp pointed tips may have been perforators or awls.

134. *Chisels.* These tools were made by working a deer tine to a flat spatulate form, and grinding a beveled blunt point as a blade. The chisel shown in Figure 48-D was 115 mm. long. The blade was cut on a tine which had not been removed from the body of the antler which was 44 mm. in diameter. Probably the antler served as an effective handle.

135. *Beads, barrel-shaped.* There seems to have been a considerable appreciation of large barrel-shaped beads, worn as the central bead of a necklace of shell beads. These were usually made of stone, coal, or the columella of large shells. A few were made of antler. The one illustrated in Figure 43-D was 48 mm. long. It had been split in half, and the halves discovered widely separated in the midden, were found to fit together perfectly.

136. *Engraved antler cylinder.* The single specimen made from the midsection of an antler tine is 4.8 cm. long and 1.8 cm. in diameter. It is cut squarely at both ends. It is hollow, having a perforation 13 mm. in diameter, and one end face is slightly reamed. The cylinder has been split longitudinally and almost one half of

it was missing. This leaves a little more than one half of its surface present. The engraved pattern is shown in Figure 53-D, and by assuming symmetry of the figure as engraved on the lost portion, the pattern was found to be continuous as it encircled the cylinder. That is, there is no reason to assume that there were any discontinuities such as endings or beginnings in the design.

It was found at a depth of 1.5 feet in the midden, unassociated. Its use is therefore problematical. However, the diameter of the longitudinal hole is very close to 13 mm., which is about the bore of atlatl weights, and bases of hooks. This suggests that it might have been a decoration for an atlatl shaft, but none such have been

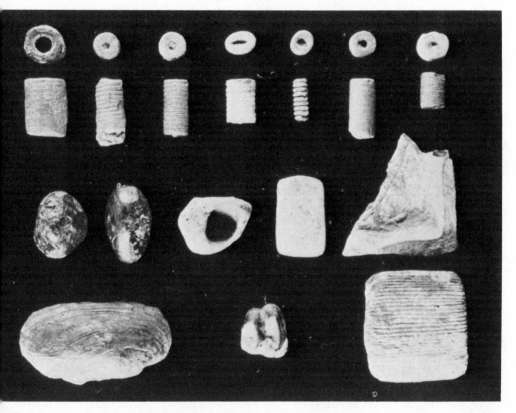

Fig. 52. Fossils and paint rocks found in general excavation. Top two rows: crinoid stems. ddle row: two left hand lumps, hematite concretions; three remaining are limonite concretions. ttom row: left, pelecypod *Allorisima;* middle, *Tapirus haysii,* extinct tapir, upper left molar ssociated with Burial No. 492): right, *Calamites,* fossil plant stem.

found in such association although bone rings have been found in such circumstances in other sites as to indicate they were probably on atlatl shafts.

SHELL ARTIFACTS

137. *Beads, small disc.* These are disc beads less than 2 cm. in diameter. This type of artifact was the most numerous; 152 strings of disc beads containing 15,620 beads were in burial association. Disc beads were worn in strings, about the neck, wrists, ankles and sometimes about the waist. They were often associated with other forms, as shown in Figures 23-25.

The method of manufacture of disc shell beads is well illustrated by the burial association of Burial 610, see Figure 23 A. The process was illustrated by finding in this grave shell bead material in all stages of manufacture. Seemingly large conchs were cut into strips of the desired width. These in turn were cut into squares, and then these squares were drilled, centrally. From these, the disc beads were formed. One wonders if any process of rotation was used in converting the square to a circular disc. The end fragments of large conch and larger sections were used for gorgets.

138. *Beads, large disc.* These are disc beads having a diameter of 2 cm. or more. They are usually not found in strings, but occur separately in the graves. Some were used as ends of hair pins. They may have served as "buttons" having been tied individually on a string.

139. *Beads, tubular.* These were made from the columella of large conch shells, and were comparatively rare in general, only a few occurring in a string of many disc beads. They were about 3 cm. long and somewhat smaller in diameter than the disc beads they accompany. In the largest group, some 35 in one string, shown in Figure 25 B, the beads had been worked down till the wall was very thin. They were thus quite fragile, were badly worn at end contacts, and had suffered damage due to decay.

140. *Beads, spherical.* These were cut and worked from the columella of large conchs. They were rare at this site, and found only in burial association.

141. *Beads, anculosa.* These seem to have been used when sewed on garments. A handful of anculosa is shown in Figure 23 A.

In Figure 21 B and D, these beads are shown in the graves in situ. It is clear that they lie in a pattern, indicating that they were attached to some form of garment.

142. *Beads, pearl.* These were rare at this site. One burial had nine beads made of slug pearl.

143. *Beads, olivella.* These were rare at this site, but were strung after grinding off one end.

144. *Beads, marginella.* These were in considerable use as decoration for garments. The shell had one end ground off to aid in their attachment.

145. *Rings.* These were shell discs of large diameter which had very large perforations, so large as to allow them to pass other beads through the perforation. They are illustrated in Figure 23 C and D.

146. *Conch containers, large marine.* These were buried with the dead sometimes unworked, but usually the columella had been removed, converting the shell to a cup or container, see Figure 21 A.

147. *Gorgets, perforated conch sections.* These were made from the large flaring lip of conch shells. In Figure 23 A is shown a large section which is believed to be an incompleted gorget. It was found in grave association with beads showing the process of manufacture. Gorgets were usually drilled with two holes in the upper margin, for suspension, and a single hole near its center. Rarely this single hole was located near the lower margin. This suggests that there may have been objects of a perishable nature suspended from these gorgets. This type of gorget is illustrated in Figure 24 A, C, and D.

148. *Pendants, broad strips, perforated or notched.* These pendants have only a single perforation and are usually found associated with beads, worn about the neck. The strips of conch shell from which they are made are usually broader at one end than at the other, giving the general appearance of a triangle. The curvature of the surface shows them to have been cut from rapidly curving outer surface of the conch shell, rather than from the flaring and somewhat flatter ''lip'' portion. The perforation near the margin centrally at an end, is made in either the broad or narrow end. This type of pendant is illustrated in Figure 23 C.

149.   *Pendants, long curved section of conch.*   These pendants were seemingly made from the edge of the curved end of conch shells. They retain the original curvature. They were worked to a tooth-like form and when perforated, at one end looked not unlike the canine teeth of large mammals. They are illustrated in Figure 25 B, C, E.

150.   *Pendants, toothshaped, occur in pairs in graves.*   These pendants worn usually as part of a necklace invariably are found in pairs. Since they seem to have been imitations of the canine teeth of large carnivora, possibly the use of them in pairs was only an extension of the imitation. Moore[2] presents in color a pair of these pendants from Indian Knoll. He reports these pendants occurring in pairs in eleven graves in his excavations.

151.   *Bars, short square in cross-section, centrally perforated.* These bars, about 2 cm. long and .5 cm. square in section, are per-

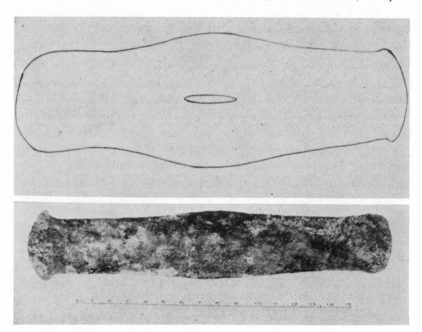

Fig. 53.   Copper bars, expanded center.   A. Outline of copper bar reported by Moore from Burial 103, Indian Knoll.   B. Copper bar from Site McL 4, Burial No. 1, McLean County, Kentucky.

[2] Moore, C. B., 1916, Plate XII.

forated centrally. They may have been toggles or buttons. They were quite rare.

152. *Atlatl weights, matched shell segments.* These weights are more fully described in the chapter on atlatls. They are illustrated in Figure 51 D. They seem to have been made by drilling a hole about 13 mm. diameter through a series of shell plates, usually eight in number, and after these were mounted on a central shaft to hold them exactly centered, the outer surface was ground down to produce a prismoidal form. Usually these composite weights are nearly right triangular prisms, but rarely they are ground with a convex surface on two faces. The third face is always flat. The central specimen shown in Figure 51 D is made of eight sections, is 81 mm. long and its maximum width is 59 mm. The maximum thickness is 23 mm.

153. *Pins, long cylindrical, expanded head.* These shell pins made from the columella of large conch were rare in this complex. Specimens are illustrated in Figure 24 A. They were unperforated, and may have been used as ear ornaments.

154. *Gorgets with burials, occur in groups of four.* This trait rests on an observation which is quite frequent at Indian Knoll. It has occurred four times at this site. It seems significant that in such cases four gorgets should be placed in the same grave. What is more, the individual gorgets usually are very similar in size, form of outline and manner of perforation. It seems obvious that a definite attempt was made to "match" the individuals in a group. These are illustrated in Figure 24. It will be noted that the form of one group differs considerably from that of another. In Figure 24 D, where only three gorgets are shown, the grave had been disturbed and fragments of the fourth gorget were found crushed too badly for restoration. Two of those shown were badly broken. The only evidence of lack of uniformity among individuals of a group is the incised gorget of this group. Moore[3] reports four incised gorgets from Burial No. 230 in his excavation.

155. *Gorgets engraved to represent turtle carapace.* This is a rare trait, but seems to have some significance inasmuch as turtle carapaces were used to cover the face of the dead when buried in shell mounds in Alabama. This trait has been reported also in

---

[3] Moore, C. B., 1916, page 472, Fig. 18.

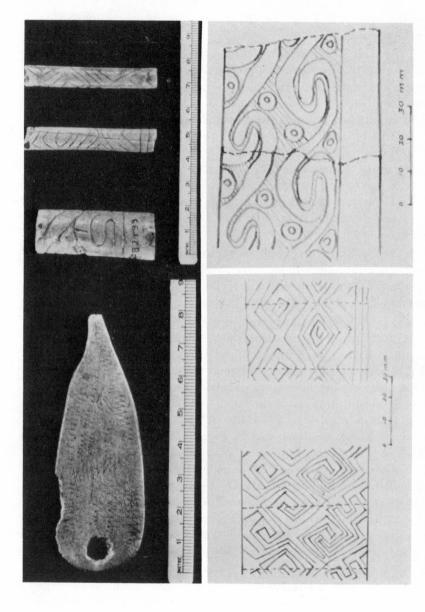

Fig. 54. Engraved bone and antler artifacts. A. Engraved scapula awl. B. Engraved cylinders of antler and bone. C. Pattern engraved on bone cylinders (full pattern shown between vertical dotted lines). D. Pattern engraved on antler cylinder.

Kentucky.[4] Frequently these carapace covers were used in connection with infant burials.

156. *Gorgets incised with equal arms cross.* While this only occurred on a single shell gorget, at Indian Knoll, see Figure 24 D, it is deemed significant inasmuch as this form of cross occurs incised on bone from other shell mounds, see Fig. 51 C. The use of the equal arm cross seems to have had much significance for later peoples, but it was clearly not unknown at Indian Knoll.

THE ATLATL, SPEAR THROWER OR THROWING STICK

It will be remembered that Moore[1] reported from the excavation of the Knoll some 28 antler hooks, 22 prismoidal stones of various materials, drilled longitudinally, and many cut antler sections also drilled longitudinally. These three types of artifacts were found in close association with the burials and because of this association, he was lead to formulate an explanation of their characteristic occurrence. Briefly, his conclusion was that the antler hooks were "netting needles" and the stones and antler sections were "sizers." They were thought to constitute a composite tool used in the weaving of fishing nets, where the mesh was made uniform by the use of the "sizers." While Moore pointed out the definite association of these types of artifact with the dead, and the apparent use of asphalt in the attachment of these artifacts to each other, he did not give sufficient details of their occurrence to enable one to draw any conclusions as to their relative position in the graves.

Reasons for the present belief that these artifacts are portions of atlatls have been previously presented,[2] together with evidence from other sites in support of that belief, which evidence will not be recited here. It will be sufficient to say that the evidence on this point, as the result of the last investigation of the Knoll, seems even more convincing than the evidence available from other sites, formerly reported, if indeed that were possible. Moore found these artifacts ("sizers" and "needles") to occur at Indian Knoll in a total of 31 burials. In another grave he found a group of 11 shell

---

[4] Webb, Wm. S. and Haag, Wm. G., 1940, p. 86.
[1] Moore, C. B., 1916, p. 437.
[2] Webb, Wm. S., and Haag, Wm. G., 1939, p. 50.

segments which, if fitted together, would form a prismoidal block of shell similar in form to his stone "sizers." To point out the regularity of the association of "sizers" with "netting needles," Moore published a tabulation of data on these occurrences. Because of the importance of this data, his tabulation has been republished herein, with slight modification. The occurrence of the shell composit artifact has been added and Moore's determination of the kind of stone used in making the "sizers" is indicated in the table. He reported the fact that many of the sizers were broken and scattered in the grave and he pointed out the obvious use of asphalt with a few. Although Moore reports 298 burials from Indian Knoll, he states that only 66 skeletons were shipped by him to the National Museum. In the course of study of this skeleton material at the National Museum, Mr. Georg K. Neumann checked the age and sex of those skeletons with which "sizers" and "netting hooks" occurred. He was able to find only 17 skeletons of those listed by Moore as having such associations. His findings have been added to this table, which thus contains the original data of Moore, the observations of Neumann, and certain interpretations by this author of the report by Moore.

In this recent excavation there were found in association with 44 burials, 25 prismoidal stones formerly called "banner stones" or by Moore "sizers," 6 subrectangular flat bars, 6 composit shell artifacts, 31 antler hooks, and 10 drilled antler sections. Among many other considerations, one very important reason for conducting this excavation was that more exact evidence might be obtained on this atlatl complex. No pains have been spared to determine the exact manner of association of "hooks," "weights" and "handles," as it now seems they should be called. All such occurrences have been photographed and many illustrations are presented in Figures 17, 18, 19 and 20, with detailed descriptions following each illustration.

From a careful study of this body of artifacts, their position in the graves, and their association with each other, the conviction has grown that *all* of these *antler hooks* are the *distal ends of atlatls.* All of the antler sections are handles, attached to the proximal end of the atlatl, and the *"banner" stones, subrectangular bars,* and *composit shell* artifacts are *all atatl weights.* This belief rests on

OCCURRENCE OF "SIZERS" AND "NEEDLES" FROM MOORE'S EXCAVATION

Burial No.	Age Group and Sex by Neumann		"Sizers" R—rough S—smooth		"Needles"	
			Stone	Antler		
2	Adult	M	Limestone	S 1		Grave disturbed
20	Child		Limestone			
28				S 1		
29	Adult	?		R, S 2	1	
34			Limestone		1	Grave disturbed
37			Claystone		1	*
45			Ferruginous Limestone		1	†
47	Adult	M	Quartz			
67			Silicious rock		1	
77				R 1	1	
82	Child		Quartz		1	
84				R 1	1	† Asphalt
87	Child		Crystalline Rock		1	*
93			Claystone		1	*
95	Adult	M	Silicious-like Jade		1	
99	Adolescent	?	Quartz			* One-half winged stone
105	Child		Banded claystone		1	†
115	Adolescent	?	Granite		1	
124	Adult	F		S 1	1	
161	Adult	F	Banded claystone		1	† Asphalt
163			Chalcedony		1	
170			Shell			Composite of eleven segments
202	Adult	M	Quartz	S 1	2	†
211	Adolescent	?	Limestone		1	
216	Child		Silicious-like Jade		1	
219	Child			S 1	1	
233	Adult	M			1	
236	Child		Gabbro		1	*
251			Quartz		1	*
259	Adult	F	Gneiss		1	*
272				R, R 2	1	Asphalt
296					1	*

* "Sizers" ceremonially broken.
† "Sizers" and "Needles" reported lying side by side.

the assumption that the body of the atlatl was made of wood, perhaps from a broad flat stave, as much as 5 cm. wide and perhaps 40 cm, or more long. One end of this wooden bar was worked to a cylinder about 13 mm. in diameter. On this end was slipped a "banner stone," having a longitudinal perforation of the proper size, and following it, an antler hook, conically reamed at its base, was attached. This was done by pointing the wooden shaft and inserting it tightly in the base of the antler hook, perhaps using asphalt as an adhesive, and binding all together. On the other end of the stave, a hand grip or finger holes or notches may have been carved in the wood to complete the atlatl. Instead of carving the handle, an excellent hand grip could have been made by drilling an antler section and thrusting into it, a spindle cut on the proximal end of the atlatl shaft, using asphalt as an aid in cementing and binding all together. A further variation may have substituted a composite shell weight, for the drilled stone weight of similar form or a polished flat stone bar, lashed to the back of the atlatl shaft, may have been used as a weight. The hypothetical construction of atlatls of various forms is well illustrated in Figure 55. These drawings by Dr. Henry A. Carey, made with the component artifacts before him, present these component parts correctly proportioned and all parts are to the same scale. The only hypothetical dimension, therefore, are the distances between the various parts. Even these distances are not entirely subjective, since account was taken of position of these specimens in the graves. Now if atlatls were made in such ways and were placed in burial associations, it would be expected that generally the more indestructable parts of stone and antler would be found together in combination of weight and hook, or handle and hook, or handle, weight and hook. Obviously, the wooden body of the atlatl, with its lashings would long since have disappeared, but the relatively indestructable portions, hooks, weights and handles would remain in association in the grave together with any asphalt which had been used in their original attachment. This seems to be precisely what has happened.

A tabulation of the occurrence of these artifacts found in this excavation shows the following facts:

In 4 graves a weight, hook and handle were together.

In 18 graves there were 20 weights, each accompanied by an antler hook.

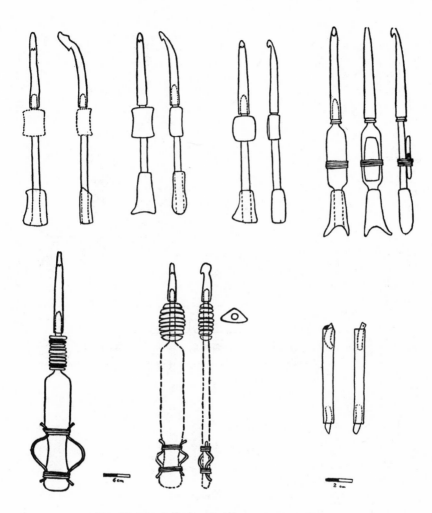

Fig. 55.   Suggested restorations of atlatl forms.
(Drawn by Dr. Henry A. Carey)

TABULATION OF ATLATL ASSOCIATIONS AT OH 2, RECENT EXCAVATIONS

Illustration Figure No.	Burial No.	Age	Age Group	Sex	Material	Form	Antler Hook	Antler Handle	Time of Placement	Remarks (For symbols see below)
19 A	39	17	A	M?	Limestone	P	1		A	‡, red ochre in grave.
12 D	55	21	YA	M	Limestone	Bar			B	Associated burials 55, 56, 58.
12 D	56	21	YA	F	Shell	P	1		A	*, shell weight 11 segments.
12 D	58	22	YA	M	Shell	P	1		A	‡
17 E	69	21	YA	M	Silicious	P	2		B	‡
19 F	92	8 mo.	I	M?	Limestone	Bar			A	*, red ochre in grave, carapace rattle.
18 D	124	28	YA	M	Granite	P	1	S	A	*†
	129	6	C	F?	Granite	P	1		A	†
20 A	140	22	YA	F	Granite	P	1		B	†*
20 E	148	35	YA	M	Banded Slate	P	1		A	‡
18 F	158	3	I	M?	Limestone	P	1		B	‡, red ochre.
	160	22	YA	F	Diorite	P			A	
17 D	217	21	YA	M	Red-brown slate	P	1		B	†, carapace rattle.
17 F	218	37	MA	M	Shell	P	1		B	‡, shell weight of 8 segments, asphalt on artifacts.
22 A	253	13	A	M?	Limestone	P	1			Disturbed burial
	308	No bones saved		M?						Many artifacts, flint, bone, shell. Black stain on bones.
21 E	339	3	I	M?	Limestone	P	1			
18 C	347	28	YA	M	Diorite	P	1		B	‡
18 E	353	18	SA	F	Syenite	P	1	S	B	‡
	396	2	I	M	Slate	Bar	1		A	‡
18 B	452	50	MA	M	Brown hematite	Bar	1	S	A	
	495	18	SA	M?	Sandstone	Bar	1	R	A?	
	503	4	C	M?		Bar				

TABULATION OF ATLATL ASSOCIATIONS AT OH 2, RECENT EXCAVATIONS—(Continued).

Illustration Figure No.	Burial No.	Age	Age Group	Sex	Material	Form	Antler Hook	Antler Handle	Time of Placement	Remarks (For symbols see below)
19 B	509	22	YA	M	Granite	P		S	B	Burial skulless.
22 B	518	21	YA	F	Granite	P	1			Antler hook broken before burial.
	544	3	I	M?	Shell	P	1		A	Carried on string of beads.
17 B	560	22	YA	F	Shell	P	1		B	Shell weight 8 segments, atlatl parts in alignment.
17 A	561	24	YA	M	Shell	P	1		A	*
20 F	577	25	YA	M	Limestone	P	1		B	†
13 C	579	9 mo.	I	F?	Brown banded slate	P	1		A	†
20 B	612	22	YA	M	Brown banded slate	P	1		A	*
	654	2	I	M?	Diorite	P	1		A	Asso. Bu. 613, 614.
	669	22	YA	F	Limestone	P	1		A	†
	687	28	YA	M	Limestone	P	1		B	†
20 C	743	8 mo.	I	M?	Black igneous stone	P	1		A	Parts in alignment, carapace rattle.
19 D	754	15	A	M	Gray granite	P	1		A	*
	760	17	A-	F	Brown banded slate	P	1	S	A	*
19 E	766	22	YA	M	Limestone	P	1	S	A	Burial disturbed.
17 C	785	7	C	M		P	1	R	A	Burial disturbed.
19 C	796	18	SA	M		P	1	R	A	‡, carapace rattle.
19 A	798	13	A	?		P	1	R	A	‡, carapace rattle.
	811	Newborn		M	Limestone	P	1		A	*
	853	23	YA	M	Gray granite	P			A	Weight of eleven segments..
	868	28	YA	M	Sandstone	Bar			A	Carapace rattle.

SYMBOLS

S = smooth   A = after body burial   * = atlatl broken and parts piled together
R = rough   B = before body burial   † = atlatl weight intentionally broken
                                          ‡ = atlatl parts in alignment

In 5 graves a hook was associated with a handle, in each grave, but no weight was found.

There were 13 weights, 3 hooks and one handle found separately in graves.

If one analyzes the tabulation of Moore and places on his finds the interpretation as above stated, regarding stone ''sizers'' as atlatl weight, antler ''sizers'' as atlatl handles, and ''netting needles'' as atlatl hooks, there were:

19 weights each associated with a single hook.
7 handles each with a single hook.
1 weight and handle together.
3 separate weights, 3 separate handles and 2 separate hooks.

It thus appears that without further analysis of the data, the important fact is at once apparent that in a large percentage of cases (42 to 77) each hook was accompanied by a weight. In other cases (13 to 77) a hook was accompanied by a handle. In the 17 cases where stone weights were found without hooks, it should be remembered that they may have been parts of atlatls made of wood, all the remainder of which has disappeared by decay.   A further study, however, of the manner of occurrence of these artifacts makes this data even more significant. It appears, as suggested by Moore, that in many cases where atlatl weights (called by him ''sizers'') were found in grave association, they had been broken, apparently by intention and the fragments more or less scattered in the grave. Moore regarded this as a ''ceremonial'' breaking, and reported it as occurring in the case of 8 out of 32 burials. Recent excavation has tended to confirm the intentional breaking of the stone weights, and the scattering of parts in the grave, another 8 instances having been found. However, having in mind the concept of an atlatl as consisting of an antler hook, stone weight and possibly an antler handle all mounted together, the implement could be effectively ''ceremonially'' broken, destroyed, or ''killed'' not alone by breaking the stone weight, but simply by breaking the wooden portion into two or more pieces. Observation seems to confirm this possibility that atlatls were sometimes broken in two, and the halves, one having a hook and the other the weight, a handle or both, were laid in the grave side by side. This seems to have been found 9 times in this recent investigation and it appears from the language of Moore that 5 of his finds may be capable of such an interpretation. Both of these two types of intentional destruction seems to have been demonstrated. They are well illustrated by many photographs, references to which are shown in the "Tabulation on Occurrence." Such intentional destruction would be expected to destroy the natural relative position of handles, weights and hooks in all atlatls so treated. This certainly offers a partial explanation for the single occurrence of some of these artifacts in graves. It is quite reasonable to suppose that in graves were "ceremonial" destruction of artifacts was practiced, oftimes not all of the parts of an artifact were buried in the grave, and if all parts were in the grave, but were scattered, the chance is large that some portions would be lost and not recovered in the excavation. It is well to keep in mind also that some hooks may have been of wood. Further, when it is remembered how much aboriginal disturbance of grave was apparent at this site as previously discussed herein, it is not surprising if parts of an artifact broken and scattered in the grave, by intention, were not always recovered by these recent investigations.

However, the most important of all evidences pointing to the existence of atlatls constructed with antler hooks, stone or shell weights, and sometimes with antler handles, is to be found in those graves where ceremonial breaking did not occur. In many graves, apparently the atlatl was placed as a burial offering, while still undamaged. Here the wooden portion decayed and in many cases the passing of the flesh of the body did not cause serious disturbance of the remaining portions of the implement. There thus results weights, hooks or handles having perforations of the same diameters, placed in alignment. The artifacts thus in juxtaposition are at distances from each other which suggest suitable dimensions for an atlatl. In spite of all the evidence of ceremonial destruction of such artifacts at the time of burial, and the very considerable amount of aboriginal disturbance of graves, there were found thirteen burials where pairs of these associated artifacts were in alignment, in proper orientation, and at such distances apart as to suggest they were parts of the same atlatls. Particular reference is made to Figure 18 A to D, inclusive, as illustrations of alignment. Of the 30 atlatl weights found in this last investigation, only one was found in such association as to indicate that at the time of burial, it was definitely not being used as an atlatl weight. Figure 22 B shows a close up of Burial 544, a male (?) infant, 3 years old. Here a highly polished "banner stone" or atlatl weight was found carried on a string of beads. The shell disk beads were relatively large, yet small enough to permit them to slide through the perforation in the stone, 11 mm. in diameter. In view of the numerous other associations of such stones with hooks, this find suggests that this stone was being temporarily carried on a string of beads as a safe place of "storage" until it could be used in the manufacture of an atlatl. If this be not a correct interpretation, it should be pointed out that not one of the other 24 similar sones was found in similar association, and out of a total of 88 strings of disk beads, large and small, from this site, this was the only one which had an atlatl weight carried in such association. Further it may be said that while such association, which is quite exceptional, does not suggest its use as an atlatl weight, neither does it suggest its use as a "banner stone"—or a "net sizer." It is interesting in this connection to recall that Knoblock[1] in his very excellent work on "banner stones," suggests such a use for the prismoidal form of stone. So far as known to the writer, Burial 544 presents the only specific instance so far reported of such association.

From the above discussion, it is apparent that in the case of a small percentage of the burials (44 out of a total of 880 if we consider only the recent investigation or 76 out of a total of 1178 if Moores figures be added), atlatls or atlatl parts were put into the graves doubtless as burial offerings. The frequent intentional breaking of this implement or its component parts would seem to suggest that such a custom had a definite significance and may well have been accompanied by some form of ceremonial ritual. Whatever the significance, if any, it must be concluded that in making these burial offerings three methods prevailed: (a) the atlatl was placed in the grave undamaged, (b) it was broken into several parts, which were usually piled together side by side—hook, handle, and weight, or (c) the stone weight was broken as if by a blow, and the fragments of stone and other parts of the atlatl were scattered widely in the grave.

Another fact should be noted, evidence of which may be seen by studying the illustrations, reference to which is made in the tabulation of the "Occurrence of Atlatl parts." This fact is that when making burial offerings, atlatls or their parts were often put

---

[1] Knoblock, Byron A., 1939 p. 53.

into the grave after the placement of the body, yet it is also known that in many instances, the introduction of the artifacts took place before the placement of the body. This applies to complete atlatls or parts as well as those intentionally destroyed. The tabulation shows that the broken atlatls or parts, 11 were or may have been deposited after burial of the body and 5 were certainly deposited before the placement of the body. Of the deposits of atlatls or their parts unbroken, 13 were made after the body was placed and 5 were made before. This seems to indicate a rather wide range of procedure and yet there is enough uniformity to suggest that the practice was following some kind of a pattern. It is not possible to obtain complete evidence from Moore's data, on this point, since he records but little details of the individual occurrence in the graves.

It may be important to note the other burial associations occurring in graves containing atlatl parts.

In the 880 burials excavated recently, 23 graves yielded 32 carapace rattles, and 24 graves showed definitely the deposit of red ochre in the grave. Of these 24 burials with red ochre, five of them were also in the group having carapace rattles.

In the 44 graves showing atlatl parts, 5 had carapace rattles and 3 had definite traces of red ochre. One of these burials having red ochre, Burial 69, had also a carapace rattle, as well as two complete atlatls. One was broken and the parts piled together *before* the deposit of the body in the pit, and the other unbroken, was placed on top of the body *after* burial. This considerable association of atlatl parts, in the relatively few graves having any artifacts whatever, with carapace rattles and the deposit of red ochre, seems significant. What such associations can mean is as yet wholly conjectural.

It would appear that Burial 69, that of a young adult male, about 21 years old, and Burial 339, that of an infant male about 3 years old, represent the typical maximum manifestation of the complex. In Burial 339 no red ochre was reported, but the bones were found heavily stained black. This is suspected to be due to deposit of red ochre at burial.

In accordance with the age and sex determination made by Neumann of the 12 skeletons sent to the National Museum by

Moore, out of the 32 reported by him as having atlatl parts in the graves, the following facts may be tabulated:

Adult, males 5
Adult, females 3
Adult, sex uncertain 4
Children (as reported by Moore) 7
Skeletons not in National Museum, age and sex unknown 13

Total 32

In the recent excavation, the distribution of atlatl parts within the age, sex groups, as reported by Dr. Snow, for 44 burials is as follows:

	Males	Females	
Middle aged adults (36–56 years)	2	0	
Young adults (21–35)	15	6	
Sub adults (18–20)	2	1	
Adolescents (13–17)	4	1	
Children (4–12)	2	1	
Infants (x–3)	7	1	
	32	10	42
New born		1	
Burial of undetermined age and sex		1	
Total			44

The results of these last tabulations seem to confirm the observation of Neumann based on the results reported by Moore.

The facts revealed are somewhat astonishing. About one-third as many graves of females contain atlatls as did graves of males. About one-third of the total were infants and children. It is hardly to be supposed that infants, children and women would have any practical use in life for an atlatl. This would seem to argue that such occurrences represent true "burial offerings" to the dead of artifacts primarily intended for the use of men. This would seem to point to some form of ceremonial ritual during which the atlatl was deposited in the grave, sometimes broken and parts either intentionally scattered, or carefully piled together, and which was accorded to a limited number of persons regardless of age or sex.

These facts pointing to the deposit of atlatl parts with all ages and both sexes, obviously after some sort of ceremonial burial pattern, has caused one archaeologist to whom these facts were presented prior to the publication of this bulletin to suggest the possibility that the atlatl, as reconstructed from the evidence obtained in this investigation, may have been merely a "ceremonial" artifact, constructed solely for such ceremonial purpose and having little or no general functional use. With this suggestion this author wholly disagrees, believing that the atlatl was a very important implement, perhaps the most important practical tool in the social economy of this people. Evidence on this point seems overwhelming, but may be summarized briefly:

1. Parts of implements, hooks, weights, and handles show wear from long continued use.

2. Often parts are found which, presumptively broken in use, were repaired by regrooving the parts for binding all together or were drilled so parts could be reunited. This is shown for atlatl hooks in Figure 48 B where a hook developed a crack and started to split longitudinally. It was grooved to receive lashings to hold it together. In Figure 37 B there are shown numerous atlatl weights, which were split longitudinally along the central bore. These show notches and grooves which seem to indicate that lashings were used to hold the parts together and thus prolong the useful life of the artifact.

3. The fragmentary remains of this implement were numerous in the midden as revealed by the general excavation. There were found 41 antler atlatl hooks, 33 antler handles, 73 fragmentary prismoidal stone weights, and 173 stone bar weights. This reveals more atlatl parts not in burial association than were found in the graves at this site and points definitely to the atlatl as a utility artifact, and to its extensive use as such.

4. The large flint projectile points as well as the antler projectile points seem adapted to the use of the atlatl rather than the bow, although it must be remembered that projectile points were also made of bone in several forms.

5. The small number of atlatls found in burial association may indicate only those implements which, because they were made with antler hooks and antler handles, were preserved. Many more, if made entirely of wood, could have been in use, but such would have long since disappeared by decay. The general digging of the midden revealed important evidence on this point.

There were found in the graves in this excavation besides 24 prismoidal stone atlatl weights and 6 composite shell weights, also 6 stone bar weights, enough stone bars to prove that they were used. Moore, of course, did not report any stone bar atlatl weights since he did not recognize the presence of the atlatl at the Knoll, but his report did indicate that he had found individual stone bar weights in grave association. On this point, he says:

Of Burial No. 52,

> "At the back of the neck of Burial No. 52 was an object of limestone, 4.1 inches in length, somewhat resembling a bar amulet, but without perforation."

Of Burial No. 134, he says,

> "Halfway down the right thigh was a blunt, celt-shaped implement of quartzite."

Of Burial No. 167, he says,

> "At the base of the skull was a celt-shaped, blunt implement without the perforation at one end that some of these tools possess, though none of the perforated kind was found in the Knoll."

It thus appears that in this language, Moore described bars of stone, believed to have been identical in form with those found in recent excavation and regarded as bar atlatl weights.

From the recent general excavation there were found 173 broken stone bars. This fact seems vary important. There were *more stone bar* fragments than prismoidal stone weights. Stone bars were adapted to use as weights on atlatls of which the body was made of wood, with the wooden hook cut out of the shaft. This large number of bars in the midden seem to demonstrate that the majority of atlatls at this site were wooden staves with (presumptively) wooden handles and wooden hooks, all in one piece, and with a stone bar as a weight. This combination has been reported by Gurnsey and Kidder[3] from White Dog Cave in Northeastern Arizona, a Basket-Maker II site which in many ways is similar to Indian Knoll. The atlatl weights found by them attached to the wooden atlatl shafts are very similar in form and size to the stone bars from this site.

These facts seem to point to the conclusion that the atlatl was usually made of wood—perhaps many without weights. When

---

[3] Gurnsey, S. J. and Kidder, A. V., 1921, Plate 33.

weights were used, most of the weights were stone bars. When prismoidal weights were drilled and thrust on the atlatl shaft, this necessitated some kind of detachable hook. Antler, because of its abundance and its properties, proved a very satisfactory substance from which to cut hooks. As has been reported, many of these atlatl combinations show no antler handle in association. Most handles or hand grips, we may assume, were thus cut on the wooden body of the atlatl. The addition of an antler handle was another step in refinement. Such highly developed atlatls were not only valuable artifacts, regarded as proper offerings to accompany the body in the grave, but being constructed largely of unperishable stone and antler parts, these parts today are found in burial association. It is thus not irrational to believe that many other atlatls, made entirely of wood, were also placed in graves, but they have completely disappeared by decay. It will be noted that Burial 55, 503, and 868 each had a stone bar in association, but no other atlatl parts.

ANIMAL BONES AS DEBRIS FROM MIDDEN

In the excavation of this site, all unassociated material found ''floating'' in the midden was collected by squares and by foot levels. After it was all washed and sorted as to kind, there remained some 380 field cartons of animal sacks of bone debris, each sack showing the square and level of its origin.

Miss Opal Skaggs, a graduate student in the Department of Anatomy and Physiology, undertook a study of this very considerable mass of bone material. This bone debris, accumulated as a result of prehistoric occupancy of this site, presents a record of animals killed and eaten as food over the years. There were relatively few complete bones preserved. The bulk of the material was broken bone fragments, some of them burned or charred in camp fires. The breakage of animal bones was largely intentional. Bones were broken in search of marrow as food, or fractured in the process of manufacture of artifacts. Many fragments were so badly broken that all identifying characters of the individual bone had been lost. Miss Skaggs sorted out of this mass of bone debris all fragments which retained identifying features.

By comparison with the bones of mounted skeletons of present day animals such as the deer, dog, wildcat, raccoon, ground hog, she was able to make certain identifications of most of this material. The residue was sent to the U. S. National Museum, where much of it was identified. A minor portion proved to be unidentifiable due to fragmentation and incompleteness. The results of the identifications and counting by Miss Skaggs were tabulated by her as follows:

	Number of Specimens
A. *Mammalia*	
1. Virginia Deer *(Odocoileus virginianus)*	
Antler	698
Astragalus	3101
Cannon Bone	
Distal	
Front	1061
Rear	1159
Proximal	
Front	693
Rear	961
Shaft	
Front	407
Rear	710
Femur	
Distal	
Left	276
Right	275
Proximal	
Left	289
Right	293
Frontal	123
Humerus	
Distal	
Left	1122
Right	917
Proximal	
Left	3
Right	5
Innominate	568
Mandible	1165
Maxilla	351
Occipital	69
Patella	29
Phalanges	
First phalanx	383

	Number of Specimens
Second phalanx	39
Third phalanx	55

Radius
  Distal
      Left 389
      Right 369
  Proximal
      Left 449
      Right 387
Ribs 1553
Scapula 1925
Tarsals
  Fibular tarsal 2519
  Fused central and fourth tarsal 874
  Third tarsal 79
Temporal 17
Tibia
  Distal
      Left 722
      Right 628
  Proximal
      Left 316
      Right 289
Ulna (Proximal extremity)
      Left 487
      Right 206
Vertebrae
  Cervical
      Atlas 293
      Axis 278
        Other cervical 403
    Thoracic 301
    Lumbar 352
    Sacral (fused) 9

2. Raccoon *(Procyon lotor)*
  Femur
      Right 4
      Left 4
  Humerus
      Left 5
      Right 2
  Mandible 260
  Maxilla 9
  Metacarpal 1

Metatarsals 3
Penis bone 33
Radius
    Left 4
    Right 3
Ribs 38
Skull fragment 1
Ulna 2
Tibia
    Left 1
    Right 3
Vertebrae
    Cervical
        Atlas 1
    Thoracic 5
    Lumbar 7

3. Opossum *(Didelphis virginiana)*
Left humerus 1
Mandible 34
Scapula 2
Skull 1

4. Dog *(Canis ——————*)*
Femur
    Proximal
        Left 3
        Right 3
    Distal left 1
Humerus
    Left 1
    Right 2
Innominate 8
Mandible 34
Maxilla 3
Metacarpals 9
Metatarsals 14
Radius 1
Scapula 3
Tarsal
    Fibular tarsal 2
    Tibial tarsal 3
Tibia
    Left 1
    Right 1
Ulna
    Left proximal 3

---

* Species indeterminate.

	Number of Specimens
Right	1

Vertebrae
Atlas	4
Axis	2
Lumbar	2

5. Ground Hog *(Marmota monax)*
Central part of skull	1

Femur
Left	2
Right	3

Humerus
Left	1
Right	2

Innominate	1
Mandible	16
Occipital	1

Radius
Left	2
Right	2

Ribs	7
Scapula	3

Ulna
Left	8
Right	6

Vertebrae
  Cervical
Atlas	3
Axis	4

Thoracic	5
Lumbar	1

6. Squirrel *(Sciurus* —————*)*
Femur	6
Innominate	1
Tibia	14
Ulna	2
Radius	1

7. Fox (————— —————*)*
Mandible	5
Maxilla	2

8. Beaver *(Castor* —————*)*
Humerus
Left	2

* Species indeterminate.

Right 2
Femur
    Left 2
    Right 1
Mandible 3
Maxilla 1
Scapula 1
Tibia
    Left 1
    Right 2

9. Bear (———— ————*)
Innominate 1
Mandible 1

10. Wildcat *(Lynx rufus)*
Fibula 1
Humerus
    Left 1
    Right 1
Innominate 2
Mandible 1
Radius, right 2
Small tarsal 1
Tibia, left 1
Vertebrae
    Atlas
    Lumbar

11. Cottontail Rabbit *(Sylvilagus floridanus)*
Femur, left 1
Humerus 1
Mandible 2
Metatarsal 3
Skull fragment 1
Teeth 2
Tibia, left 1

12. Skunk *(———— ————*)*
Femur 1
Mandible 1

13. Chipmunk *(———— ————*)*
Femur 1
Humerus 1

14. Mink *(———— ————*)*
Skull fragment 1

---

* Species indeterminate.

B. *Aves*

    1. Wild Turkey *(Meleagris galopavo)*

Breast bone	42
Coracoid	167
Femur	7
Humerus	403
Radius	45
Scapula	1
Tibia	297
Tibio-tarsus	291
Ulna	28

    2. Goose (———— ————*)

Breast bone	14
Coracoid	57
Femur	10
Humerus	63
Radius	8
Scapula	13
Tibia	54
Ulna	29

    3. Turkey Vulture *(Cathartes aura-septentrionalis)*

Femur	1
Humerus	1
Ulna	2

    4. Sandhill Crane *(Grus canadensis)*

Fragments of humerus ...... possibly	3

C. *Reptilia*

    1. Common Box Turtle

Plastron	250
Carapace	120

    2. Chelydra

Carapace	37
Large foot bone	3
Plastron	109
Portion of ilium	12

D. *Pisces*

    Buffalo mega

Part of skeleton, not identified	6

    Drumfish (Aplodinatus grunniens)

Head	305

---

* Genus, species indetermined.

Of the 25,756 fragments identified 23,177 are bones of the Virginia Deer. This shows the dominant place held by the deer as a source of meat for the inhabitants of Indian Knoll. The very considerable use of deer bone in the manufacture of artifact is indicated in the tabulation of bone artifacts.

In her final report on miscellaneous bone count, Miss Skaggs says in part:

> "Considering the number of astragali identified, it appears that at least 1,551 deer were present, since each animal has one of these tarsals in each pelvic limb, and it is not very likely that only one limb of the animal would be utilized by the tribal inhabitants after the animal had been secured. For that reason, the total number of astragalus in the data has been divided by two, giving the above figure. Seemingly, the irregular surfaces prevented the usage of the astragalus for artifacts.
>
> In the case of the cannon bones, the count in Table 1 shows a decided prevalence of the cannon bones of the pelvic extremities over those of the thoracic. However, the artifacts identified as being cannon bones reveal the preference of the thoracic extremities for various implements."

It is to be noted that on this large site, from some 380 cartons of broken bone recovered from the general excavation, not a single identifiable fragment of Wapiti (Elk) or of Bison (Buffalo) bone has been found or any artifact made from them. Only two bones of bear have been found on this site, and they may possibly have been the contribution of later times. No bones of bear were found in burial association, and no artifacts made from them.

A STUDY OF THE DOG SKELETONS FROM INDIAN KNOLL WITH SPECIAL REFERENCE TO THE COYOTE AS PROGENITOR

By OPAL SKAGGS

Twenty-one dog skeletons, 17 sufficiently well preserved for measurement and study, were obtained from Indian Knoll on the Green River, in Ohio County, Kentucky. This yield merits careful investigation not only because it is from one of the largest known sites of its kind, but also because the dog skulls suggest that they may be derivatives of the coyote rather than of the wolf.

Scientific studies regarding the origin of dogs present a wide diversity of opinion. Allen (1920) and others maintain that the dog was the earliest domesticated animal; however, no historic study has revealed the true wild ancestry of the dog. It is universally agreed that the Egyptians and the Chinese had domesticated dogs as early as 5000 B.C. Lowie maintains that in the beginning of Neolithic or even as early as Mesolithic times, dogs or some indication of their presence have been found. More uncertainty arises from the possibility that the progenitor of the dog may not be a single species; instead, a number of species of wild canine may have been involved in the origin of the various dog breeds recognized today.

Relatively few investigations have produced any conclusive evidence on prehistoric canine osteology. Thus, the purpose of this study is to describe and to present the results of a series of measurements that would be essential in any comparative study of the osteology of the dog. Although much is still lacking in the knowledge of this subject, the approach indicated seems to serve as a logical contribution from which may be analyzed the significance of the coyote in its relationship to the dog of Indian Knoll. By means of such measurements and comparisons, productive knowledge of the ancestry of dogs in general may be more fully comprehended, and, at the same time, any deviations from an original pattern to bring forth a distinct species may be determined.

In an attempt to establish a more direct relationship between the dog of Indian Knoll and the coyote and to illustrate that such a relationship does not exist between this kind of dog and the wolf, measurements were obtained from each dog skull and the average for each sex was calculated, Table I. A male (125498) and a female (1879173) wolf *(Canis lupus nubilus)* were procured from The Smithsonian Institute, and a male (3465) and a female (3464) coyote were obtained from The Colorado Museum of Natural History; these skulls served as type specimens for the comparison with the average Indian dog of each sex, Table I.

Because of the individual size differences of the dog skulls concerned, it was necessary to establish some means by which proportions could be designated. Consequently, indices, or the ratios of one measurement to another, were used. In this manner, significant comparisons can be recognized, Tables II, III and IV.

Only a few of the measurements considered need any explanation to an individual with an elementary knowledge of mammalian osteology, because, for the most part, the measurements are designated by the anatomic landmarks from which the dimensions were obtained, e. g., condyle to symphysis in reference to the mandible. It is essential that all breadth measurements indicate maximum widths in order to avoid confusion of indefinite points. On the ventral aspect of the skull, the basal length indicates the distance from the foramen magnum to the alveolar processes of the median incisors; primarily, it represents the total skull base. To indicate the distance from one tooth to its opposite or in obtaining the length of the tooth row, the distance between alveolar processes is the most accurately fixed point in cases where the teeth may have been disturbed from their natural setting or may be entirely absent.

Measurements of the extremities of the dogs are included, but their significance cannot be determined because the coyote and the wolf extremeties were not available for comparison, Table V.

All measurements were recorded in the centimeter scale, and the percentage of error was kept at a minimum.

The interrelations of the measurements of the dog skulls do not show unusually wide variation (Table I); this congruity is accepted to indicate that all the dog skulls observed are of the same species.

The Indices presented in Table III seem to be most significant in establishing the attempted differentiation; however, other indices might be equally important or perhaps even more indicative. Also to be considered is the fact that only one coyote and one wolf skull of each sex were used for comparison with the averages obtained from the two groups of dogs, but, as previously stated, the coyote and wolf specimens appear to be typical of their respective species.

Table IV may be of little or no significance; yet, by dividing each dog and each coyote measurement by the corresponding wolf measurement, the ratio of the measurement of one species to that of another may be obtained. For example, the basal length of the male coyote is seventy-three percent of the basal length of the male wolf. This figure shows that the coyote measurement is approximately three-fourths the corresponding wolf measurement. And, in the same manner, the basal length of the male dog skull is fifty-seven per cent or approximately one-half that of the male wolf. Then, after computing the poroportions for the occipito-premaxillary length, an index, or the ratio of the larger number to the smaller number, may be determined. In this case, the indices 94 and 93.4 are obtained. By the same method, indices for the female coyote and the female dog are 71 and 75 respectively. A difference of 4 units may not be significant, yet it does indicate that the braincase of the female coyote is absolutely longer than that of the female dog.

The most comprehensive difference between the male dog and the male coyote occurs in the ratio of the breadth of the orbitals to the breadth of the zygomatic arches. The difference of 34 units clearly shows that the zygomatic arches of the coyote are narrower or have less sway as compared with the dog and the wolf.

The male dog has a shorter and relatively wider cranium, while the situation is reversed but less prominent for the female species. From Table IV it is also evident that the female dog and the male coyote possess wider and less elongated palates than the male dog and the female coyote as compared with the wolf. Similarly, in the ratio of the pterygoidal height to the width at the parietals, the male coyote is greater by 10 and the female coyote is less by 9. From the ratio of the breadth of the parietals to the breadth of the zygomatic arches, the zygomatic width is half the parietal breadth of the male coyote, and the two measurements of the female dog are approximately the same, as compared with the wolf.

To further elucidate the comparison, Table IV should be consulted. From this chart, it is not difficult to comprehend that the coyote and the dog indices are more compatible than those of the dog and the wolf, with one exception.

The ratio of the occipito-premaxillary length to the basal length determines the length of the braincase in proportion to the length of the head. The dog indices more closely approximate those of the coyote than those of the wolf.

The index obtained from the ratio of the palatal length to basal length is a sort of measurement of the snout. The differences in the dog and the coyote indices are negligible, but the wolf indices are conspicuously smaller.

The ratio of the orbital breadth to the breadth of the zygomatic arches indicates that the eyes of the dog and the coyote are more closely situated relative to the size of the head than is the case of the wolf.

The index for the breadth of the parietals to the dorsal length (occiput to nasals) is the ratio of the breadth of the cranium to the entire length of the skull. In all cases, the indices for the female are greater than those for the male; this indicates that the female possesses a larger cranium.

The relation of the width of the palate at the first molar to the palatal length indicates that the dog, in this instance, has a relatively shorter and broader palate, and the coyote palate is absolutely wider like the palate of the wolf.

The height at the pterygoids and the basal length are measurements to show the relationship of the maximum height to the maximum length. The indices for all the animals considered approximate the same value; however, there is less difference between those derived from the coyote and the dog than those of the wolf and the dog.

The ratio of the height to the width is shown by the index obtained from the height at the pterygoids to the width of the parietals. Sex difference is very obvious and relatively the same between the species; however, the difference between the dog and the coyote is less marked than that of the dog and the wolf.

The ratio of the breadth of the parietals to the breadth of the zygomatic arches gives the transverse cranio-facial index. As is evidenced in most vertebrates, the male has a better developed muscular system. The sway of the zygomas will decrease the index; consequently, the number is relatively larger for the female.

Although no comparison can be formulated, it is interesting to note in Table V that the limb bones of the left side of the animal are longer than those of the right. It is probable that the left side is more centered, and the line of the body is toward the right; consequently, the dogs studied may not have been ambidextrous canines but, as is evidenced in human beings, used the right extremities with more dexterity than the left.

Accepting the data procured as valid evidence, it seems highly probable that a distinct species of domesticated dog lived with the human inhabitants of Indian Knoll.

As shown in the Comparative Table this type of dog appears to have a greater similarity with the coyote than with the wolf. Therefore, it is believed that the dog from Indian Knoll may have been derived from a coyote-like ancestor rather than a wolf.

It may be pertinent to remark that the dog as a domesticated form probably accompanied his hunter-master when he arrived in the New World from the Asiatic Continent, and therefore, may have been a type of Asiatic origin.

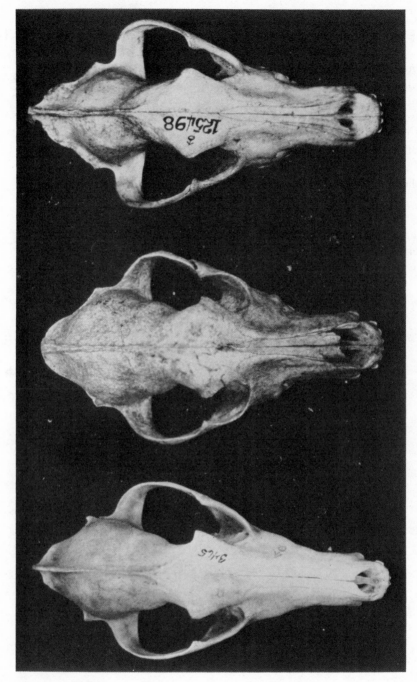

Fig. 56. Top views of the crania of male canines, all reduced to the same size: left, Coyote; center, Indian Knoll Dog; right, Wolf.

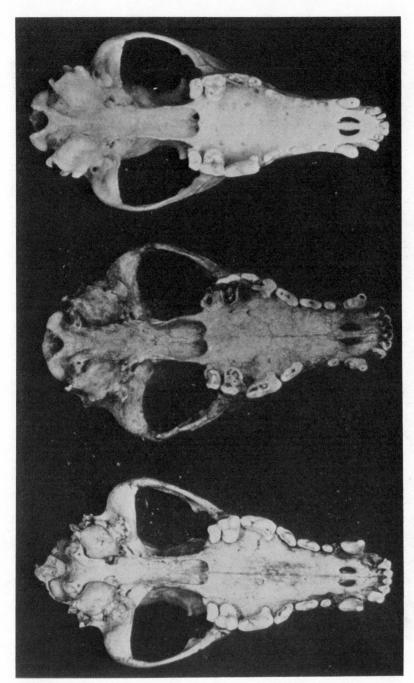

Fig. 57. Ventral views of the same crania, Coyote, Indian Knoll Dog, and Wolf arbitrarily reduced to same scale.

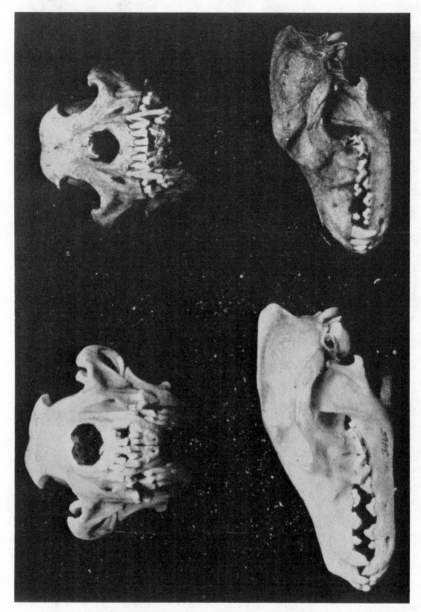

Fig. 58. Front and side views of the skulls of the Coyote (left) for comparison with the Indian Knoll Dog. Both male specimens to relative size.

TABLE 1

DOG SKELETONS FROM INDIAN KNOLL

INDIVIDUAL AND AVERAGE DOG SKULL MEASUREMENTS COMPARED TO COYOTE AND WOLF

	MALES											FEMALES											
	1-4	1-129	1-34	1-31	1-7	1-117	1-56	1-55	Dog Ave.	Wolf	Coyote	Coyote	Wolf	Dog Ave.	1-26	1-12	1-8	1-24	1-9	1-60	1-35	1-3	1-30
Length-occiput to outer alveoli at I⋅C Dorsal	14.80	14.45	14.15		14.99	13.90	14.60	12.80	14.23	25.70	18.60	17.65	24.65	13.38	13.50			13.80	13.70		13.80		12.10
Basal length	14.48	14.20	13.66		14.33	13.49	14.36	12.44	13.85	24.34	17.54	16.98	21.82	12.92	12.76	12.49		13.70	13.42	12.80	13.55		11.72
LENGTH																							
Occipito-premaxillary	9.09		8.90		9.40	8.30	9.32	8.34	8.95	14.56	11.30	10.67	19.25	8.39	8.22	7.90		8.80	8.74	8.60	8.77		7.70
Palatal length	7.90		7.59		7.90	7.30	7.74	6.80	7.54	12.62	9.69	9.32	11.12	6.99	7.16	6.64	7.09		7.28		7.45	6.67	6.40
Between outer margins of mastoids	5.34	5.37	4.96	4.45	5.19		5.36	4.58	5.04	6.30	5.33	5.24	5.95	4.66	4.57	4.44		4.94	4.89	4.55	4.74		4.48
Between outer margins of paraoccipital processes	4.33		4.15	3.64	4.25		4.40	4.00	4.13	8.20	4.74	4.68		3.74		3.74			4.03				3.46
Between outer margins of occiput	5.86	5.90	5.56	4.96	5.65	5.60	5.89	5.24	5.58	8.17	6.05	6.00	7.45	5.21	5.20	4.97		5.37	5.35	5.33	5.45		4.80
Between outer margins of zygomas	9.25		8.80	7.93	9.38		8.80	8.57	8.83	14.04	10.00	9.60	12.45	7.76	7.83	6.96		8.26	8.03	7.74			
Between outer margins of pterygoids	1.87		1.64		1.84	1.83		1.76	1.79	1.61	1.54	1.59	1.49	1.61	1.55	1.51			1.65	1.54	1.63		1.73
Alveolus of i¹ to orbit	6.14	6.09						5.60	6.25	11.46	8.74	8.55	9.96	6.38					6.38	5.45		5.07	4.67
Median length of nasals			5.80			5.54	5.80	4.69	5.68	9.85	8.05	7.44	7.90	5.04	5.46	4.78			5.45	4.80			
Outer width of occipital condyles	3.45	3.24	3.17	2.62	3.22	3.25	3.40	2.99	3.17	4.51	3.37	3.14	4.40	3.02	2.95	3.00		3.13	3.10	2.96	3.19		2.79
Inner width of occipital condyles	1.76	1.62	1.30	1.62	1.77	1.87	1.44	1.63	1.63	2.32			2.00	1.55	1.57	1.59		1.59	1.52	1.54	1.68		1.37
Height of occiput	2.63	2.74	2.74	2.15	2.69	2.53	2.46	2.96	2.63	4.05	3.24	3.00	3.64	2.30	2.34	2.08		2.44	2.35	2.42	2.39	2.00	2.08
Breadth of parietals	4.79	5.10	5.10	4.80	5.14	5.25	4.93	4.95	5.26	6.59	4.05	5.94	6.35	5.07	5.67	4.62		5.23	4.94	5.40	4.99		4.64
Breadth of orbitals	3.35	3.35	3.00	2.65	3.30	3.19	3.19	2.85	3.07	4.63	3.34	3.40	3.97	2.66	2.73	2.38			2.01	2.92	2.65		2.67
Breadth of supra-orbital processes	5.84	4.68	4.00	3.84	4.60	4.60	4.50	4.05	4.50	6.71	4.77	4.74	5.40	3.54	3.35								3.73
Width of palate at canines	2.05	2.12	2.00		2.06	2.05	2.16	1.94	2.05	2.90	1.94	1.95	2.34	1.86	1.83	1.65			1.98	1.90	1.83	2.00	1.80
Width of palate at molars¹	3.16	3.25	2.98	2.73	3.17	3.00	3.25	2.78	3.04	4.35	3.27	3.16	4.34	2.78	2.78	2.52	2.84	3.04	2.70	2.90	2.69	2.95	2.66

UPPER JAW and LOWER JAW measurement table (values in order of the 22 specimen columns, left to right):

Measurement	1	2	3	4	5	6	7	8	9	10	11	12	13	14	15	16	17	18	19	20	21	22
Width of palate at molars³	3.26	2.99	2.76	2.54	3.01	2.87	2.93	2.48	2.91	4.04	2.94	3.04	3.84	3.04	2.57	2.50	3.00	2.55	2.66	2.73	2.80	2.48
Height at pterygoids	4.70	4.83	4.89	4.50	4.92	4.85	4.65	4.70	4.75	8.85	5.90	5.80	7.70	4.40	4.63	4.00	8.00		4.55	4.45		4.35
UPPER JAW																						
Length of tooth row	8.07	7.60	7.06		8.10	7.75	7.83	6.80	7.60	11.96	10.28	9.70	10.73	7.26	7.56	6.90	8.00	7.04	7.16	7.95	6.90	6.60
Length of premolar row	2.60	2.60	2.65		2.69	2.65	2.64	2.14	2.56	4.14	3.60	3.50	3.65	2.30	2.50	1.94	2.69	2.30	2.57	2.70	1.79	2.36
Length of molar row	2.74	2.80	2.46	2.40	2.77	2.65	2.76	2.69	2.66	4.22	3.84	3.55	3.90	2.64	2.64	2.46	2.78	2.78	2.69	2.76	2.94	2.33
Alveolar breadth at i³	1.45	1.32	1.24		1.34	1.25	1.28	1.28	1.31	1.95	1.30	1.10	1.58	1.33	1.40	1.24		1.26	1.90	1.40	1.37	1.34
Alveolar breadth at canines	2.05	2.12	2.40		2.06	2.05	2.16	1.94	2.11	2.90	1.80	1.10	2.30	1.85	1.83	1.60	1.98	1.98	2.10	1.83	2.00	1.80
Alveolar breadth at pms.¹	2.26	2.23	2.13		2.17	1.82	2.34	2.00	2.14	3.25	1.94	1.03	2.74	1.96	1.78	1.80	2.00	2.10	2.55	1.97	2.13	1.92
Alveolar breadth at pms.³	2.77	2.74	3.00	2.46	2.83	3.00	3.25	2.78	2.72	3.90	2.56	1.83	3.45	2.33	2.37	2.14	2.35	2.55	2.90	2.33		2.23
Alveolar breadth at molars¹	3.16	3.25	3.00	2.73	3.17	3.00	3.25	3.04	3.04	4.35	3.27	3.70	4.33	2.77	2.57	2.50	2.70	2.90	2.66	2.69	2.95	2.66
Alveolar breadth at molars³	3.26	2.99	2.84	2.54	3.01	2.87	2.93	2.48	2.86	4.05	3.05	3.70	3.85	2.66	2.57	2.49	2.55	2.55	2.66	2.73	2.80	2.48
Alveolus of i¹ to m²	7.14	6.95	6.25		7.35	6.90	5.59	5.33	6.65	10.70	8.86	8.24	9.77	6.34	6.59	6.06	6.75	6.51	6.36	6.80	6.10	5.54
Alveolus of c to m²	5.55	5.50	5.40		5.69	5.46	4.84	4.69	5.41	8.50	7.25	6.28	7.52	5.03	5.65	4.77	5.53	5.14	4.93	5.15	4.74	4.50
Alveolus of pm¹ to m²	4.77	4.60	4.33		4.86			4.04	4.57	6.60	6.00	6.28		4.18		3.40	4.80	4.54	4.54	4.36	3.58	3.99
Alveolus of pm² to m²	3.69	3.64	2.24		4.05	3.77	3.90	3.34	3.52	5.41	4.64	6.15	5.15	3.18	3.60	2.50	3.76	2.78	3.53	3.50	2.50	3.28
Alveolus of m¹ to m²	1.83	1.92	1.74	1.74	1.94	1.90	1.93	1.73	1.95	2.64	1.78	1.60	2.80	1.82	1.84	1.76	1.95	2.00	1.90	1.70	1.79	1.62
Length of pm³	0.49	0.57	0.59	0.51	0.54	0.56	0.69	0.58	0.57		0.56	0.70	0.56	0.56	0.55		0.60	0.59	0.54	0.57		0.52
LOWER JAW																						
Length of tooth row	8.27	8.10	8.10	6.84	8.41	8.00	8.44	7.46	7.95	12.45	10.10	9.68	11.05	7.44	7.50	7.05	7.60	7.76	7.82	7.23	7.12	7.12
Length of premolar row	3.34	3.20	3.40	2.80	3.30	3.30	3.35	3.14	3.29	4.90	4.74	4.50	4.63	2.92	3.24	2.55	3.14	2.74	3.10	2.56		3.08
Length of molar row	3.29	3.10	3.10		3.12	3.05	3.12	3.12	3.09	4.63	3.76	3.56	4.10	2.98	3.14	2.74	2.89	3.04	3.19	2.90		2.96
Alveolar breadth at canines	1.00	1.14	1.30	0.89	0.96	1.93	1.06	0.97	1.16	1.63	1.05	1.10	1.25	0.95	0.91		0.95	0.96	0.92	1.05		0.99
Alveolar breadth at pm₁	1.24	1.35	1.20	1.00	1.10	1.40	1.27	1.14	1.21	1.83	1.10	1.00	1.60	1.26	1.12		1.17	1.37	1.24	1.57		1.10
Alveolar breadth at m₃	2.15	2.42	2.04	1.70	2.25	2.08	2.63	2.43	2.22	2.96	1.87	1.83	2.72	2.07	1.77		1.96	2.14	2.00	2.64		1.90
Alveolus of i₁ to m₃	8.28	8.10	8.09	6.84	8.41	8.00	8.25	7.33	7.91	12.45	10.00	9.73	11.24	7.52	7.50	7.05	7.60	7.76	7.82	7.30		7.12
Alveolus of c to m₃	7.59	7.37	7.27	6.66	7.46	7.30	7.64	6.75	7.25	11.05	9.40	8.70	9.87	6.79	6.70	6.64	7.23	7.00	6.96	6.55		6.44
Alveolus of pm₂ to m₃	5.90	5.66	5.75	4.23	5.61	5.61	5.95	4.37	5.54	8.70	7.28	6.78	7.90	5.04	5.40	5.41	4.59	4.64	4.77	4.41		5.19
Alveolus of pm₃ to m₃	4.95	4.61	4.80	3.35	4.65	4.65	4.83	4.44	4.64	7.15	5.75	5.39	6.55	4.22	4.50	4.55	4.53	4.64	3.84	3.50		4.12
Alveolus of pm₄ to m₃	3.80	3.69	3.63	2.62	3.75	3.69	3.79	3.35	3.64	5.45	4.39	4.10	5.13	3.53	3.24	3.50	3.66	3.60	3.10	2.70		3.42
Alveolus of m₁ to m₃	2.28	2.20	2.33		3.05	3.00	2.20	2.96	2.58	4.57	2.65	2.36	4.45	2.52	2.26	2.15	2.24	2.25				2.93
Length of pm₄	0.57	0.63	0.55	0.59	0.62	0.60	0.64	0.65	0.61	1.09	0.99	1.00	0.50	0.69	0.70	0.69	0.70	0.59	0.74			0.60
Number of premolars	4	4	4	3	4	4	4	4	4	4	4	4	4	4	4	4	4	3	4	3	3	4
Condyle to symphysis	11.65	11.80	11.15	9.50	11.74	11.23	11.80	10.09	11.12	10.86	14.20	13.44	15.80	10.39	11.50	9.56	10.96	10.72	10.47	9.93	9.93	9.57
Outer inter-condylar width	7.81	7.70	7.40		7.64	7.53	7.46	7.03	7.51	11.23	8.10	8.22	10.10	6.59	6.60		6.74	6.24	6.66	7.03	7.03	6.27
Inner inter-cordylar width	3.86	3.50	3.42	3.00	3.60	3.02	3.33	3.28	3.38	4.05	3.89	4.20	4.45	3.37				3.01	3.60	3.90	3.90	2.96

TABLE II

SKULL INDICES OF INDIVIDUAL AND AVERAGE DOGS COMPARED TO COYOTE AND WOLF

	MALES											FEMALES											
	1-4	1-129	1-34	1-31	1-7	1-117	1-56	1-55	Dog Ave.	Wolf	Coyote	Coyote	Wolf	Dog Ave.	1-26	1-12	1-8	1-24	1-9	1-60	1-35	1-3	1-30
Occipito-premaxillary length																							
Basal length	62.78		65.15		65.60	65.23	64.90	67.04	65.12	59.82	64.42	62.90	88.22	64.82	64.42	63.25		64.23	65.13	67.19	64.72		65.69
Palatal length																							
Basal length	54.56		55.56		55.13	54.12	53.90	54.66	54.65	51.44	55.25	54.88	50.96	54.62	56.11	53.16			54.25		54.98		54.61
Breadth orbitals																							
Breadth zygomas			34.09	33.41	35.18		36.25	33.25	34.44	32.98	33.40	35.42	31.89	32.95	34.87	34.19		25.03	37.72				
Breadth parietals																							
Dorsal length occiput to nasals	32.36	35.29	36.04		34.29	37.77	33.77	38.67	35.46	25.64	29.84	33.65	25.76	38.23	42.00	38.66		38.18	36.06		36.16		38.35
Width at molars[1]																							
Palatal length	40.00		39.26		40.13	41.09	41.99	40.88	40.56	34.47	33.75	33.91	39.03	39.40	38.82	37.95			37.09	35.55	36.11	44.23	41.56
Height at pterygoids																							
Basal length	32.46	34.01	35.79		34.33	35.95	32.38	37.78	34.67	36.36	33.64	34.16	35.29	34.76	36.29	32.03					32.84		37.11
Height at pterygoids																							
Width at parietals	98.12	94.71	97.84		95.72	92.38	94.32	94.95	95.22	134.29	106.30	97.64	121.27	87.09	81.66	86.58				84.26	89.18		93.75
Breadth parietals																							
Breadth zygomas	51.78		57.95	60.53	54.79		56.02	57.76	56.47	46.94	55.50	61.87	51.00	61.52	72.41	66.38		63.32	69.77				

TABLE III

COMPARISON OF DOG, COYOTE AND WOLF SKULL INDICES

	MALES					FEMALES				
Measurement	Number	Dog Range	Dog Average	Wolf	Coyote	Coyote	Wolf	Dog Average	Dog Range	Number
Occipito-premaxillary length										
Basal length	6	62.78-67.04	65.12	59.82	64.42	62.90	88.22	64.82	63.25-67.19	6
Palatal length										
Basal length	6	53.90-55.56	54.65	51.44	55.25	54.88	53.64	54.62	53.16-56.11	5
Breadth orbitals										
Breadth zygomas	5	33.25-36.25	34.44	32.98	33.40	35.42	31.89	32.95	25.03-37.72	4
Breadth parietals										
Dorsal length occiput to distal nasal tip	7	32.36-38.67	35.46	25.64	29.84	33.65	25.76	38.23	36.06-42.00	6
Width at molar[1]										
Palatal length	6	39.26-41.99	40.56	34.47	33.75	33.91	39.03	39.40	36.11-44.23	7
Height at peterygoids										
Basal length	7	32.38-37.78	34.67	36.36	33.64	34.16	35.29	34.76	32.03-37.11	5
Height at pterygoids										
Width at parietals	8	92.38-98.12	95.22	134.29	106.30	97.64	121.27	87.09	81.66-93.75	5
Breadth parietals										
Breadth zygomas	6	51.78-60.53	56.47	46.94	55.50	61.87	51.00	66.68	61.52-72.41	5

TABLE IV
COMPARISON OF INDIAN DOG AND COYOTE TO THE WOLF

	MALES				FEMALES			
	Coyote / Wolf	Index	Dog / Wolf	Index	Coyote / Wolf	Index	Dog / Wolf	Index
Occipito-premaxillary length	77%		61%		55%		49%	
Basal length	73%	94	57%	93.4	78%	71	59%	75
Palatal length	77%		59%		84%		63%	
Basal length	73%	94	57%	96	78%	93	59%	94
Breadth orbitals	72%		66%		86%		67%	
Breadth zygomas	43%	60	63%	95	77%	90	62%	91
Breadth parietals	84%		79%		90%		62%	
Dorsal length occiput to distal nasal tip	72%	85	59%	70	72%	80	54%	87
Width at molar[1]	75%		70%		72%		64%	
Palatal length	77%	97	59%	84	84%	86	63%	98
Height at pterygoids	67%		54%		75%		57%	
Basal length	73%	92	57%	95	78%	96	59%	97
Height at pterygoids	67%		54%		75%		57%	
Width at parietal	84%	80	79%	70	90%	83	62%	92
Breadth parietal	84%		79%		90%		62%	
Breadth zygomas	43%	51	63%	80	77%	86	62%	100

TABLE V

INDIVIDUAL AND AVERAGE POST-CRANIAL MEASUREMENTS OF INDIAN DOGS

Cat. No.		MALES									FEMALES							
		1-4	1-129	1-34	1-31	1-7	1-117	1-56	1-55	Average	Average	1-12	1-8	1-24	1-9	1-60	1-35	1-26
Tibia	Left	14.30	13.95	11.95	14.10	13.30	14.30	12.85	12.85	13.54	12.84	11.75	12.80	13.80	13.00	12.70	13.35	12.50
	Right	14.15	13.90	13.80	11.90	13.90	13.30	14.30	12.80	13.88	12.66	11.70	12.75	13.65	12.85	12.65		12.35
Femur	Left	13.80	13.95	13.50	11.75	13.65	12.90	14.20	12.75	13.31	12.81	11.50	12.80	13.65	12.95		13.35	12.60
	Right	13.70	13.85	13.50	11.70	13.65	12.90	13.90	12.70	13.24	12.48	11.50	12.70	13.85	12.89	12.10	11.80	12.55
Immominate	Left	12.00		11.70		11.15		12.20	10.85	11.58	9.90	9.05	8.95	11.10	10.49			
	Right	11.49		11.60				12.10	10.80	11.50	10.11	8.95		10.99	10.40			
Radius	Left	12.80	12.65	12.70		12.95	12.20	12.90	11.62	12.55	11.77	10.65	11.95	12.50	11.95	11.80		
	Right			12.70		12.95	12.20		11.60	12.36	11.69	10.60	11.85	12.45	11.80	11.75		
Ulna	Left		14.85	14.80		13.65	14.50	15.60	13.75	14.52	13.52	12.50	14.00	14.80				12.80
	Right		14.75	14.80			14.50			14.68	13.73	12.45	14.00	14.75				
Humerus	Left	13.05		11.70		12.85	12.05	13.35	11.95	12.49	11.92	10.65	11.90	12.65	11.85	12.85	12.30	11.65
	Right	13.00		11.60			12.05	13.30	11.90	12.37	11.72	10.60	11.75	12.60	11.70	11.40		
Scapula	Left			10.30		10.40				10.35	8.75	7.70	9.45			8.50		9.35
	Right			10.30		9.95				10.12	8.42	7.65			8.35	8.40		9.30

POTTERY FROM INDIAN KNOLL

By Wm. G. HAAG

Pottery from Indian Knoll is represented by 792 sherds of two general types, shell-tempered and grit-tempered. None of the sherds is associated with any material of the typical shell heap component. All of the sherds were found in depths down to five feet, but 662 sherds or 76% of the total were concentrated in the upper one and one-half feet.

The chart shows the distribution of the types by one-half foot levels. The shell-tempered wares total 621 sherds or 78.5% of the total and grit-tempered sherds total 171 or 21.5%.

SHELL-TEMPERED WARES

Shell-tempered pottery predominated at the site. Of the 621 sherds of all types, 575 were plain wares. These shell-tempered wares may be readily classified into the following types, but their mode of occurrence and lack of stratigraphic position hardly warrant the designation of pottery types in this study.

PLAIN HEAVY

Paste:—Coiled; temper consists of rather coarse, crushed-shell fragments with occasional inclusions of smooth, round pebbles, temper 30 to 40% of paste; texture medium to coarse; hardness 2-3; paste core gray or brown fired to buff or brown on inside and outside.

Surface:—Smoothed on inside and outside.

Form:—Wall thickness 8.5 to 19 mm. One vessel a large bowl or jar of 30 cm. diameter. Other features unknown.

Of the 72 sherds of this type found, 62 were in the one-half foot level and may have belonged largely to one vessel. Similar sherds have been found at a number of sites in Kentucky, namely, the Williams Site, CH 2, and Flanary Site, Cn 2. Although none was found at Oh 2, the large double lugs illustrated in Figure 23 of the Williams Site report[1] are from sherds of this heavy plain type. Much of the potsherds from the Williams Site may be assigned to this classification.

---

[1] The Williams Site, by W. S. Webb and W. D. Funkhouser, Reports in Arch. and Anthr., University of Ky. Vol. 1, No. 1, 1929.

CHART OF DEPTH DISTRIBUTION OF POTTERY TYPES

Depth in Feet	Shell-tempered													Grit-tempered							Totals
	Heavy		Medium			Fine			Net-impr.		Cord-mkd.		Rough	Plain			Simp.-stp.		Cord-mkd.		
	Body	Rim	Body	Rim	Handle	Body	Rim	Handle	Body	Rim	Body	Rim	Body	Body	Rim	Handle	Body	Rim	Body	Rim	
.5	61		52	11		10	3		2	4			1	7	1		7		41		200
1.0	2		145	8	2	10	2		5	2			1	11	1		10	1	17	1	217
1.5	1		116	17	1	10	2		9	2			1	7	1		16	2	1		185
2.0	1	1	12	4		3			1				1	7			1		2		36
2.5	1		10					2						1			6				19
3.0	1		10			1			1								1				13
3.5	2	1	21	4		3			1				1	8					2		43
4.5			1											1			1				3
5.0			2																		2
?	2		33	4		4			5		7	2		2		1	13			1	74
Totals	70	2	402	48	3	41	7	2	24	8	7	2	5	44	3	1	55	3	63	2	792

PLAIN MEDIUM

Paste:—Coiled; temper material consists of crushed shell particles with occasional round ferruginous sandstone pebbles as large as 4.5 mm diameter; the aplastic is 40 to 50 percent of the paste; texture medium to coarse; hardness 2-3; paste core gray to black, often fired on exterior only to buff, tan, or dirty brown, frequently fired on inside and outside to brown, or buff-cinnamon.

Surface:—Smoothed, exterior and interior. One specimen had on the shoulder at an unknown distance from lip a row of dots 8 mm between centers made by a hollow cane 3 mm in diameter.

Form:—Lip—flattened to rounded; when flattened, it is at right angles to the wall surfaces; when rounded there is usually a bulging or thickening of the wall just beneath lip. Rim—straight walls or sometimes slight thickening of rim for two or three cms below the lip; occasionally an outward roll at the lip produces a slight shelf. Body—large jars with mouth of 9 cm diameter; others of 20 cm at mouth, 24 cm at shoulder or 26 cm mouth and 30 cm shoulder or some of 40 cm at neck with flaring mouth. Many other shapes probably are represented, but only one rim sherd was found that was of a bowl. Base—convex. Thickness—4.5 to 10 mm at lip, 5 to 6 at rim, 5.0 to 8.5 wall. Appendages—strap handles 25 mm wide and 6.5 mm thick and 20 mm wide by 14 mm thick.

The shell-tempered pottery called Plain Medium is the most common ceramic remains at Oh 2. Four-hundred and fifty-three sherds were found at various depths although they occurred in greatest numbers in the one-half, one, and one and one-half foot levels. This is 73% of the shell tempered sherds and 57.2% of the total sherds found at the site.

This ware is found at many sites throughout the Mississippi Valley with only local variations in temper and paste. It has been found in large numbers of sherds at the Williams Site and at Tolu[2] and McLeod's Bluff.[3] The Flanary Site[4] pottery remains were almost entirely of this ware. These sites are all Middle Mississippi domiciliary mound and village sites. It can be assumed that this ware is of widespread occurrence in this area on sites of Middle

---

[2] The Tolu Site, by W. S. Webb and W. D. Funkhouser, Repts. in A & A Vol. 1, No. 5, 1931.
[3] The McLeod Bluff Site, by Webb and Funkhouser, Repts. in A & A, Vol. III, No. 1, 1933.
[4] The Tolu Site, page 407.

Mississippi classification as well as on sites like Indian Knoll and other shell heaps and some rock shelters in the Green River country. It is probably the utilitation pottery of a widespread group of peoples who occupied the middle reaches of the Mississippi valley late in prehistoric times.

PLAIN FINE

Paste:—Probably coiling was technique used in manufacture; temper of finely crushed shell constituting about 10% of the paste, to produce a very compact paste; rarely large grit particles are included in the otherwise fine paste; hardness 2-2.5; paste core black to dark gray fired to buff or tan, sometimes no evidence of surface firing but burnished to black shining surface, sometimes fired throughout.

Surface:—Smoothed exterior and interior, sometimes burnished. One sherd, a shoulder fragment of a jar, had two parallel incised lines 15 mm apart.

Form:—Lip—Rounded; one specimen had lip extended as a shelf at right angles to the rim with outer margin of shell scalloped. Rim—straight walls; slight outward flare near lip; one specimen had crenulated lip produced by rounded stick impressions regularly spaced along margin. Body—bowl usually with mouth smaller than greatest diameter of the vessel with diameters of the order of 14 cm at mouth and 22 cm at greatest width of body; rarely bowls with flaring mouth; jars with narrow mouth and high rim forming abrupt angle with flaring shoulder. Thickness—5 to 6.5 mm rim and wall.

Only 50 sherds of this ware were found at Oh 2. However, it too, is a pottery type of rather widespread distribution throughout the Southeast with only minor local variations in paste and temper. It has been found in small quantities at the Williams Site, at Tolu, and at McLeod's Bluff.

NET-IMPRESSED

The net-impressed potsherds found at Oh 2 were of two varieties, namely, a large mesh and a small mesh. Both were fabrics on heavy, coarse shell-tempered sherds from shallow bowls or "salt pans." Net-impressed pottery has a distribution throughout much of Western Kentucky, being found at Tolu, William's Site, and the Flanary Site. A few sherds of this ware were found at the Chiggerville Site, Oh 1.[5]

---

[5] The Chiggerville Site, by W. S. Webb and W. G. Haag, Repts. in A & A, Vol. IV, No. 1, 1939, fig. 17.

CORD-MARKED

These nine sherds are in most characters similar to the Medium Plain shell-tempered ware. The surface has been malleated with a cord-wrapped paddle. Since so few sherds were found, it is difficult to make any definite statement of the character of the type, but the closest description is that given for Fox Farm Cord Marked by Griffin.[6] The two rim sherds show the characteristic partial smoothing.

All of these sherds were found in the pit above Burial No. 285 and the exact depth at which they occurred is not known. The burial was deposited at a depth of 7.2 feet from the surface and had the sherds occurred at this lower level, it might mean that the burial had actually been made after the sherds had dropped on the surface. It is assumed that subsequent disturbance of the upper levels of the pit carried the sherds to a lower depth.

ROUGHENED

The five sherds of this type seem worthy of mention since they constitute so distinctive a type. The paste is generally like Medium Plain and the surface has been roughed either by closely placed punctations from a blunt stick or by repeated paddling with a crudely made check-stamp paddle. The William's Site had a few sherds of this general type but the suggestion of a check stamp is more pronounced there. Three of the sherds from Indian Knoll have large, subrectangular punctations which rather definitely appear to have been made individually.

GRIT-TEMPERED WARES

One hundred and seventy-one sherds of the total found at the site were grit-tempered sherds. This number constitutes 21.5% of all types found and, considering the location of the site and its relation to the area of Middle-Mississippi sites, the grit-tempered wares are of no mean importance. From the chart it is apparent that the vertical distribution of grit-tempered sherds closely parallels that of the shell-tempered wares.

PLAIN

Paste:—Method of manufacture unknown; temper of rather fine sand or limestone constituting about 20% of the paste,

---

[6] Griffin, J. B., The Fort Ancient Aspect, University of Michigan Press, Ann Arbor, 1943, p. 347.

occasionally contains a few large flakes of shell; texture medium; hardness 3-3.5; paste core black or gray, when black the outer surface is fired to a light yellow-buff, or gray, or mottled brownish-black to a depth of one mm or less, when gray the outer surface is fired to a bright orange-buff.

Surface:—Smoothed on inside and outside.

Form:—Bowls only known from Oh 2. One specimen 14 cm at mouth with body somewhat larger. Lip—flattened or rounded. Rim—straight side walls; one specimen has a semi-circular lug 7.5 mm thick extending 23 mm from the outer wall flush with the lip. There are two perforations in this lug, 15.5 mm apart. Thickness—6.7 at lip, 3.5-7.5 wall.

SIMPLE-STAMPED

Paste:—Similar to the plain ware.

Surface:—Covered from base to lip with shallow grooves 2-2.5 mm wide, four grooves in 14.5 mm, haphazardly applied.

Form:—Bowls and flaring mouth jars. Lip—rounded. Rim— one specimen has short parallel lines about 4 mm long and 4 mm apart incised just beneath the lip at right angle to lip. Thickness—3.5 to 6.5 mm. Appendages—one sherd has two five mm high conical feet, 34 mm center-to-center; fragment broken in such a way as to preclude possibility of a tripodal base.

This simple-stamped ware is in many respects similar to Bluff Creek Simple Stamped.[7] So few rim sherds were found at Oh 2, it is difficult to definitely describe the ware, but sherd comparisons with samples of the Bluff Creek Simple Stamped show that the pottery is of one tradition. The occurrence of this type pottery is similar in stratigraphy and other relationships at the particular sites on which it is found.

CORD-MARKED

Paste:—Similar to plain grit-tempered ware, but temper is largely broken potsherds constituting about 10% of the paste. Also includes crushed limestone.

Surface:—Covered with malleations from a cord-wrapped paddle. Cord apparently a twisted fiber.

Form:—Only one rim sherd gives much evidence of the form of this type ware. This sherd was from a jar about 18 cm diameter at the neck and the lip was carinated with five mm

---

[7] Haag, W. G., A Description and Analysis of the Pickwick Pottery Pottery, in An Archaeological Survey of Pickwick Basin in the adjacent Portions of the States of Alabama, Mississippi and Tennessee, by W. S. Webb and D. L. DeJarnette, BAE Bull 129, 1942, pp 513-526.

high points about six mm between centers. Walls range in thickness from 4 to 10 mm.

Mulberry Creek Cord Marked pottery found in Pickwick Basin[8] is nearly identical with the body sherds found at Oh 2. A nearly complete vessel of this type has been excavated at a site in Western Kentucky, which can be classified as Woodland.[9] This site was only a few miles from Oh 2.

In general, the grit-tempered wares found at Oh 2 are of types which are usually found associated with one another at many sites in the southeast. Geographic and temporal variations merely enhance the basic importance of the types as markers of the widespread distribution of a peoples with a generalized Woodland culture type. What other artifacts might be taken as associations of the grit-tempered pottery is not known at this time, but obviously the peoples responsible for the accumulation of the bulk of the midden of Oh 2 were not the manufacturers or users of the grit-tempered pottery.

CONCLUSIONS

From the nature of the occurrence of the potsherds at Indian Knoll, it is apparent that the concentration of the bulk of the material in the upper one and one-half feet of the midden indicates that the manufacturers of the pottery were not Shell Heap Peoples. Further, since the site has undergone such an extensive period of cultivation and occupation during historic times, and since it was previously excavated in part, it is believed that these potsherds were originally all surface deposits.

Observations at the site during its excavation showed that potsherds had a surface distribution of greater extent than the shell midden. At a distance of about 500 yards, a rather extensive Middle Mississipi component was test-trenched and the same kind of shell-tempered wares were found here as were found at Oh 2. Hence, it is concluded that the occurrence of potsherds at Indian Knoll is the result of temporary occupancy of the site by transient aboriginal visitors and that no part of the ceramic remains may be considered as culture elements of the Shell Heap People.

---

[8] Ibid., p. 518.
[9] The Ashby Site, Mu 4, Muhlenberg County, Ky. Unpublished manuscript.

REPORT ON CHEMICAL ANALYSIS OF STAIN ON BONES

By JOSEPH H. GARDNER

Graduate Assistant, Department of Anatomy and Physiology

OBJECT:

To determine whether or not the stains (black, brown, red and green, mostly black) on the human bones from Site Oh 2 are due to iron or copper (rarely).

METHOD:

The human material to be tested was scraped from the stained area on the bone. A similar test was made from an unstained area on the same bone.

Since human bone contains iron, a dilution threshold was predetermined. That is, a point of dilution was reached where the normal amount of iron found in bone would not give the iron test. It was found that by dissolving 25 miligrams of bone in 0.5 milli-leter of (dil.) HCl and then diluting this to 3.5 millileters the iron test would not occur. Thus the bones from site Oh 2 were tested using this dilution factor.

TEST FOR IRON:

Twenty-five milligrams of material was dissolved in 0.5 milli-leter of (dil.) HCl. The solution was heated, then centrifuged and decanted. The decant was then diluted to 3.5 millileters. To this 1 to 3 drops of NH_4SCN was added, if a red color occurred iron was present.

TEST FOR COPPER:

Twenty-five milligrams of material were dissolved in approximately 1 millileter of (dil.) nitric acid. The solution was heated, in order to speed up the reaction, then it was centrifuged and decanted. The decant was made alkaline by adding ammonium hydroxide and then centrifuged and decanted. The decant was made just acid by adding acetic acid and then a few drops of potassium-ferro-cynide $[K_4Fe(CN)_6]$ were added and the solution was centrifuged. If a reddish brown precipitate occurred copper was present.

SUMMARY AND CONCLUSIONS:

The data thus obtained indicated that whether the bone is stained or not, upon testing for iron, a positive reaction will result. This may be explained on the basis that the soil surrounding the bones during their burial period contained more than the normal content of iron. It was found in testing soil from site Oh 2 and comparing it with control soil, that the Oh 2 soil gave a more positive iron test. The stains found on the bones varied from light, medium and dark brown to red, yellow, green, purple-black, gray and black. All of these color stains gave the iron test; black and green giving the most positive tests. The test for copper was difficult to obtain and only a very few bones gave a positive test which was repeated as a check.

It is concluded that the stains appearing on the human bones were brought about by an increased amount of iron and copper in the soil, and that at the point of the stain the concentration of the iron or copper in the soil was greater than that around the unstained areas.

BIBLIOGRAPHY

BURNETT, E. K.
  1946   Personal Communication, Museum of the American Indian, Heye Foundation, New York, New York.

FOWKE, GERARD
  1928   Archaeological Investigations, Forty-fourth Annual Report, Bureau of American Ethnology, Washington, D. C.

GURNSEY, S. J. AND KIDDER, A. V.
  1921   "Basket-Maker Caves of Northeastern Arizona," Peabody Museum Papers, Harvard University, Volume VIII, Number 2.

HOFFMAN, WALTER JAMES
  1896   "The Menomini Indians," Medicine Bags, Fourteenth Annual Report, Bureau of American Ethnology, p. 261.

KIDDER, A. V. WITH GURNSEY, S. J.
  1921   "Basket-Maker Caves of Northeastern Arizona," Peabody Museum Papers, Harvard University, Volume VIII, Number 2.

KNOBLOCK, BRYON W.
  1939   "Bannerstones of the North American Indian," LaGrange, Illinois.

MOORE, CLARENCE B.
   1916   "Some Aboriginal Sites on Green River, Kentucky,"
           Journal of the Academy of Natural Sciences of Philadel-
           phia, Second Series, Volume XVI, Part 3.

MOOREHEAD, W. K.
   1917   "Stone Ornaments of the American Indian," The Andover
           Press, Andover, Massachusetts.

RITCHIE, WILLIAM A.
   1932   "The Lamoka Lake Site," Transactions of the New York
           Archaeological Association, the Lewis H. Morgan Chap-
           ter, Rochester, New York.

TYZZER, E. E.
   1943   "Animal Tooth Implements from Shell Heaps of Maine,"
           American Antiquity, Volume VIII, Number 4, p. 354.

WEBB, WM. S.
   1939   "An Archaeological Survey of Wheeler Basin on the
           Tennessee River in Northern Alabama," Bulletin 122,
           Bureau of American Ethnology, Washington, D. C.

WEBB, WM. S. AND DEJAINETTE, DAVID L.
   1942   "An Archaeological Survey of Pickwick Basin," Bulletin
           129, Bureau of American Ethnology, Washington, D. C.

WEBB, WM. S. AND HAAG, WM. G.
   1939   "The Chiggerville Site, Site 1, Ohio County, Kentucky,"
           University of Kentucky Reports in Anthropology and
           Archaeology, Volume IV, Number 1.
           "Cypress Creek Villages, Sites 11 and 12," University of
           Kentucky Reports in Anthropology and Archaeology,
           Volume IV, Number 2.

WILLOUGHBY, CHARLES C.
   1935   "The Antiquities of the New England Indians," The Pea-
           body Museum of American Archaeology and Ethnology,
           Harvard University, p. 217.